A Cruel Deception

KIM BOOTH

First published by Effield Press in 2018.

ISBN: 9781793044525

To Joan and Ted a promise fulfilled

TABLE OF CONTENTS

It has been said that fraud is a victimless crime. A determined fraudster will display no conscience, show no pity and conceal a total ruthlessness and disregard for their victim. The difference between fraud and other crime is that the victim of a serial fraudster is abandoned in a financial position from which they are unlikely to recover. The effect can be devastating in the knowledge that their financial future is entirely re-mapped and that whatever was intended to be left for loved ones has gone forever. The accumulated wealth worked for and intended for the comfort of retirement has been unlawfully appropriated by the fraudster and in a majority of cases has been frittered away never to be recovered. Only those who have never encountered a genuine fraudster and witnessed its repercussions would call it a victimless crime.

FOREWORD

This is the true story of a very calculated fraud, there are no bare chested heroes swaying a scythe, no super heroes urgently looking for a phone box to rush into and get changed in a flash, and no stereotyped Detective Inspector who has an immense drinking habit, broken marriage and lives on his own but is dedicated to "his job" (Well not in this investigation!). Instead this is the story of a true in-depth fraud investigation from the start to the finish. It is not solved within an hour with two or three minute breaks for commercials but is investigated over a period of 18 months or so. Frauds can differ immensely, some frauds can last minutes or as in this case can last six or seven years being controlled throughout the period by the fraudster. For a fraud to last seven years is very rare but does demonstrate the determination, greed and disregard for others shown by the fraudster. The offence can know no bounds and the effect on the victim in my mind can be as damaging as other serious offences. Throughout my thirty year investigative career I have encountered victims who have lost everything including their marriage and their health. In some cases they have taken their own their life as a result of the consequences.

The uniqueness of this offence comprises of several factors. Usually the fraudster commits the offence and makes good their escape; in this case the fraudster has remained in contact with the victims over a period of nearly 7 years perpetuating the fraud. The fraudster has involved other individuals who most of the time unwittingly assisted in the offence not knowing the importance of their involvement. Furthermore the offender has not been deterred by the involvement of the police but has actually made arrangements in the event of discovery or over the course of the fraud to continue to the point that the victims literally do not have any more money to give.

One can only speculate as to when and how this fraud would have eventually ended and at what further "cost." Fraud is a crime that is relentless in its nature and will only come to an end either by the intervention of the police or other authority or due to the fact that the victim is of no financial use to the fraudster who will then move on.

If a person is the victim of a robbery where their handbag or wallet is stolen and they are assaulted then within a short period of time they have recouped their financial loss, their clothes if damaged have been replaced and in the fullness of time hopefully if not injured too seriously during the offence their injury will have healed. Eventually their confidence to "go out" again will return. In some frauds as a result of the fraudster the victim has been cheated out of all their savings. In a number of cases the victims are retired, whereby their capacity to earn and recoup their loss has declined or is non-existent. They rarely regain their financial security for the time they have left. In a lot of cases the victim is unable to regain their confidence. Fraud cases involving the elderly in particular can leave the victim devastated fearing callers at the door never leaving the security their house again. In the past, victims frequently knew the offender. However in recent times alongside globalization and the vast reach of the internet, the fraudsters are increasingly faceless. They may even be in another country using a laptop to perpetrate the crime by building relationships involving vulnerable individuals who are "looking for love". Never underestimate the effect fraud can have on a victim - come with me on a real investigation to understand the high points and the low points, the effect it can have on the victims, and observe to what lengths a fraudster is prepared to go to achieve their aim. Make no mistake: the fraudsters are still out there searching for their next victim. and I sincerely hope that their next target is not a close friend or relative for I know first-hand the cruel torment and manipulation fraudsters are capable of.

Chapter One: The story unfolds

Market Rasen is a pleasant market town in Lincolnshire nestling at the edge of the Lincolnshire Wolds. On market days it becomes quite a busy place with local farmers and merchants displaying their wares for sale. As well as a market it is also a weekly meeting place where individuals who live out in the more rural areas gather to catch up with the local gossip and stand around talking.

On certain days it can become a very busy place due to the regular meetings at the local Market Rasen racecourse where on race days one can hardly move, or the peace and tranquility can be disrupted by either the large gatherings of motorcyclists that congregate at Willingham Woods just down the road. On bike nights in the area, bikers can be seen riding through the town on rather immaculate and expensive motorbikes that are in some cases stood in the garage at home until there is a nice day for a ride to "Willingham woods".

From a crime prospective Market Rasen is a nice place to live and generally the more serious crime that is committed within the area is due to "imports passing through", that is to say that the offences are committed by people visiting the area who have a good look around then come back to commit burglaries and the like. Sometimes the visitors arrive on race day or stop off travelling along the main A631 on route to the eastern coastal area.

There have been several instances where the more serious criminal has tried his hand at committing crime in Market Rasen thinking that the local police walk around with "straw in their teeth" only to find out later that the police together with members of the public in some of these rural communities are not as daft as they thought. For instance, the target criminal from the Leeds area who thought that it would be a good place to commit offences of dwelling burglary only to be identified by a farmer who realised that the stranger was not local and took the registered number of the offender's

3

vehicle. The scenario resulted in a criminal who had been busy committing offences nationwide being sentenced to 6 years imprisonment, or the travelling burglar who always travelled with his wife and young child in the car. The wife would remain in the car with their child while her husband went about his business of burglary. If he had not returned within a couple of hours they would drive away, so they could return north to dispose of the stolen property. The father was arrested and refusing to give his details to the arresting officers, giving his wife time leave the scene. If in the event the burglary was successful and he had stolen either cash or jewellery he would put the proceeds in a stamped address jiffy bag with his home address on and place it in the nearest post box just in case he was stopped by the police in the area.

On the occasion that he visited the Market Rasen Police area he had committed a burglary at a detached dwelling house in a rural village. He had broken in to the house through the rear patio doors forcing them in the process, he had also visited all the rooms in the house removing jewellery from the master bedroom and on the way out visited the child's bedroom where he broke and emptied her money box of an amount of bank notes. He left the premises and travelled with his wife and child towards Lincoln where he came across another large detached dwelling. Having parked the car up the road leaving his wife and child he again after having checked no one was at home entered the premises by forcing a rear window. Quickly he went to the master bedroom and stole a handful of jewellery, but unknown to him, he had been seen by a neighbour. The Police attended and he attempted to escape by running at, and breaking through a patio door. After a fight with two police officers he was arrested and detained.

At the police station he refused to provide his details knowing that if he delayed the process his wife would realise that he had been arrested and make her way home to await the arrival of her husband.

Eventually after a couple of hours he disclosed his identity, only a matter of minutes later a solicitor from up north contacted the charge room enquiring if his client was in custody (obviously contacted by the burglar's wife when she had safely returned home!)

Upon searching the offender after his arrest he was found to have in his possession a number of bank notes. It was known that earlier in the day a similar "Modus Operandi" had been used at another burglary twenty miles or so away. The money in his possession was seized and fingerprinted. He vehemently denied during his interview any offence of burglary other than the offence that he was caught committing by the police.

The occupants of the previous burglary were visited and elimination fingerprints were taken from the child of the house (who thoroughly enjoyed the experience!) and were found to be on the bank notes seized from the burglar. He soon realised as youngsters tend to do, that this one was no exception. The parents had lost count of how many times their child had emptied the money box and counted how much was in it leaving fingerprints all over the notes. The burglar really had to grit his teeth and he had great difficulty pleading "Not guilty" to that one! (He knows who he is!)

Shortly after he disclosed his identity a visit was made to his home address a nicely furnished detached bungalow in South Yorkshire where, to the surprise of both he and his wife the garden was dug up and a further stash of stolen jewellery was found that was identified as coming from house burglaries around the UK including the Market Rasen area.

***

In another case, one Saturday afternoon a report was received at Market Rasen police station from the local vicar to the effect that he had returned home to the vicarage to find that it had been broken into and a quantity of jewellery had been stolen, and it had only happened within the last half hour. A few minutes later another telephone call had been received to the effect that an elderly rather itinerant looking man aged around seventy years old had been in the local pub selling jewellery. The first thought was that this was too good to be true but upon attending the pub we found a rather untidy elderly male in discussion at the bar. The witness who has made the telephone call discreetly pointed the man out who was responsible for selling the jewellery. After a short protest and upon searching the man a pocketful of jewellery was found on him that did not fit the profile of the individual, and roughly fitted the description of items stolen from a local vicarage. He was arrested, insisting that he had purchased the jewellery from "a man down the road who he did not know."

Upon interview over a period of hours he persistently denied the offence of burglary stating *"If you found me stood over a dead body holding a smoking gun I would say that the man who gave me the gun went that way!"* making a pointing gesture. It soon became apparent that this man had played the game before!

There was no way he was readily going to admit the offence, even after the jewellery in his possession was identified as having been stolen from the vicarage.

Eventually after a few hours he relented and admitted the offence. It was at the conclusion of his written statement and whilst reading it over he held the statement to his face only a matter of inches away. When asked, he stated that he had been serving prison sentences for over fifty years and that during a term of imprisonment after the war he was sentenced to hard labour with periods of stitching mailbags by gaslight, which had detrimentally affected his eyesight.

Upon further interview he disclosed that during the war as a youngster he had been evacuated from east London to the Lincolnshire area where he was placed under the care of a local priest. During that period he was, on a regular basis both physically and sexually abused by the priest until he ran away, this being the reason why over a period of forty of so years had travelled the length and breadth of the country breaking into vicarages. He in his own mind saw that committing offences of burglary was a way of extracting some form of revenge. Upon interviewing him and getting to know him, one couldn't help but like him a little despite being a burglar and a persistent one at that!

On his later appearance at Crown Court he was charged with several offences of burglary, the defendant's barrister described him as a "recidivist criminal" whose career went back to his teenage years. During that time he had been subject to every type of sentence available with the exception of a Conditional Discharge. His barrister asked the learned judge to consider any sentence handed out in a term of months rather than years to which the judge replied after giving a flicker of a smile "You will go to prison for a term 38 months."

The defendant as he was being taken down the steps shouted to the judge, "You bastard judge I'll never do it!" to which the judge replied with a wry smile, "Just do as many as you can!"

So, on the whole it is the visitors from away that commit the more serious crime in and around Market Rasen, and as always, hope to get away with it.

Chapter Two: The Enquiry Begins

It was early April 1983 and I was the local detective constable in Market Rasen covering what was, and still is a very large area, which has a quite varied amount of crime. I occasionally had another Detective to "assist with my enquiries" but on the whole worked alone on a regular basis. It was a great place to work but with it comes an amount of responsibility. When the crime figures and the amount of detected offences are good everybody at "the nick" gets a pat on the back, from the sergeants, constables down to the cleaner. When of course the crime figures were suffering, the Detective Chief Inspector would appear ranting and raving *"the bloody crime detection figures for Market Rasen are rubbish what the bloody hell are the CID doing about it!"* It must be mentioned that in the past and in the absence of a National Police Fingerprint database, crime detection was more difficult even if fingerprints were found at the scene of a crime. The investigating officer had to either have a good idea who the offender was, or from which police area he was from so the fingerprints found at the scene could be compared manually against the database of another police force.

One particular day whilst sitting at my desk doing my paperwork, the weather was fine and sunny. I was performing the usual routine of keeping one eye on the task in hand such as the paperwork and the other on my other allocated task. The "other task" was usually dumped on me dependent on which Police Officer was engaged on office duties i.e. dealing with enquiries from members of the public who came into the police station. On this particular day the constable in question was, and still is an avid ornithologist who in his spare time engages in the pastime of ringing birds for the British Trust for Ornithology. As usual, provided there were no bosses shown on the duty roster, the first thing he would do upon his arrival at work would be to put his nets out on the police station lawn to catch a variety of birds which when they entered his very

8

fine almost invisible net were carefully removed and "ringed". When erected in the most favorable spot on the police station lawn the net was just out of his sight but was below my office window. The officer would therefore rely on me to telephone down to the enquiry office with the message "You've got one!" The constable in question would run out with his little box, very delicately remove the poor unsuspecting bird from the net, remove his pliers from the box, identify and attach the appropriate ring to the bird's leg, check it, then release the bird which would fly away obviously somewhat puzzled at their new appendage attached to their leg. The constable would quickly gather his box of rings and run back to the enquiry office to resume duties!

This particular day the nets were out as usual and I was keeping half watch whilst doing my paperwork. Due to my mounting cost of having either a pub meal or local fish and chips for lunch (and very good they were too!) I had the previous night decided to take a pack up containing cake and sandwiches.

I was interrupted from my work by the local civilian police driver who travelled around the police stations delivering the mail, which also included anything that needed taking from place to place. He came into my office and said, "This one's for you - it's been around the houses a bit I've seen it before" and handed me a report. Upon looking at it closer and the signatures I could see that it had been to various CID offices around the force. It had been to police headquarters marked "Not ours" Lincoln CID marked "not our area" Bracebridge Heath CID marked "Try Gainsborough" and then finally endorsed by a Detective Sergeant "Rasen area- Det Cons Booth to deal".

The report had originated from a neighbouring force and was entitled ALLEGATION of FRAUD. I started to read the report and was basically perplexed with what I was reading. It all seemed very strange really. I carried on reading whilst eating my sandwiches and was suddenly interrupted by the very large voice of the constable in the enquiry office shouting up the stairs, "*I thought you were supposed to be keeping an eye out for me, my bloody nets are ruined*!" and with that I heard the very solid police station door slam shut and the commotion continued outside onto the lawn under my office window. On the lawn I saw a white shape flapping about in the process of ripping the bird ringing nets to pieces with a police officer diving onto the flapping net attempting to subdue the bird. Whilst I had been so engrossed in reading the report and at the same time throwing my uneaten crusts out of the window onto the lawn for the birds, a seagull had swooped down to get the crusts and had become entangled in the nets and wrecking them in the process, needless to say I was not asked anymore to keep an eye on the local bird ringing activity from my office window!

Having tendered my apologies and survived the onslaught of *"You can't trust the bloody CID to do anything"*. I continued to read my report of fraud and began to wonder what it was all about. I could see why it had bounced around so many CID offices and came to the realisation that basically to sort it out was down to me. The report read as follows;

HUMBERSIDE POLICE
Division Hull East Station. Tower Grange
Date   10th Nov 1983
Subject Alleged Deception
Marked Received Lincs Police 8th Nov 83

Sir,
On Thursday, 8th September 1983, I was on crime patrol and asked to attend Ilkley Villas, Eastcourt Street, Kingston upon Hull. I there saw Terence George WARNER, 54 years, and his wife who related to me a lengthy story involving his family, a summary of which is as follows;

Terence WARNER has two elder brothers Laurence, 63 years, who died in January 1983, leaving a widow living at 11 Arkley Close Brough, North Humberside, and Edward, 62 years, living with his wife at 25, Ryland Road Dunholme, Nr Lincoln.

About 7 years ago, Edward and his wife went on holiday to Scotland and met a couple that they got to know as Mr. and Mrs. HENDRY. As a result of the continued friendship at the end of the holiday, subsequent holidays were taken by swapping homes between the HENDRYS and Mr. Edward WARNER and his wife.

At some time, it is not known exactly when, it transpires that Mrs. HENDRY has revealed to Edward and his wife that she was the illegitimate daughter of the Duchess of Argyll, Margaret, and the fact that she had a large amount of money and jewellry left to her in a will from an uncle. The Duchess of Argyll was preventing Mrs. HENDRY getting the money because she was living with a man whom the Duchess disapproved of. She also had a number of debts to pay off before she could inherit this large amount of cash and jewellry.

It appears that Mr. and Mrs. Edward WARNER then began giving Mrs. HENDRY various amounts of cash in order to assist them pay off debts so the will could be resolved.

It appears to the complainant, Mr. Terence WARNER, that when his brother had exhausted all his savings and could borrow no more, Edward began approaching other members of the family. He approached Lawrence WARNER and his wife living at Brough. He related the same story and Mr. Lawrence WARNER and his wife parted with £300. In December 1980, Mr. WARNER and his wife, in company with Mr. and Mrs. HENDRY from Scotland, visited Mr. and Mrs. WARNER at Brough. Again the same story was pursued but no request was made for money. Later, in January 1981 a number of

payments of money were either sent direct to Scotland or cash given to Mr. Edward WARNER for onward transmission to the Hendrys. Payments were repeated in this way in July, August, September and October of 1981 and a total amount of £3,736 was handed over in this way by Mr. and Mrs. WARNER at Brough. Payments stopped when they exhausted all their savings.

It is believed that payments have continued by Mr. WARNER in Lincoln by borrowing and obtaining loans. Terence WARNER states his brother in Lincoln is destitute and believes he has parted with a minimum of £10,000 to Mrs. HENDRY and the amount could be as much as £20,000.

Mr. Terence WARNER has attempted to persuade his brother of the fact that he has been conned but he refuses to accept this, believing it will all come true one day and that he will be repaid although many promises have not been kept. He brought this to our attention for investigation as to any offences committed by Mrs. HENDRY.

It would appear that any deceptions have been committed in Lincolnshire on Mr. Edward WARNER and his wife. Any other evidence available is hearsay and without their full co-operation no prosecution would be successful.

I submit this report and attached statement in order that enquiries can be made with Mr. WARNER at 25 Ryland Road, Dunholme near Lincoln.

Detective Constable

***

Having read the above report it all seemed a bit hard to believe but having read it twice I decided to carry on with my paperwork and I returned to it a few days later after having given it some thought and read over the report again.

On 11th September 1983, I went to Arkley Close, Brough and spoke to Mrs. Evelyn WARNER. She confirmed the payments as indicated by her brother-in-law and was able to produce receipts from the Inland Telegraph Service for various amounts and dates which showed various paying offices in Scotland with Mrs. HENDRY as the payee. She was also able to give an address for Mrs. HENDRY obtained from Mr. Edward WARNER and this was Burnside Bungalow, Keills Bridge, Craighouse, Isle of Jura Argyleshire. I recorded a statement from Mrs. Evelyn Warner.

I made brief enquiries with the Scottish Police covering the area and was informed that there was talk of a woman who in the past was known for using this "*modus operandi*" and that she was no relation to the Duchess of Argyll It was not known if she had been prosecuted for any offences.

I informed Mr. Terence WARNER of this and he asked for a few weeks before any action was taken to try and persuade his brother to co-operate with any police enquiry.

On 2nd November 1983, I was again contacted by Mr. Terence WARNER and asked if the enquiry could now go ahead.

The following week after having finalised the work in progress, I decided to make some tentative enquiries. I had been visited by a Detective Sergeant who was the supervisor covering my patch in the absence of my own and mentioned the report to him. He laughed and said, " *Oh I wondered where that one would end up and you've got it*" He stated that he had seen the report previously and advised me not to spend too much time on it as it appeared to be a waste of time and there was other crime that wanted sorting out. The matter was beginning to bother me in that if in fact the allegation was true and there was any foundation in it then the matter needed dealing with.

Later the following day I decided that I would take a further look at the matter and would attempt to identify this "Mrs. HENDRY" using the Police National Computer (PNC). I realised that it would be a difficult task as the only details I had at that time was a name but without a date of birth, place of birth or indeed description. After a few hours the result was negative and I was no further on. I referred back to the report and the mention of Scotland surely if a woman is capable of a deception to this degree she has previously come to the attention of the police!

Eventually after numerous telephone calls over a period of weeks I made contact with an old police sergeant in the Loch Gilphead area who seemed to recollect a woman with a connection to the Duchess of Argyll although the name HENDRY did not seem familiar to him. The sergeant said he would make a few enquiries and come back to me with any results.

A matter of a couple of weeks went by when I received a call from the sergeant to the effect that the woman he had in mind was not called HENDRY but was in fact called MORRISON. She had lived for a time in the area but had a number of years ago moved on leaving a trail of debt. He seemed to recollect that she made reference to her being related to the Duchess of Argyll and that the woman in question had been prosecuted for offences and that he seemed to think that she had previously had dealings with the police for other matters. He did not know her first name but her surname was certainly MORRISON and he gave an approximate age. Her current whereabouts were unknown. He would make further enquiries try and dig out the paperwork bearing in mind that this all happened ten years earlier in 1972, it was unlikely that any paperwork was still in existence. I informed him it would be very much appreciated if he could try and find any. He assured me that he would and if successful would send me a report. Deep down I knew this was a long shot but would keep my fingers crossed in hope.

The name MORRISON was a start. I went back to the police computer and was assisted by a police woman operator (who I subsequently married!) She was provided with the details, as I knew them and given the task of attempting to identify the woman in question.

The searches on the computer provided a whole array of females partially fitting the brief details and would require an immense amount of searching to eliminate red herrings. The matter was left in her capable hands. In the meantime I decided to dip a toe in the water and call to see Mr. and Mrs. WARNER at their home address to see what they had to say about the matter. Bearing in mind that it would be a situation where I would be probing into their private affairs but had decided that it had to be explored just in case they were in the process of being victim of a deception, on the other hand having researched the rather colourful background of Margaret Duchess of Argyll the version of events as claimed was not beyond the realms of possibility!

What if what was claimed was in fact true and anyone

14

wanted to complain about the police sticking their nose into matters of a private nature? What if in fact it was true and any police activity compromised any private arrangements that had been made? I had made a decision it had to be done to hell with the consequences! I also had the mumblings of my Detective Sergeant in my ear saying "*If you look at this one,* (meaning the allegation) *you had better be right, or you will be back shaking door handles!*" And yes, the police did actually used to do that whilst walking around the beat on nights.

One cold Wednesday evening I decided to visit Mr. and Mrs. WARNER at their home address. I knew that I had yet to correctly identify "Mrs HENDRY" and did not know the circumstances of their relationship. As I drove along the country roads I was thinking to myself just what I was going to say. I had not met Mr. and Mrs. WARNER before but from the small amount of enquiries I had made did not result in the revealing of anything untoward. Both were in fulltime employment without having either any previous convictions or in fact any dealings with the police previously. Edward as far as I could establish worked in an office at a large local factory and his wife Joan worked at the local social services but in what capacity was unknown.

I arrived at the address during the early evening, the premises were on the outside a very well presented mid terraced house in a row of about five. The door was answered by a man of about 60 years with a very slight build with short and neat grey hair. I introduced myself showing my identification card and was very politely invited in. After a small hallway I was invited into a lounge that was sparsely furnished but very clean tidy and presentable, also in the lounge was a woman who appeared of younger years sat in a chair that Mr. WARNER introduced as his wife Joan. It seemed almost surreal to be sat opposite a very friendly couple that could still be in the process of being duped.

Mr. Warner, "I am here to discuss with you what I would describe as a very delicate situation. It is not my intention to pry into your private affairs but as a result of concerns raised by another person I have come to see you about what I consider to be a possible fraud that you may or may not be a victim of. I understand that you and your wife have formed a relationship with a woman called Barbara Hendry and that you have been sending her amounts of money over a period of time. Is his correct?"

Both Mr. and Mrs. Warner looked at each other but did not reply.

I was at this point still weighing the situation up and was treading carefully as I did not want to upset them, as I needed their assistance at this stage.

I went on to say, "If this is not the case then fair enough but I would ask that you assist me is evaluating the circumstances just to make sure that all is in order."

Mr. Warner said, "May I ask where you have got your information from, officer?"

I replied, "This has come to the attention of the police from somebody who is concerned about your welfare and is obviously worried about what is going on".

I was really attempting to be very polite and Mr and Mrs Warner were sat in the lounge listening intently to what I had to say, to such a point that I was running out of words. It felt to me that I was intruding into their world and basically sticking my nose into their business.

Eventually I had to say "Well, that's the reason I am here, people have genuine concerns, what have you both got to say about it?"

Mr. WARNER appeared somewhat put out at the suggestion but appeared defiant.

Mr. Warner said, "I do appreciate your concerns Mr. Booth but I can only reassure you that everything is in order and that this is not a police matter. We both know what we are doing but it does cause me some concern that the police have become involved. It really does not warrant this."

Since I have started the ball rolling I decided to probe a bit and find out what I could.

"Is this woman called Barbara Hendry?" I asked. "How long have you known her?"

Mr. Warner replied, "Mr. Booth, I appreciate your concern but it is a private matter between us. Rest assured that we know what we are doing but I am not happy with the fact that the police have become involved there is nothing to worry about. We have known the person involved for a number of years and we are more than happy with it she is an extremely good friend." At this point Mr. Warner looked towards his wife Joan who nodded in agreement.

It was obvious to myself that Mr. WARNER or indeed his wife were not going to discuss the matter and in all of thirty years I have never been so politely told to basically mind my own business.

Both Mr and Mrs Warner were resolute in not wanting to discuss the matter and were very confident that they knew what they were doing.

I turned to ask Mrs Warner if they were in possession of any paperwork that Mrs Hendry had given them or that would corroborate the story. Mrs Warner looked at Mr Warner and said that they were in possession of paperwork. I paused then asked Mr Warner if they could provide me with details of Mrs Hendry so I could check her out. Mr. Warner again explained that this was a very personal matter of a very delicate nature and to rest assured that they were in full control and knew what they were doing. I was not convinced that all was in order my feeling was that they were being deceived by this woman.

Although very personable and polite they were both determined and resolute and could not be persuaded to disclose any details whatsoever. They were extremely nice people but I had grave concerns that all was not well.

I decided that I ought to leave the house with at least something, I enquired again as to the identity of the woman in question. I was informed by Mr. WARNER that both he and his wife were happy with the identity of this woman who they had known over a period of years and considered to be a family friend and for reasons that they were not prepared to discuss the matter further and certainly would not disclose her identity.

I asked, "Have you been sending this woman money?

Mr. Warner replied, "Mr. Booth we would prefer it if we did not discuss this matter any further. Thank you."

This was clearly going nowhere. The Warner's had confirmed this woman existed and hadn't denied sending her money. It hardened my resolve to get to the bottom of it. But how could I do it?

It was obvious to me that this situation was going nowhere but deep down due to the fact that both Mr. and Mrs. WARNER has firstly confirmed the woman existed, and secondly whilst not confirming the sending of money and had not exactly denied it, hardened my resolve to get to the bottom of just what was going on, but how was I going to do it? I had left Mr. and Mrs. Warner my telephone number that they could call if they had any concerns, they would always be able to get in contact with me. Days turned into weeks and I was no further closer to identifying Mrs. Hendry. I had at one point been in Lincoln and seen Mr. Warner coming out of a post office clutching a piece of paper which I had convinced myself was a money transfer receipt. I went into the post office after he had left the area and in fact confirmed that he had arranged a money transfer to a post office in Scotland. I came out of the post office after confirming the transaction shaking my head to myself thinking where do I go from here?

Chapter Three: The Puzzle begins

It was a matter of weeks later when I received a call for the Criminal Records Bureau to the effect that a woman had been identified in Scotland who was considered to be a possibility, in fact she was one of three hundred that the system had thrown up. Her name was Barbara Elizabeth WRIGHT BAIN or FERGUSON or MORRISON @ Countess De LEONE @ Madam FELLONA Bn 17.1.30 at Glasgow. Further enquiries revealed that she had previous convictions for fraud and extortion and had in the past been sentenced to 15 months imprisonment. Despite having a name and some dubious aliases just would not be enough to confront the Warners with, such was their determination and confidence in what they were doing. Despite not having a reasonably positive identification at this time the "Countessa" element was looking promising to the enquiry. I first had to establish which court had dealt with her, identify the previous officer was who dealt with her and then track him or her down. This was going to prove to be a difficult task but again it had to be done.

In crime enquiries all is not what it seems, I have a name of an individual who was looking quite interesting but whether it is the person who is linked to Mr and Mrs Warner is a different matter. So often in the past not only in our police area but nationally promising leads have turned out to be red herrings and cannot in the end be linked despite outstanding coincidences.

Hence the following example from firsthand experience.

In 1981 a series of arson attacks occurred at rest homes in and around Hull North Humberside. All available resources were deployed in the investigation. The investigation into the offences, turned out to be very labour intensive and during the enquiry a murder and an attempted murder occurred one night in Scunthorpe. Since the two offences were of a serious nature and together with the fact that the majority of the detectives in Grimsby and Scunthorpe were investigating the arson offences in Hull resources available in Scunthorpe were depleted. As a result the Humberside Force asked Lincolnshire Police for assistance it was decided that 15 Detectives would travel to Scunthorpe from Lincolnshire to assist with the murder investigation. Some Lincolnshire detectives were only to keen to be given a chance to work on old "stomping ground" as Scunthorpe prior to the creation of Humberside came under the Lincolnshire Police area and some Detectives considered it "going home."

I was one of the Detectives fortunate enough to be selected and travelled to Scunthorpe for a briefing before commencing enquiries. It soon became apparent that this at Scunthorpe was a very serious situation indeed. The circumstances were that on the previous night at about 11pm in the evening an "Old soldier" was returning from a services club when persons unknown grabbed him from behind and he had a knife drawn across his throat and his throat cut. He was thrown into the gutter and left to die. It was only when a surgeon passing in his car returning from duty at a local hospital stopped and gave first aid that saved the old man's life.

Earlier the same evening a middle aged man was walking down a local footpath between houses known as the "Frodingham footpath" on his way home from work when he too was approached from behind and was stabbed in the back. On this occasion the man was not so fortunate, no assistance was available and he died on the footpath only to be found a short time later by a passer-by.

It was noticed the deceased as he died – eyes wide open had in his hand an amount of privet hedge that he had grabbed on his way down to the floor. A witness was traced who stated that he had seen a man in a green fluorescent type jacket running away from the area. A search of the area revealed a green fluorescent jacket found a short distance away in a large dustbin. The jacket had blood on one of the sleeves and a name was found written inside the jacket. A team was dispatched to the house of the owner of the jacket who was arrested and detained for interview.

The word got round the incident room that the murder and

the attempted murder the previous night were detected and the "Lincolnshire Lot" could get off home (all in jest!). I was not convinced, as were others it all seemed too cut and dry for me!

The individual arrested was interviewed and actually admitted the murder but denied the offence involving the "old soldier". He described how he had used the knife from behind and even admitted how the deceased had died with his eyes open and clutching a piece of privet in his hand. The case seemed to be detected or did it?

Celebrations were in their infancy and the general thought was that it was only a matter of time before the person detained for the murder admitted the other offence. It was announced shortly afterward that the man arrested had retracted his confession and denied all knowledge of the murder despite the compelling evidence against him, i.e. the blood on the jacket, the man fitting his description running from the scene and his name in the bloodstained jacket where another witness had said he was wearing at work that night. The evidence was put to him again and he admitted the offence, all was back on track, or so it seemed.

Since the individual had declined a solicitor he was appointed one who attended the police station and he was interviewed again, he denied the offence. Hours later the truth was out. What had happened was that the individual arrested for the murder left work and as usual walked home eventually walking along the Frodingham footpath. If he timed it right we would be travelling down the footpath at about the same time that a local bus conductress having finished for the night was getting ready for bed as usual with her bedroom curtains open. The man, as he had previously done climbed the fence of her garden and watched her getting undressed in her bedroom window.

It was whilst he was watching the bus conductress undress he heard a scuffle on the path next to the rear of the garden and looked through the hole in the fence to see the deceased falling to the ground after having been stabbed from behind. He heard two people running away and climbed over the fence onto the footpath where he saw the deceased lying on his back with a fatal injury. He approached the body to check how seriously injured he was only to find no response. He observed that the eyes of the deceased were open and that on his journey to the ground, and in a desperate attempt to stay on his feet had grabbed a handful of privet hedge, which he was still clutching. The man panicked and ran away towards home and on seeing he had blood on his jacket removed it and put it in a nearby dustbin. After placing the jacket in the dustbin he continued to run away only to be seen by a witness on the way.

The moral of the story and the advice for any budding detective is to not take the obvious as being the truth but bear everything in mind and evaluate the evidence available, as what appears obvious is not always the case.

The undetected murder and the attempted murder, enquiries continued and eventually two local names were put into the frame. Enquiries were made to establish the movements of the suspects on the night of the two offences.

Two local men were later charged with the murder and attempted murder on the same night and were sentenced to life prison sentences.

A month or two had passed but no further progress had been made in the enquiry. All enquiries in an attempt to trace an officer who had dealt with the "Countess" in Scotland had proved negative at this stage. There was a possibility that due to the passage of time the officer(s) had retired and taken their knowledge with them or even died such was the possibility.

I had the suspicion that the so called "evidence" I had revealed would not be enough to persuade Mr and Mrs Warner to either allow me to investigate or make a complaint such as their faith in Mrs. Hendry. I was undecided at this point whether, in the absence of concrete evidence to visit them again. I was also mindful that all I had at this stage was circumstantial and there was always a possibility I could be wrong.

My resolve was further hardened one day when I was in Lincoln shopping. As I passed the National Westminster Bank I saw Ted Warner coming out of the door. He did not see me but I followed him from the bank to a nearby post office. I stood and watched him go in and stand at the counter to be served. What was Ted Warner doing in the post office? I could only conclude that he was still sending money to Mrs Hendry in Scotland. I didn't wait to find out but decided to make a mental note of what I had seen and try again later to see Mr and Mrs Warner to confront them with my evidence.

Later that week I travelled to the home of Mr and Mrs Warner to confront them with my suspicions.

I arrived at their home early evening and was invited in. As usual the reception was very friendly. I was offered a cup of tea and was aware that both Mr and Mrs Warner were anxious about hearing what I had to say. I decided that I would tell them straight away and wait for the response.

I informed them that as a result of my enquiries I had found a Scottish woman who had previously been prosecuted for fraud and extortion number of years ago and that she has been using the name of Barbara Morrison or Countess De Leone. I further told them that I had reason to believe that his woman was the same woman as Barbara Hendry and that I was concerned that she was deceiving them. After disclosing my somewhat circumstantial revelation it was taken very well by both Mr and Mrs Warner. I was very politely told that they were more than satisfied with the arrangement with Mrs Hendry and respectfully informed me that the evidence was at the best circumstantial. I did get them to confirm that they possessed a large amount of paperwork including certain legal documents that verified their story. We did reach an agreement that on the condition that my enquiries were discreet I could continue as they had been sworn to secrecy and that if it was known the police were involved it could compromise what they were attempting to achieve.

Mr. Warner said, "Mr. Booth, we have known this woman over a number of years and we have become firm friends, there is an inheritance involved that is being blocked by the Argyll family and if it became known that Mrs. Hendry has ether borrowed money or been in contact with the police then it could invalidate the releasing of the inheritance. That is all I can tell you at the moment but we both appreciate your concerns."

It did not seem right to me and I had decided in my mind that they were being deceived and that I would continue anyway either with or without their permission such was my resolve. I was frustrated however that despite being very receptive and polite neither Mr or Mrs Warner would not entertain the possibility that there was a deception going on, anyway, to be fair, at this stage the evidence was not exactly overwhelming!

I still had not received any results from other officers who had dealt with this Countess De Leonie and the trail was getting cold. Mr Warner went on to say that the problems being encountered by Mrs Hendry were that the Argyll family was in denial that she is the illegitimate daughter of Margaret. At this point Mr Warner was interrupted by his wife Joan and told him he had already said too much.

I again attempted to explain that we knew who she was and it was unlikely that it was true. I asked how much money had been sent to Barbara Hendry but was informed that it would not be discussed.

Both Mr and Mrs Warner remained polite throughout our conversation but resolute. It was obvious that they had total confidence in this Barbara Hendry but I was not convinced. I again attempted to get the Warner's to make a complaint, which would warrant me mounting and investigation but again they declined. I told them that I was pretty certain that they were the victims of an elaborate deception but they both remained to be convinced.

I asked them to retain all of their paperwork and I would discreetly look into things a little bit further as I was concerned regarding their finances. I again asked them to contact me if they had any further questions.

After the discussion we parted on good terms and as I sat in my car outside came to the opinion that Mr and Mrs Warner were the nicest people one could ever wish to meet, albeit somewhat naive, or were they? Or in fact had I got it wrong? They certainly seemed quite confident and happy with the way things were. I must admit due to the high level of confidence of Mr. and Mrs. Warner I was starting to have slight doubts myself. When I sat and looked at the paperwork I was certain that a fraud was being practiced but after a few minutes in the company of the Warners I had my doubts! I also thought that I am on the verge of encountering an interesting adversary. Firstly, she had sworn the Warners to secrecy about their dealings and the legacy and secondly she had anticipated the fact that at some time her past would be revealed and that she needed to negate any suspicions.

I did however still think that this was a deception and a sophisticated one at that. It makes a change to come across an offender who actually gives things a bit of thought! I really thought that this visit would resolve the matter, but it didn't and I was wrong. As I drove away I thought to myself, what is the next step?

I was becoming rather concerned that if Joan and Ted Warner were being the victim of a scam, then my lack of action made us all vulnerable. Both Joan and Ted were sending what was thought to be large sums of money that they could hardly afford to this woman in Scotland, and I knowing about the situation was helpless to do nothing whilst it continued. I had considered going to see their relatives but the ones I knew already suspected something was wrong and I did not know any other relatives. If Joan and Ted had confided in their closest relatives then by the fact that they had loaned them money they also believed the story. I also considered that if Mr. and Mrs. Warner found out that I had been to see their relatives without informing them, then any goodwill I had with them would be lost. I felt that I needed some advice where to go with this enquiry and how to expose what was going on.

I did feel that this could not possibly carry on any longer, and that it has run its course I only had to wait for Joan and Ted to contact the police and report a fraud. What I did find of concern was the financial damage that was happening to Joan and Ted who obviously firmly believed in what they were doing and as far as I was concerned were being firmly deceived and it had to stop.

Chapter Four: Frustrating times

Christmas 1983 -84 came and went but I again visited Joan and Ted over the Christmas period to see if all was well. As usual Joan and Ted were very hospitable, very polite and talkative until I broached the subject, only to be informed that all was progressing well and that in the not too distant future all would be resolved which would save me a lot of time. I informed them that I sincerely hoped that would be the case but couldn't personally see it. Ted approached me on the way out saying "I'm sure it will be alright and if that is not the case we will assist you in any way we can."

I was reassured by this but concerned of the financial damage that would continue to occur. I just hoped that I was wrong.

I had more or less through various processes identified a possible suspect but two small problems remained, firstly I had to be certain that the individual identified was in fact the offender and secondly I had to prove it!

Around the first week in January 1983, I returned to my office to find a report lying on my desk. I immediately saw that it had originated from Lothian and Borders Police in Dalkeith and was sent to the Chief Constable of the Lincolnshire Police for my attention.

Subject BARBARA ELIZABETH WRIGHT BAIN or FERGUSON or MORRISON @ COUNTESS de LEONE @ MADAME FELLONA

I refer to telephone communication dated 16th inst from DC Booth Lincolnshire Police Market Rasen, Lincolnshire, relative to the above person who is the subject of enquiries by him into a number of frauds committed in that police area, when she allegedly obtained sums of money amounting to £30,000 from various persons on the pretext that she is the *illegitimate daughter of Margaret, Dowager Duchess of Argyll, and that she has a trust fund of four million pounds in her name deposited by the said Duchess for her in a bank in Zurich Switzerland.*

During the months of September and October 1972 I made enquiries into a series of similar frauds committed by this person in Edinburgh and Midlothian and during these enquiries I was able to establish that the suspect had no connection whatsoever with the family of the Duke of Argyll but that her mother was Janet McGlone or Campbell or Bain who at that time resided c/o Harvey, at 35 Linn Walk, Garelochhead, Dunbartonshire and that her father was James Bain, a journeyman baker, who was since deceased. I was able to obtain from Registrar House in Edinburgh a copy of the accused's birth certificate, giving her place and date of birth and details of her parents.

During these enquiries it also came to light that she was responsible for defrauding the DHSS of approximately £900 between July 1970 and July 1972, by making false claims for benefits to which she was not entitled.

As a result of these enquiries the above named appeared at the Sheriff Court, Edinburgh on 8th February 1973 when she pled "Guilty" to a number of charges of fraud amounting to £5,670 and as a result was sentenced to 15 months imprisonment.

At the request of DC Booth and to assist him in his present enquiries, forwarded herewith are photocopies of the accused's birth certificate together with copies of press extracts referring to the above case, and a copy of the relevant police reports to assist him in the compilation of evidence in his current investigation.

After reading the report I realised this was a real breakthrough. I was now certain that this was the same woman and I was impressed that the Sergeant in Scotland had obviously kept his word, located the necessary paperwork, compiled a report and sent it to me for my attention. All I had to do now was to prove it and get Mr. and Mr. and Mrs. Warner on my side and finally bring this matter to a close. I also realised that this would involve a large amount of work. The individual concerned, as I suspected, had used this M.O. before and had obviously been through the police system. There was a nice press cutting enclosed that gave me a good impression of my adversary, a rather seasoned individual but not having a good hair day! I was now was satisfied that I had identified "Barbara", she had previous convictions (Which did not surprise me knowing how she had operated with Joan and Ted Warner!) I also had her birth certificate together with some newspaper cuttings of her previous court appearances together with a photograph!. I was sure that this would do the trick. When I showed it to Joan and Ted Warner surely that would realise now it was all an elaborate deception and support a prosecution. I decided that as soon as I could I would visit Joan and Ted Warner and inform them of what I had found out. I really did not think that I would get anywhere but I had to try all the same. I carried on with my other duties and called a couple of times without success.

On 28th February 1984 two senior officers from the Trustee's Savings Bank attended Lincoln Police Station to report a set of circumstances which they were beginning to consider to be fraudulent, Heads of Inspection were their titles. They had first seen a uniformed officer who as soon as he heard the word "Deception" decided that whatever it was, it was a matter for the CID.

Fortunately I was in the building in the process of interviewing a couple of burglars who had tried their luck out at Market Rasen. The visitor's presence was brought to my attention, mainly because it was becoming a bit of a joke with my CID colleagues that I was pursuing the Duchess enquiry and was flogging a dead horse! Upon walking around the police station and especially within the CID office I would be greeted with taunts of "Morning Milady" or individuals bowing towards me and touching their forelock whilst walking past. It was all in good spirit but they all knew it was water off a ducks back and had absolutely no effect whatsoever. I however held a different view that if it was a deception and the lengths that the offender had gone to were true, then it needed pursuing.

I saw the two inspectors from the bank and listened to the story that they had to tell. Two of their customers had been obtaining loans from the Trustees Savings Bank in Lincoln to assist a friend in Scotland. The Inspectors identified the customers as one Edward and Joan Warner, which as far as I was concerned was just what I needed. Despite the Warner's being very good customers the bank manager Mr Leslie Smith had become extremely suspicious and had reported his concerns to his seniors, as a result it was a matter which they decided deserved the attention of the police.

The bank were of the opinion that an offence of deception was being committed - the Warner's had obtained an overdraft in excess of £13,000. The reason that they gave for wanting the overdraft was that they were helping a friend to release a sum of money that had been left to her.

The loans by way of overdraft had been available from October 1983 until January 1984, which was when the manager became suspicious.

Throughout the interviews with both Joan and Ted Warner and with Mrs Hendry the manager had kept comprehensive notes. Towards the end of the loans period the manager of the bank had requested that the Warner's provide some documentary evidence to support their reasons for wanting the loans.

The loans had been collected from two banks - one in Glasgow and one in Fareham Hampshire. Upon releasing the money, the individuals collecting it had signed receipts and names and address had been provided. The first thing I requested was to see the receipts in question and was told that they would be sent for.

Both Joan and Ted had upon request from their Bank manager produced two letters from different solicitors in Scotland stating that Mrs Hendry had given to them to support her claims. The suspicions were that the both letters appeared to have been typed on the same typewriter.

The suspicious bank manager had written to both of the solicitors concerned who did not have any knowledge of a Barbara Hendry and having checked their records confirmed that the letters in question had not originated from their offices. The letters appeared to be forgeries. It was at the time of this meeting it was disclosed Mr Warner had again been into the bank attempting to borrow a further £400.

I felt this was a breakthrough.

The Bank Inspectors informed me that permission had been given for the Bank Manager in question to attend Lincoln Police Station at a date to be arranged to make a written statement. All cooperation would be given.

Chapter Five: The enquiry starts

Having seen the representatives from the bank and armed with all the new information I again visited Joan and Ted Warner at their home address. I informed them that I had seen the representatives from the bank and that they had made enquiries concerning the paperwork that they had been provided with from Joan and Ted and as a result of that, they had been informed by the solicitors the letters in question were forgeries. The room went quiet and Joan who was the first to respond by declaring that she was most unhappy with the bank for not taking them at their word and making enquiries about the letters which they had provided to support their claim. I informed them of the coincidences that I thought that Mrs Hendry was the same woman who I thought had a conviction for fraud but using another name. I tried to impress on both Joan and Ted that I was convinced that they were being deceived I had all the newspaper cuttings. I decided not to show them at this stage as it could be detrimental to the case in the future if the matter of identity became an issue. I certainly did not want to compromise anything as the individual responsible certainly needed prosecuting for this and besides I was looking forward to meeting her! So many times in the past had cases been compromised by police officers not sticking to the rules.

It was all a bit too much for Joan and Ted to take in but I had noticed that in between my visits Ted's health had appeared to have deteriorated and he seemed rather frail to me. I did not push the point at this stage taking into consideration that both Joan and Ted had lived with this since 1976!

As I left the house we agreed that firstly, they would not mention my visit to Barbara Hendry and secondly that I needed to know over the next couple of days if they would assist me in a prosecution and thirdly no matter whatever the reason not send any further money to Barbara Hendry. Both agreed that they would comply with my two requests and that the third was easy to comply with because they did not have any further money to send! I left to the words of Ted saying, "We will be in touch either way".

I had considered alternative courses of action in the event that Joan and Ted declined to make a complaint. Due to the nature of the offence and that the bank had been provided with forged letters on which an overdraft facility had been obtained that we could mount a prosecution using the bank as a complainant as opposed to the Warners. It was a possibility, but we really needed the co-operation of Joan and Ted and the only course of action was to wait and see.

As with all crime investigations it takes time to collect the amount of evidence needed. If the defendant pleads guilty then the case does not have to be fully proved but if a not guilty plea is entered and a court appearance transpires then the prosecution has to prove the offence alleged " beyond all reasonable doubt" which includes seeing all the witnesses and taking statements. It is not like you see on the television that the crime, no matter how large it is, is solved within an hour and with two commercial breaks in between!

Fraud offences can be notoriously time consuming and sometimes boring to investigate and fraud investigators need to be a certain type of individual. They need to be very thorough and patient as some investigations can take months or even years to complete but they also need to be seasoned investigators. I was satisfied that I now had enough evidence to confront the Warner's with. I had not seen Barbara Hendry myself but was satisfied that this was the woman involved albeit the photograph was a number of years old. I decided that as soon as I could I would again visit Mr. and Mrs. Warner. After a few days the opportunity arose to visit Mr. and Mrs. Warner. As usual I turned up early evening at their door. Again, I was offered every hospitality. I first asked them how they were and both appeared to be alright. I also asked them if the existing arrangements with Mrs. Hendry were still progressing to which they replied they did not have any concerns whilst at the same time wanted to know what I was again doing at their house.

I informed that that I still had the same concerns about their friend Barbara Hendry and possessed new evidence that would support my view. I realised that this was going nowhere. There was no doubt in my mind that there was no question of either Joan or Ted not knowing Barbara so the question of identity was not an issue. I decided to take the bull by the horns and tell them what I knew. This would resolve the matter..........................or so I thought!

I explained that the woman Morrison had previously come to police notice for fraud and extortion and I had been able to obtain a news cutting of the case together with her photograph. After a sharp intake of breath and quietly confident that I was now in possession of material that would solve the problem, I produced the newspaper cutting and showed it to Mr and Mrs Warner to which Mrs Warner replied, "That's an old photograph."

I was slightly taken aback but before I went any further decided to get confirmation that this was actually the woman we were all talking about.

"Yes," replied Mr Warner "that's Barbara."

I asked, "That is the woman who you have been dealing with then?"

"Yes that's her," replied Mr Warner.

"Well now that you have seen the photo and we are both satisfied it's her, how do you feel?" I asked.

"Barbara told it would come to this," replied Mr Warner. "She said that this would happen, you see it is all because of the Argyll family are trying to discredit her."

I was taken by surprise by the reply "What do you mean?" I asked.

Mr Warner replied, "Barbara told us that the police would come to visit us at some time, and that there would be a possibility the police would rake up bad press against her. You see because she is trying to claim her inheritance she is encountering all sorts of obstacles along the way, and it is because of the Argyll family causing these problems.". I was slightly aghast at what I was hearing and for a change I didn't really know what to say! I was now convinced that there was a deception being carried out. After I had got over the shock I informed Joan and Ted Warner that I was satisfied with the enquiries I had made and that the convictions "Barbara" had were genuine. I was gaining the impression that Both Joan and Ted had been told that if the subject of previous convictions surfaced then it would be a case that Barbara had been subjected to being framed.

I tried again to explain that I was satisfied it was all-wrong and that we had now established that Barbara Hendry had come to the attention of the authorities previously but both Joan and Ted were satisfied with the explanation they had been given was convinced that the financial damage had now been done. We parted amicably as there was not a lot else I could say except asking them both to think about our discussion and contact me with their decision if they wanted to pursue a prosecution. It didn't look hopeful though.

***

A few days later, I was contacted by Ted Warner who stated that at that time they did not want to make a complaint. They had discussed the matter and decided that things were still progressing as planned. Ted stated that he did not want to take the chance of ruining things as they were of the opinion that they would be getting their money back at some time in the future. I asked Ted if either he or Joan had spoken to Barbara Hendry since my last visit. Ted hesitated and said that both he and Joan had spoken to Barbara who was most incensed at the involvement of the police but stated it didn't come as a surprise to her as it would no doubt be "the family" causing problems. She reassured Joan and Ted that things were still in hand and it would all be sorted out and when it has been sorted out she would be "dealing with the police" for interfering in her business (no surprises there!). Upon hearing this, both Joan and Ted told Barbara that the police had their welfare at heart but they would appreciate it if this matter were not pursued. Reluctantly Barbara agreed.

I could not believe what I was hearing, my first thought was "The bloody cheek of it!" Here we have a couple being deceived, parting with large amounts of money to their own detriment and the suspected offender was in effect going to sort me out! Hearing this only made me more determined, the offender whoever she really was had made a big mistake.

It didn't bother me how long it took I would get to the bottom of it sort it out and her as well! Even if I had to do it in my own time!

Chapter Six: Back to the drawing Board

It is not unknown for seasoned fraudsters to take the lead in these types of enquiry as they are by nature, very confident individuals. Normally when conducting an interview with a suspect the interviewer can observe "indicators" given by the suspect as to their truthfulness these are known as "liesigns" and "bysigns" or what is also known as "Body Communication Leakage" (BCL). These signs if given out during an interview are not an exact science and should not be treated as a direct indication that the suspect is being untruthful, if these signs are mainly absent and the individual will attempt to establish some type of rapport with the interviewer combined with a display of a high degree of self-confidence. The same modus operandi will exist between the offender and their victim who will no doubt take to offender into their confidence i.e. the phrase "Confidence Trickster."

Upon being confronted with authority the experienced confidence trickster will attempt to "bluff it out" or alternatively go on the attack. I have encountered situations where the offender about to be arrested has quoted the name of a Senior Officer stating he or she is a close personal friend and they "would be hearing about this!" On one occasion the offender under arrest said, "I am a close personal friend of Detective Chief Superintendent 'so and so' and I can assure you he will be hearing about this! You haven't heard the last of this!" Nevertheless I had total confidence in the enquiries that I had made and was certain that the individual concerned was not who he claimed to be and subsequently arrested him, despite his protestations. His conduct displayed a total air of absolute confidence, which even took me by surprise and for a brief moment began to wonder.

On route to the CID car after making the arrest even my Acting Detective Sergeant whispered in my ear "I hope you have got your facts right here or we are both in the crap." He was obviously seeing his potential CID career disappearing into the ether of civil litigation for a case of unlawful arrest.

The individual concerned later admitted that upon moving into a new area for the purpose of committing deception offences he would scan the local papers to obtain the names of senior police officers he could quote later in the case of encountering the local CID or fraud squad.

The above concept is again demonstrated by personal experience of the following case.

In Oct 1992 whilst working evenings as a duty Detective Sergeant in Lincoln CID, a telephone call was received from the proprietor of a local guesthouse in the city. He rang police to express concerns about a resident that recently booked in for a week's accommodation. The owner stated that the man who had booked in had given the name "Mr Parish" but was overheard during phone calls made from the guesthouse to be using several other names.

During night patrol a visit was made to the guesthouse for the purpose of making further enquiries.

Upon arriving the proprietor gave a description of the resident but went on to say that he had not seen him since lunchtime earlier in the day. Consent was given to have a look in the guest's room by the owner. Upon entry all was in order. In the wardrobe was found a couple of expensive suites hanging up shaving kit and toiletries in the bathroom. Also found under the bed was a combination briefcase which was found to be a "conman's" kit. The case contained three passports in different names, two or three bank books in different names, credit cards, building society passbooks and a number of photo booth passport type photographs. As a result of finding the briefcase I informed the proprietor that I would be taking it to the police station for safe-keeping and when the guest returned that he should contact me on the telephone number provided on my card which I gave to the guest house owner. I also asked him that should the guest return that he should ring me and I would return.

I left the guesthouse around 9pm and awaited a call. I returned to the police station with the briefcase.

I had only been in the CID office for a matter of minutes when the telephone rang. I answered the phone to a man giving his name as Mr Parish.

"Hello, this is Mr Parish, Is that Detective Sergeant Booth?"

I replied "Yes Mr Parish that is I."

Mr Parish enquired in a very polite manner if I was the officer who had taken his briefcase. I replied that I was and had taken it for safekeeping to which he replied, "I bet! You have got no right to enter my room where I am staying without my consent. I will be taking this further I can assure you. I will be making a complaint to your superiors, I am going out now so if you return it to the guesthouse I will collect it later and we will say no more about it!"

I replied, "Oh dear Mr Parish there's no need to take that attitude I was only hanging onto the briefcase for safe keeping you know. You can come in and collect it I will wait for you."

Mr Parish realising that I would not be intimidated by his threats replied, "Oh yes, I bet I can. You got lucky this time!"

I again told Mr Parish that he was more that welcome to attend the police station to collect his briefcase.

Mr Parish replied, "I don't think so on this occasion Mr Booth I bid you farewell."

I signalled my colleague to ring the guesthouse and find out if Mr Parish was still there and the man said, "Don't bother to ring the guesthouse I have already left and I will post you the keys if you can take them back for me please?" and with that the man rang off.

We searched the railway stations bus stations and Taxi ranks without success.

From the items contained within the briefcase it was obvious that Mr Smith was involved in credit card and mortgage fraud in and around Lincoln to the value of £300,000.

A few days later envelope arrived to the CID office posted in the Lake District, within the envelope were a set of keys from the guesthouse with a note from Mr Parish saying, "Mr Booth as promised, hope you are keeping well." Signed Mr

Parish.

During the following months and as a result of my enquiries it became apparent that Mr Parish had been very busy in the area. He had negotiated to purchase a plot of land re-mortgaged it without first completing the purchase and obtained £175,000. He had lined up another two possible mortgage frauds and was near completion but had been interrupted by our visit.

Further enquires revealed that Mr Parish (not his real name) had been frequenting local nightclubs and wine bars where he had been well received. He was described as being extremely smart and presentable and had even been associating with members of the local football team.

Mr Parish had in his short time in Lincoln met several girls and stayed a couple of nights with them wining and dining them along the way. Mr Parish was -described as "strikingly looking and knew how to treat a lady." At this pace I would be struggling to find a female who would be prepared to give any details about him, all of them were concerned about his welfare and all without exception wanted to see him again!

After a couple of weeks I received a post card from Blackpool it read: Mr Booth, hope this postcard finds you in good health! I am keeping OK by the time you receive this I will have moved on! No hard feelings! Mr Parish.

Over the following six months or so I received several postcards from various locations over the UK. All were from Mr Parish but the time I received them he had in fact moved on.

I noted that three of the postcards were from Blackpool and if running true to form there would be a woman involved along the way, wine bars and the like.

I had by this time identified Mr Parish as being an individual who had previously been convicted of offences of deception and had served a prison sentence. I circulated details of him around Blackpool and a week or so later received a telephone call from Blackpool police stating that they had Mr Parish in custody.

Mr Parish was conveyed from Blackpool to Lincoln Police

station for interview.

The following morning I attended the interview room where with a colleague I saw Mr Parish.

I was confronted with a 6'4'' inch male with black well-groomed hair dressed in what appeared to be a very expensive suite, bearing in mind he had spent the night in police cells he looked very fresh and ready for interview.

His first words were "Hello Mr Booth, we meet at last. Did you like the postcards?"

He introduced himself and stated that he did not want the services of a solicitor.

He was interviewed regarding the offences he had committed firstly wanting to know what the evidence was against him.

He said, "Mr Booth if you hadn't gone down to that guest house that night I would have got away and you wouldn't have a clue who had done all this. Like I said you got lucky and my luck ran out!"

He asked if I had returned the guesthouse keys and about the welfare of his girlfriends, "I got a call from a couple of the girls saying that you had been round asking."

I had previously asked two of the girls if they were able to contact Mr "Parish" to which they had replied "No."

Mr Parish after being informed of the in-depth enquiries said, "Well it would appear that you have done your homework."

The interview took 4 hours or so to cover all the issues.

At the end of the interview he said, "I would like to thank you for the most thorough and in-depth criminal interview I have ever had!" and laughed.

He concluded saying that he had committed the offences but that no one had been hurt and the only crime he commits is against credit card companies and building societies "Because it doesn't hurt anyone."

Mr Parish admitted the offences, as he knew that he had been evidentially caught, if the evidence was not there he would not have so easily admitted them.

I found Mr Parish to be very amenable, polite and to possess a good sense of humour he was very intelligent and articulate. During interview he was very relaxed and laid back and could visually be seen assessing his situation. He was however a criminal and no doubt could look after himself if he needed to.

Mr Parish was charged with four offences of mortgage fraud with a view, due to the value of the offences, remanding him in custody. He appeared before the magistrates, represented himself before a female magistrate who subsequently granted him bail and released him. He later that day attended the police station and thanked my colleague and myself for dealing with him. "No hard feelings," he said, "but when I saw it was a lady magistrate I knew I was in luck!"

Two months alter I received a call that Mr Parish had been found dead in a hire car in the midlands. He had connected a pipe to the exhaust and killed himself. He left a letter apologising to his wife and asking to be remembered to his children saying he always loved them. At the end of the letter he added…and please don't forget to tell Detective Sergeant Booth at Lincoln CID that I won't be answering my bail!

Upon being informed of his death I couldn't help but think that the criminal world of the conman would be a sadder place without Mr Parish albeit a criminal in the eyes of the law he was a likeable one, and to some females a very loveable rogue! But in his own mind during his very accomplished and very profitable criminal enterprises he had never hurt anyone furthermore he genuinely believed that in committing frauds against banks and building societies that the banks could afford the loss and if they were so stupid to fall for his frauds and believe his "cons" then any losses were their own fault.

***

For the next few weeks I pondered about my next step in the Warner case. I was satisfied that I had identified the correct woman and was also satisfied now that it was she who had the previous convictions for using the same modus operandi in the past. What I had not expected was, that when I confronted Joan and Ted Warner that Hendry had already anticipated my move. She had realised that at some time in the future even the most dedicated friend would start to have reservations and either they or a relative would call the police. Bearing in mind that she had used the M.O. previously was this the reason for shrouding the story in secrecy and swearing the victims to that secrecy for fear of a compromise in the "legacy's" success? If that was the case then the victims were sworn not to tell relatives what was going on, thereby lessening the chance of the police being informed too early in the offence?

It seemed to be working, had I actually made the mistake of underestimating the opposition? The fact was that this offence could not continue, it had carried on for a number of years and was it now coming to an end? My main concern was for the welfare for Joan and Ted Warner as I knew by now that their financial situation was dire. I could not allow it to continue it was going to have to be brought to an end. But I needed some kind of support. I had to find somebody in the police who would back me up. Being a junior officer I needed the support of a more senior colleague who would evaluate my evidence and give me the support where and when needed and especially if it transpired that I was wrong.

I submitted a report outlining the circumstances to the local Detective Chief Inspector.

From: Detective Constable BOOTH   Market Rasen
To: D.C.I. Lincoln   26th March 1984

Suspected Fraud Enquiry – Mr E.V. and Mrs J. WARNER

On 18th November 1983, a report was received from the Humberside Police. The circumstances that they had received a complaint from Mr Terence George WARNER 54 years of Kingston Upon Hull to the effect that he considered his relations are currently being the victims of an elaborate fraud.

Terence WARNER has two older brothers, Laurence aged 63 years who died in January 1982 leaving a widow Evelyn. (Please see statement attached) and Edward WARNER 62

43

years who lives with his wife at 25 Ryland Road Welton Nr Lincoln.

Some seven or eight years ago Edward and his wife Joan went on holiday to Scotland, whilst there, Mr and Mrs WARNER met a Mrs Barbara HENDRY. They became friends and subsequently spent some holidays with Mrs HENDRY, who at the time was living on the Isle of Jura. Mrs HENDRY claimed to be the main beneficiary to an estate of a James CAMPBELL, a property owner of immense wealth who lived on the continent. Mr CAMPBELL died around 1978 and left such a complicated will and such vast assets that it was taking several years to wind up the estate. Mrs HENDRY alleged that one of the clauses in the will is supposed to have insisted that none of the beneficiaries must borrow money to assist in the winding up of the estate until the final distribution take place.

Mrs. Hendry alleges that her mother, Margaret CAMPBELL allegedly the Duchess of Argyll is a trustee of the estate, but unfortunately, Mrs HENDRY does not get on with her. The feeling was supposed to be mutual and so the Duchess is always delaying things. The clause in the will about borrowing meant that everything had to be done in utmost secrecy and as a result of their assistance and co-operation the WARNERS were supposes to receive £885,000 out of the inheritance due to Mrs HENDRY alleged to be around £11 million pounds.

Mr. Terence WARNER in Hull was concerned regarding the whole circumstances as he considered it suspicious. He confronted his brother Edward at Dunholme about it, they had a disagreement and now do not speak very often. After giving the matter some thought Mr Terence WARNER contacted the police.

In late November 1983, I visited Edward and Joan WARNER at Dunholme regarding the compliant made by his brother in Hull.

He confirmed that both he and his wife had been sending money to a woman in Scotland but who they wouldn't name and have been doing so for a number of years. Although very polite and friendly, Mr and Mrs WARNER would not furnish any details about the woman or about the amounts of money involved.

Despite numerous visits to the home of the WARNERS since November 1983 Mr. and Mrs. WARNER would not provide any details and have not done so to date.

Enquiries were commenced and it was established that Edward Warner had over the years borrowed a large sum of money from relatives and sent it to Scotland to assist in financing Mrs Hendry in her pursuit of her forthcoming inheritance. Mr Warner had borrowed £3,736 from his sister-in-law (wife of the late Laurence Warner) in Hull and from other relatives. This had virtually left Evelyn Warner penniless.

Information was received that Mr and Mrs Edward Warner were still obtaining money from another source, a further visit was made to see them, but they refused to divulge details of where the money was coming from, going to, or about Mrs Hendry and the inheritance.

Further enquiries were made and "Mrs Hendry" was identified as being Barbara Elizabeth Wright BAIN @FERGUSON @ MORRISON @ Countess De LEONE @ Madam FELLONA Born 17.1.30 @ Glasgow. It has been established that BAIN @ HENDRY is an experienced criminal and has served two prison sentences of 3 months and 18 months in Scotland for extortion, theft and several offences of fraud, (news cuttings attached). These offences involved her purporting to be the illegitimate daughter of the Duchess of Argyll.

Over the Christmas period and New Year 1983-4, the Warners were again visited and stated that the money would be coming through "any day now", three months later the money has not materialised.

Around 28th February 1984, Inspectors from the Trustees Savings Bank attended Lincoln Police Station to report a set of circumstances of which the bank were very concerned. It transpired that the manager of the Lincoln branch of the TSB had been granting loans to two of their customers and the bank were concerned that an offence of deception was being practiced. The customers involved were a Mr and Mrs Warner of Dunholme near Lincoln, who had obtained an overdraft facility in excess of thirteen thousand pounds. The reason given for the overdraft was that they wanted the money to help a friend to release sum of money that had been left to her.

The loans by way of overdraft had started in October 1983 and had continued up until January 1984 when the bank manager became suspicious and contacted his seniors at the bank.

Throughout the interviews with Mr and Mrs Warner the manager a Mr Smith has kept a very comprehensive note of the conversations with his clients. Towards the end of the loans in January 1984 Mr Smith the manager requested that Mr and Mrs Warner produce some documentary evidence to support the reasons for the loans. The Warners as a result of his request produced two letters from two different solicitors allegedly connected with the inheritance based in Scotland. Mr Warner stated the letters had been provided to him, by Mrs Hendry. Close examination of the two letters show that they appear to have been typed on the same typewriter.

Mr Smith has provided a witness statement scheduling details of the loans provided.

Through correspondence with the solicitors by the TSB it has been established that the solicitors in question have no knowledge of a Mrs Hendry, in effect the letters produced are in fact forgeries.

Finally I am satisfied that a deception is still in progress against Mr and Mrs Warner by Hendry. The Warners still do not accept that it has been perpetrated in the first instance by her, as they find it extremely hard to believe that anyone could be capable of it, however they agree if it proved to be correct then they would support a complaint. It would appear that as best that can be established at this stage a sum of between twenty and thirty thousand pounds has been given by the Warners to Hendry.

Both Mr. and Mrs. Warner are in their sixties and in full time employment. They live in a rented council house, have no phone and do not possess a car, and they still have a black and white television. The house is clean although sparsely furnished and nearly all of their income goes to pay off debts incurred by this situation. Mr Warner is in poor health and his health has deteriorated since November, he admitted that he and his wife made a tin of corned beef last for three meals.

I feel that they are reluctant to complain (Hendry says that any police involvement could jeopardise the inheritance) I would suggest that proceedings be taken against Hendry @ Bain for the offence of obtaining overdraft facilities by deception, using the TSB as complainants, as I consider that if the situation is allowed to continue, at the end of it Mr and Mrs Warner will be ruined.

At the time of compiling this report the Warner's have been making enquiries with the TSB for a further £400 loan.

I submit this file for further direction and advice.

Detective Constable K Booth

The CID in the nearby City of Lincoln supervised the area of Market Rasen in those days and there were a number of very efficient detective sergeants. Nearly all were of the "old school".

By sheer chance I began to be supervised by another detective sergeant by the name of Norman Norris - a slim very studious officer sporting what could be considered to be a very well-groomed beard. I did not know Norman ever so well but I did know that he had previously served on the fraud squad and was regarded as a very thorough, diligent and knowledgeable officer who when considering matters would evaluate all the options in a slow but methodical process. I appreciated that this offence was not the crown jewels but would ask him to have a look and see what he thought. I did think that he might consider that it was a bit small for him to deal with, but how wrong could I have been.

***

Detective sergeant Norris came to see me on a supervisory visit to Market Rasen, the object of the exercise was to have a day out away from the city and to see what work I had on. I considered this visit as a good opportunity to explain the Duchess saga to him and obtain what I considered to be his valued opinion. I explained to him that I had "got this job on" to which he replied *"Get the kettle on lad, let's have a cup of tea and tell me all about it."* I was quite impressed with his degree of interest and felt reassured that here was the person with the necessary experience to bring this whole situation to a halt.

I really could not wait to see what Norman had to say. I let the tea bags brew and took them out poured the milk in, and dumped the teabags in the sink only to hear from the detective sergeant "I'll have mine strong!" I looked down at the tea, which appeared very weak, and not wanting to upset my advisor took both the teabags out of the sink and placed them in his cup of weak tea. After a minute or so the tea strengthened up and looked a great deal stronger. I was sure that would do.

I returned to the CID office and Norman was sat waiting for his tea he said, "I've heard a bit about this Duchess job, tell me all about it."

I started the story and after a few minutes Norman interrupted and said, "This is a good cup of tea lad!" (I always think of this moment when I see the Yorkshire Tea advert!) I grinned and continued with my story.

At the end of the conversation Norman took away the paperwork and said "I will read all that you have got and will ring you later.

The following day I started work at about half past eight and had just sat down at my desk when the phone rang. It was detective sergeant Norris.

"Is that you Kim he asked?"

"Yes," I replied, "What do you think?"

"Well I think that you have got a deception and it needs stopping, I can see what has been happening and it is obviously her (Hendry) the only thing that we need now is some evidence."

"How do you want to pursue it?" I asked.

"Well, the way I see it Mr and Mrs Warner are not going to complain at this time so we will have to look somewhere else, I noticed that you have considered using the bank as complainants. That's a workable idea but not as good as the Warners making a statement but we can see about that. I suggest that you go and see the bank manager that has dealt with the Warners and get a witness statement from him, and then we can see where we are with that."

"Ok," I replied

"Is there anyone else involved in this?" asked Norman.

"I'm not sure," I said, "I will give you a call when I have seen the bank manager again."

I put the telephone down feeling very reassured that detective sergeant Norris had reviewed my paperwork and agreed with my feelings. I knew that I now had all the support that I needed. As expected Norman had shown interest and discussed it in a very matter of fact manner and pointed me in the right direction all I had to do now was to get on with it and see where it took me. Little did I know how the story would unfold or indeed where it would take me?

Things were beginning to come together. I decided to make an appointment to interview the bank manager involved, in fact I could not see him quick enough and get the enquiry going on a solid footing.

After a phone call in which I very adeptly demonstrated a "sense of urgency", I attended Lincoln police station the following day where I saw the manager of the Lincoln branch of the Trustees Savings Bank Leslie Smith.

Chapter Seven: The story deepens

At this stage in the story it is important for the reader to understand a small part of police procedure involved in the making of statements to be used in a trial. The individual making the statement will have usually "seen" something that is of interest to the investigator or found something of interest such as the murder weapon that has been thrown away. The details of which will be included in the statement provided by the witness. In addition to things "seen" the maker of the statement may wish to include in the statement a document(s) or items of relevance to the investigation. These items being either documents or other things to be included are given what is called an "exhibit number" this number is usually the initials of the person making the statement who "produces the item" as in gives it to the police or person recording the statement. The exhibit number will remain the same number for the duration of the investigation and up to and mostly including any subsequent trial. For example:

Marleen Suzanne Miggins is a store detective. She is on duty one day working in a store when she observes a female Sandra Smith a local drug addict acting suspiciously. She watches her and sees her place a bottle of expensive perfume into the lining of her coat. Marleen Miggins follows Smith to the door of the premises and stops her outside, identifies herself as the store detective, searches Smith and finds the bottle of perfume. The police are called and Smith is arrested.

The store detective Marleen Suzanne Miggins provides a statement to the police. In the statement she refers to finding the perfume inside the lining of Smiths coat. The perfume is given and exhibit number of **MSM1 (Police item MSM 1)** the initials of **M**arleen **S**uzanne **M**iggins. The police officer dealing with the theft of perfume needs to prove that it came from the store where Smith was detained and arrested. The statement will read...... I am the manager of "Betterbuys" and I have been shown by Police Constable Dixon one bottle of perfume **Police item MSM 1** and I can identify it as being property of Betterbuys from the serial number (or batch number as shown on the packaging or the price label whichever is present) and that no-one has any right or authority to remove it from the premises of "Betterbuys" without firstly going through the normal channels of payment.

Cases can have numerous Police exhibits that form part of the case. The current case of R v Hendry for instance has 130 exhibits produced by different witnesses. These exhibits will be shown to different witnesses in the building of the case to either prove or disprove various parts of the case under investigation. Each witness will sign the exhibit label attached to the exhibit during the making of the statement. Some cases will only have one or two exhibits produced by the witnesses. The largest number of exhibits in a case I have personally been involved with was 4.2 million exhibits and 400 or so witnesses.

Mr. Smith had worked for the TSB for over forty-three years and was approaching the end of a very distinguished career at the bank. He was a graying senior type of figure who if he had not been a bank manager one would have probably guessed that was his position. I got the impression that he was expecting to see a more senior rank in the police force rather that a Detective Constable but he did not appear unduly disappointed. He did keep looking at the door expecting to see some sort of senior officer walk in and take charge. It wasn't to be I was it!

I also got the impression that judging by the amount of notes that he had in his hands this was not going to be a quick statement to record but I was ready for it and as it happened so was he and he had quite a story to tell but it was going to take some time.

I decided that I should be committing something to paper before anybody changed their minds.

I said to Mr Smith, "We need to get everything in some sort of chronological order so that I can begin to record your statement what have you got with you?"

Mr Smith explained that he had all his interview notes from seeing his customers Mr and Mrs Warner, together with the notes of conversations he had with other individuals involved.

"Other individuals involved?" I asked.

"Oh yes," he replied. "I have spoken to Mrs Hendry's solicitor Mr Spiers, her doctor, Doctor Turner, and the security guard Mr Wilson."

"What security guard?" I asked.

"The Security Guard that is employed to ensure the security of the painting," he replied.

"What painting?" I asked.

"The Rembrandt of course!" he said in a manner assuming that I knew of the existence of any such painting. "The Rembrandt is part of the inheritance," he replied, "It's being kept safe because of its value. It's in a secure vault in Glasgow but I haven't seen it." I had no doubt in believing what Mr. Smith was saying but I was rather surprised that there appeared to be other people involved. This was the first I had heard of a solicitor, doctor or even a security guard. To my mind the involvement of other individuals led me to two options, these being that the other persons involved were jointly concerned in the offence or the other option, which is very rare, that the other persons had become involved unknowingly. For a fraudster to involve other people unknowingly denotes a high level of determination and experience on behalf of the fraudster. I will just have to wait and see where this takes me.

"So how do you contact these other people?" I asked.

"They have always contacted me, I only have Mr Wilson the security guards telephone number." He consulted his notes and recited a telephone number, which I wrote down.

"It can be difficult contacting him." said Mr. Smith, "As he works shifts."

I was beginning to wonder just what I had become involved in. I decided to record the statement with the thought that if I was wrong and there was a legitimate legacy I would never hear the last of it.

STATEMENT OF WITNESS

Leslie SMITH
Trustees Savings Bank Lincoln

I am employed by the Trustees Savings Bank (England and Wales) in the capacity of Branch Manager. I work at the bank's premises situated at 12 Bank Street Lincoln, and have worked for them for forty-three years. Amongst the regular customers at the bank are a Mr. Edward Warner and his wife Joan. Mr. Warner has a savings account and a cheque account with our branch. Mrs. Warner has her own cheque account.

ON 20th February 1981 I was consulted by Mrs. Warner with regards to her obtaining a personal loan the purpose of which was to repay her daughter.

Mr. Warner had previously informed me that she would be receiving a large legacy amounting to some £885,000 towards the end of February from a Mrs. Hendry in Scotland. I was later informed by Mrs. Warner that this would not be forthcoming in the immediate future because other arrangements had been made. The £500 loan that Mrs. Warner was requesting was refused due to the absence of documentary evidence to support the actual existence of the said legacy. Two similar requests for loans were made by Mrs. Warner during December 1981. These were also refused.

On 4th August 1982 Mr. Edward Warner came to the Trustees Savings Bank alone and requested a personal loan for a holiday and car repairs. Mr. Warner stated that the holiday was to visit a friend, called Mrs. Hendry in Scotland, and that he was expecting to receive a large sum on money in a few weeks time from the same Mrs. Hendry. This loan request was refused.

On 6th August 1982 Mr. and Mrs. Warner both came to the bank to enquire as to why the loans had been refused. They were informed that it was due to the lack of documentary proof in support of the alleged legacy.

On 18th October 1983 Mr. and Mrs. Warner again came to the bank to see myself for a personal loan of £650. I enquired what the loan was for and was told it was to assist their friend Mrs. Hendry who lives in Glasgow to meet final court fees in connection with litigation of an estate valued at £855,000 or more. The Warners went on to say that Mrs. Hendry was in poor health and the large cost of the litigation is such that Mrs. Hendry had been unable to afford the solicitors fees and continue her claim. The Warners informed me that for the past five years they had borrowed money from other sources such as finance companies and had paid it back. This money had gone to Mrs. Hendry to assist her in paying legal fees. It was at this time I requested that since money was to be loaned that some documentary evidence should be furnished such as a court receipt or something like that to support the loan.

On 7th November 1983, Mr. Warner came to the bank and produced some form of legal bill. He handed it to me to retain on his file. I produce this letter to Detective Constable Booth of the Lincolnshire Police (Police Item LAS1) I saw that the receipt was for £775.05. Mr. Warner informed me that the sum of approximately £125 had been met by the Warner's and Mrs. Hendry. At the same time I was informed by Mr. Warner of a compensation claim that an injunction had been taken out to prevent the release of the inheritance until a debt of £500 had been paid.

Mr. Warner handed me a solicitor's letter stating that the payment of £500 should be paid in order to that no further delay of the payment would be incurred. Since Mr. and Mrs. Warner had complied with my request I agreed to facilitate the loan for £500 as requested. I now produce this letter (Police Item LAS 2) I also produce TSB cheque No 000171 for £500 dated 5th November 1983 drawn by E V Warner on his account LAS 3)

On 18th November 1983 Mr. Warner came to the bank and showed me a letter that purported to have come from the Sheriff's office Buchannan Street Glasgow that indicated that payment of £500 was required this being the confirmation of the request of 7th November 1983. Mr. Warner had not *received a receipt from Mrs. Hendry at this time. At the same time Mr. Warner produced a solicitor's letter showing that a writ would be served further delaying payment unless £483 was paid to a Trustee prior to his discharge as a Trustee to the estate. Mr. Warner requested an advance to cover this amount and it was granted. I now produce TSB withdrawal slip for £500 signed by E V Warner (Police item LAS 4)*

On 2nd December 1983, Mr. Warner came to the bank and showed me a letter, a small portion of which I was allowed to photocopy. He told me that it was part of a letter from Judge Morrison to Mrs. Hendry's solicitor. Judge Morrison was supposed to be an uncle of Mrs. Hendry's who was advising her indirectly regarding her divorce, but it had been discovered that the decree absolute had never been obtained. (Police item LAS5)

Solicitors had advised Mrs. Hendry that decree absolute ought to be obtained to prevent any future claim by her ex-husband.

The sum of £850 was advanced to Mr. Warner, £775 being the amount required and £75 personal expenses to enable him to travel to Glasgow. I now produce withdrawal lip for £850.00 signed E V Warner (Police item LAS6)

On 6th December 1983 Mr. Warner telephoned me at the bank. He told me he had received tragic news from Glasgow to the effect that on the night of 2nd December 1983 the Lawyer who received the letter containing the £775 had had a heart attack whilst driving to see Mrs. Hendry at her home. He was taken to hospital and died during the night. The private court hearing scheduled for the Saturday morning was cancelled and a further hearing was arranged for the following Monday. At this hearing an adjournment was arranged and Mrs. Hendry would have to appoint another solicitor to represent her. Mr. Warner informed me that this would involve extra court fees amounting to £550. I made this amount available to him. I produce withdrawal slip dated 6th December 1983 signed E V Warner (Police Item LAS7)

On 9th December 1983 Mr. Warner called to see me at the bank and informed me that the decree absolute hearing had *taken place on Tuesday 6th December 1983 and this had been granted, However the Judge indicated that after a study of the papers he felt that some token provision ought to be made to Mrs. Hendry's 15 year old daughter who lives with her father. The Judge set this amount at £2000 and ordered that the money be paid into the Court. I was given to understand that Mrs. Hendry had managed to accumulate £1400 but was still £600 short of the required amount. At Mr. Warner's request I agreed to make this £600 available for collection by Mrs. Hendry from the Springburn Branch of TSB in Glasgow Scotland. It was arranged with the manager of that branch that Mrs. Hendry should be allowed to collect this amount at 16.15 hours the same day. I produce TSB cheque No 463094 drawn on TSB Lincoln (Police Item LAS8) and withdrawal slip for £600 signed by myself (Police Item LAS 9) the money was made available by the cheque being posted to Scotland and the money paid out by the Scotland Branch which was re-imbursed by cheque the day after the money had been collected.*

On 13th December 1983 Mr. Warner came into the bank and informed me that the hearing had been arranged for Saturday 9th December but the Judge in Chambers did not attend, he had been traced to Aviemore and he finally agreed to hold a meeting on Monday 11th December 193. The £2000 was paid into Court, but the Judge declined to complete the formalities until the cost of the court fees, £512 was paid. Mr. Warner informed me Mrs. Hendry had obtained this cost in writing and was sending a letter down to him.

On 13th December 1983 the £512 plus £50 expenses was made available to Mr. Warner, which was again sent by arrangement to the Springburn branch of the TSB in Glasgow. I now produce TSB withdrawal slip dated 13/12/83 signed E Warner for £562.00 (Police Item LAS10) and TSB cheque No463114 for £562.00 that was sent to TSB Springburn Glasgow (Police Item LAS 11)

On 15th December 1983 Mr. Warner came to the bank and saw myself. He informed me of a sitting of the Court had been arranged for 10am Friday 16th December, and that a senior

Judge of the court had declared that there would be no further delays and no further court fees would be required from Mrs. Hendry. Mr. Warner went on to say that unknown to Mrs. Hendry who had been staying in a flat with her daughter for the past 15 weeks that the flat belongs to her mother (the Duchess) who is now demanding a rent of £60 per week by 12 noon today otherwise and injunction will be filed. Mr. Warner informed me that Mrs. Hendry had been able to raise £340 and he requested to be allowed a facility of £560. I agreed and arranged for it to be collected at the Springburn branch in Glasgow. Ted 15th December 1983. I produce TSB withdrawal Slip for £560.00 (Police Item LAS12) and corresponding TSB cheque for £560.00 dated 15th December 1983 (Police Item LAS13)

On 21st December 1983 Mr. Warner came to see me at the bank. He told me that he had a "phone call" arranged at 11am that day to Mrs. Hendry. I suggested that this call should be made from my office and Mr. Warner used the phone and dialled a number. He spoke to the person at the other end for a few minutes then he handed the phone to me. I said "Good morning Mrs. Hendry" and introduced myself,

The woman at the end of the phone who I took to be Mrs. Hendry replied, "Everything is now finalised regarding the divorce and all the papers have now been accepted by the court." Mrs. Hendry went on to say that the release of the money was "under the Trustees signature" of her mother who is against the transfer of the money to Mr. and Mrs. Warner, however a board is to meet tomorrow (Thursday 22nd December 1983) to "set aside" Mrs. Hendry as Trustee due to her mis-management of her Trusteeship.

Mrs. Hendry said it was expected that this hearing, again in private sitting in Glasgow would enable money to be finally transferred to Mr. and Mrs. Warner. She told me that cost was again involved and that the total amount was £1680, she had been able to obtain £1050 but was £630 short of the amount needed. I said that I would discuss the matter with Mr. Warner.

I handed the phone back to Mr. Warner who finished the

call. I then discussed making the amount available to Mr. Warner and pointed out to him that the total amount being advance was becoming very large.

Mr. Warner said that he wanted the money making available which I arranged.

The £630 was again collected from T.S.B Springburn Glasgow on 22nd December 1983. I produce TSB withdrawal slip dated 22/1/2/83 for the amount of £1630.00 signed E V Warner (Police Item LAS14) and corresponding TSB cheque No 463173 dated 12/12/83 (Police Item LAS 15) The £630.00 was collected from TSB Springburn Glasgow on 22nd December 1983.

Shortly after Mr. Warner came to see me at the bank. He informed me that Mrs. Hendry in her distressed state and obviously very ill had misunderstood the total cost of the legal fees and required another £260. Mr. Warner authorised me to forward this amount from his salary and requested that the money be sent to Dennistoun branch of the T.S.B. Duke Street Glasgow. I contacted the manager of the branch and made arrangements for the amount to be collected. The settlement cheque was forwarded to T.S.B. Dennistoun at midday the same day. I now produce TSB withdrawal slip dated 22nd December 1983 signed by myself on behalf of Mrs. Warner (Police Item LAS16) and corresponding TSB cheque No 463179 for £260.00 dated 22/12/83 (Police Item LAS17)

On 23rd December 1983 Mrs. Hendry telephoned me at the bank. She told me that the hearing had gone in her favour and that she now had to go to Edinburgh for the final release of the money. She further stated that £775,000 would be forwarded to the bank on 28th December 1983 this would be followed by a further £5,075,368 and later by £3,500. She said that there was a final account to settle for four solicitors of £485.00. After consultation with Mr. Warner I made this amount available to Mrs. Hendry at T.S.B. Springburn. I telephoned the branch and asked them to make the cash available to Mrs. Hendry at 1.30pm. I produce TSB withdrawal slip dated 23/12/83 for 485.00 signed by J Warner (Police Item LAS 18) and corresponding TSB cheque No 463190 for £485.00 dated

23/12/83 (Police Item LAS 19).

At 6pm on 24th December 1983, Mr. Warner telephoned me at my home. He said that he and his wife had been in contact with Mrs. Hendry and had been informed of the most distressing sequence of events. Mrs. Hendry had gone form Edinburgh to Glasgow to see the four Solicitors and to obtain certain documents from each of them. The first two had been cooperative, the third was a bit off hand and reluctant but eventually completed his part. The fourth and the most senior Solicitor left the office whilst she was still on the premises and knowing that she was there. He did not return so Mrs. Hendry went to his home. He had not arrived there at 4pm when she arrived so she waited for him.

Mrs. Hendry said that he did not arrive until 11pm then refused to do anything to assist and said he would only transact business at his office on Wednesday 28th December. Mr Warner said that Mrs. Hendry had told him that the Solicitor had "Showed her the door" without even offering her a drink of tea, into the pouring rain knowing that she had neither money nor transport. She set off walking to the hospital 14 miles away where she was having medical treatment, and after finally getting a lift arrived there at 3am.

She was totally exhausted and spent most of Saturday and Christmas day recovering. The same fourth Solicitor claimed that his fees as the senior were greater than the amount of the other three. She had taken £120 to him at his home, which he kept. He claimed a further £531 being the amount due to him. Mr Warner then told me that Mrs. Hendry had said that she had consulted a "gentleman of law" on the Island of Lewis and informed him of the situation.

On Tuesday 27th December 1983 I was in Dunholme with my wife visiting relatives when I saw Mr Warner walking along the road. I stopped and talked to him in the car and we went back to his house where we had a cup of tea. We talked about Mrs. Hendry and the situation from 11.30 am until 2.15pm.

At 1pm the same day and during our conversation I drove Mr. Warner to the telephone box in Welton and awaited a call from Mrs. Hendry. The phone rang and Mr Warner answered it and spoke for a while. He then passed the phone to me and I spoke to Mrs. Hendry. She told me that she had had treatment at the hospital, which was having an effect on her. She also said she was in pain but despite this Mrs. Hendry mentioned to me that £531 was due to be paid to the fourth solicitor and she required the money. I told her I would discuss this with Mr. and Mrs. Warner. Mrs. Hendry said she would telephone Mr. and Mrs. Warner at the telephone box at 10.30pm. My wife and I then left the Warner's house an hour or later and went home.

At 10.40 pm the same day Mr. Warner rang me at home and asked me to make available £600 to Mrs. Hendry at Trustees Savings Bank Dennistoun which I arranged the next morning. I produce TSB withdrawal slip for £600.00 dated 28/12/83 (Police Item LAS20) and TSB cheque No 463193 for £600.00. (Police Item LAS21) the £600 was subsequently collected from the Dennistoun branch of the TSB Duke Street Glasgow.

The following day I received a telephone call from Mrs. Warner at 10.30 am to inform me that she had received a telephone call from Mrs. Hendry to say she was on her way to the Trustees Savings Bank Duke Street Glasgow to collect the money with a man called Mr. Legget who was another solicitor.

On Wednesday 29th December 1983 I was still on holiday at home and at about 11 am the telephone rang. I answered the phone to find that it was Mrs. Warner who told me that Mr. Legget, the London representative of the Board of Trustees had obtained the discharge of the fourth solicitor and was on his way back to London. It was understood the first cheque would be forwarded straight to the bank immediately he had delivered these documents. Mrs. Warner said it appeared that Mrs. Hendry in her confused state due to the treatment and the drugs had misunderstood the amount required and a further £400 was needed plus £50 to cover rail or air flight to Lincoln. I made arrangements for this to be made available and the money was collected from the Trustees Savings Bank at Dennistoun Glasgow. I produce TSB withdrawal slip dated

29/12/83 for £450 signed J Warner (Police Item LAS22) and one TSB cheque No 463204 for £450.00 dated 29/12/83 (Police Item LAS23) The money was again collected from TSB Dennistoun branch Glasgow.

During the following few days I received telephone calls from the Warner's to the effect that all was proceeding normally towards the release of the money and that arrangements were in hand for a solicitor to ring me at the bank.

At 4.15pm on Monday 9th January 1984 I received a telephone call from a man called Mr. Spiers who introduced himself as a solicitor and one of the four Trustees appointed in connection with Mrs. Hendry's inheritance. He told me that he was flying to Zurich on Wednesday 11th January and would be returning on 16th January. His visit was for the purpose of attending the Kantonal Bank to obtain final details of their costs and the release of the funds held by them. He informed me that the amount to be sent direct to Mr. and Mrs. Warner was £775,000 and that details of other remittances would be made known to me upon his return from Zurich.

On 11th January 1984 Mrs. Warner contacted me and informed me that there had been a terrible misunderstanding between Mrs. Hendry and her mother and that Mrs. Hendry had been charged with theft and fined £350. Also there was a debt of £450, this resulted in Mrs. Warner wanting £850 to be made available to her. This I did and the money was paid through the Springburn Branch of the Trustees Savings Bank. I now produce TSB withdrawal slip dated 12/01/84 for £850.00 (Police Item LAS24) and one TSB cheque No 463305 dated 12/01/84 for £850.00 (Police Item LAS25)

At 3pm the same day I took a call from the solicitor Mr. Spiers. Mr. Spiers said that he was in Zurich. His words were "Mr. Smith upon my arrival here in Zurich this morning I made it my first priority to ensure that I should be able to bring the money back with me. You have my categorical assurance the cheque will be in your hands Thursday 19th January. I will be sending it direct to you and not Mrs. Warner. I will complete any further business with Mrs. Warner when I come to Lincoln to see her."

At about 10pm on 12th January 1984 I was at home when I received a telephone call from Mr. Warner. He said that both he and his wife had been speaking on the telephone to a Doctor Turner. This was a lady doctor who had attempting to obtain ambulance transport through the National Health Service, but this was not available until the following week. However, a private ambulance with an attendant nurse could bring Mrs. Hendry to Lincoln the following day. The cost would be £250 to £300. Mr. Warner requested that I make this amount available, which I did on 13th January 1984. I now produce TSB withdrawal slip dated 13/01/84 for £300.00 (Police item LAS26) and one TSB cheque for £300.00 No463318 dated 13/01/84 (Police Item LAS 27)

Due to the weather over the weekend of 14th/15th January 1984 the ambulance failed to arrive due to heavy snow. Attempts were made to obtain a flight but the first on that could be arranged was on Monday 16th January 1984. I arranged to drive up to Humberside Airport to meet Mrs. Hendry and bring her to the Warner's home at Dunholme. The plane was delayed and did not arrive until 2.15pm. When the plane did arrive I waited with Mrs. Warner and met Mrs. Hendry in the reception lounge. Mrs. Warner introduced me to Mrs. Hendry and I drove them both to Dunholme near Lincoln. On the way Mrs. Hendry produced a letter saying that she had not had time to open it. She opened the letter in our presence during the journey and read it to Mrs. Warner. I dropped them both off at Dunholme and returned to the bank.

At 3.15 the same day I was at the bank when I received a telephone call from Mr. Spiers who said that he was still in Zurich and that he had been attempting to contact Mrs. Hendry by phone the previous night but had lost the connection before he was able to tell her that she must be in the Probate Court, High Street Edinburgh on Thursday 19th January 1984 to sign final papers. He asked me to inform her and find out whether this was possible. I telephoned Mr. Warner at his office and told him. I also mentioned to Mr. Warner about the two letters Mrs. Henry had brought down with her and that I would like to take a photocopy of each of them.

The following day, 17th January Mr. Warner came to the bank and brought the two letters from Mrs. Hendry.

The first letter I saw was on the headed notepaper of a firm of Solicitors called Ross Harper and Murphy Solicitors and Notaries of 232 St Vincent Street Glasgow. The letter read;

ROSS HARPER & MURPHY
Solicitors and Notaries
232 St Vincent Street
Glasgow G2 5RH

Kantonal Bank Head Office Zurich Ref/5639/26 15/1/1984

Dear Mrs. Hendry,
The Kantonal Bank has been in touch with us today also Mr Spiers, you will have to attend the Probate Court on 19th January to finalise and sign all papers transferring the money into the names of Joan and Edward Warner Dunholme Lincoln also Mr. Spiers has an appointment and a promise to see Mr. Smith of the Trustee Savings Bank in Lincoln, and he wishes to settle financial side, in the interests of the Warner family and the above gentleman to be settled no later than the 20th completed as proposed by your own requests.

Mr. Spiers will be in possession of the cheque on 17th, your birthday which has to be handed over on that date, only the Kantonal Bank knows the reason for that! The cheque is for the full amount of £9,858,005p (Nine million eight hundred and fifty eight thousand and five pence. Also you have the interest of the shares to be added on. Mr. Spiers will attend to all transactions with Mr. Smith, as I do not want to know if you broke the will or not, as I feel you have gone through enough of late. I would say a certain party has cost you your life and health, but in the end God pays them back, but knowing you, you would not wish that on anyone, but I'm afraid we are not all built with that very humane kindness to one's fellow man that you have, and the few trusted people in

63

this office will not forget you and Mr McGrouther for the agony you went through.

Enclosed is a letter from Mr Mellick nasty to say the least!

We all wish you free from pain and peace and laughter with your kind and trusted friends in Lincoln, it was one of life's pleasures meeting you.

Yours very Sincerely
Signed (unreadable)

The second letter provide by Mr Warner was from a firm of solicitors in Glasgow called Joseph Mellick. The letter read.

JOSEPH MELLICK   160 HOPE STREET

  Solicitors   Glasgow

and Notaries Public   G2 2TL

Dear Madam,

Your presence is required at the Probate Court on 19th Jan, as we expect Mr Spiers to be back in the UK on Tuesday or Wednesday morning with the cheque from the will the full amount apparently. It has just been brought to my attention that we are not handling the financial side of the money or any investments on your behalf, this I have learned today from Zurich and you are now dealing with an English Bank also you have the full approval of Mr Spiers and the Kantonal Bank which is not to my approval so therefore I feel it is my duty to notify the Probate Court of you and Mr McGrouther breaking the terms of the late James Campbell's will, in the circumstances put before me, as I personally was out £1050 for court expenses in cash so it was not traceable and I also in receipt of it in your handwriting. If I am not in possession of my money by Wednesday first at 6pm when I call at your house at that time (in cash) I shall speak up at court on Thursday when everything is recorded this I feel is my right as I have lost a very wealthy client, and you will receive not a penny. I'm giving you that amount of time only because of your terminating illness and also the fact that Mr. Spiers is the Senior Partner.

I shall return your receipt when and if you have the cash. I want it paid before the finalizing takes place and you are in funds, also the interest as agreed of 5%

Signed

Joseph MELLICK

I made copies of the letters and gave them back to Mr Warner. I now produce the two letters (Police item LAS 28)

Mr Warner informed that he and his wife had discussed the contents of the second letter fully and they felt that this amount must be met, but when this is all completed they will have to take advice as to whether the contents of the letter are in any way actionable.

Mr Warner asked me if I would agree to advance the amount mentioned in the letter of £1102.50 a return air flight of £108.00 and incidental expenses of £39.50. I agreed to do this and he took the whole amount £1250.00 in cash. I produce TSB withdrawal slip for the amount of £1250.00 dated 17/01/84 (Police Item LAS 29)

Mr Spiers contacted me and said that he would be collecting the cheque later that day and it would be drawn on a London bank. He also confirmed that he would be travelling down with Mrs. Hendry.

On 18th January, Mr Spiers telephoned me and told me he was back in Scotland and confirmed all was going well and that he was going to finalise details at the Probate Court in Edinburgh that day.

At 3.30pm the same day he phoned me again and said that as a result of his visit to the Probate Court he had been misled regarding the fees for the Probate Court final appearance as he had been given to understand that these would be deferred until after the money had been released but had now been informed they were due at the hearing itself, the amount being £1500.00.

I contacted Mr Warner and told him about the fees and he again requested that I make the funds available, which I did. I produce TSB withdrawal slip dated 19/01/84 for £1500.00 (Police Item LAS30) and one TSB cheque No 463359 dated 19/01/84 for the amount of £1500.00. (Police Item LAS31)

The £1500.00 was collect from Trustees Savings Bank Springburn Branch Glasgow.

At 5.10 pm the same day Mrs Hendry telephoned me to say she had just come out of the probate Court and all was in order. She and Mr Spiers would be flying down at 9.30 am 20th January.

At 7.30 on the morning of 20th January Mr Warner telephoned me at home. He said that he had been advised that there had been a last minute hitch after leaving the Probate Court. Mr Spiers had visited an Accountant for the final release as Mrs Hendry did not have any funds of her own, the money being all tied up in the inheritance to be passed to the Warner's. Mr Spiers felt that he was justified in asking for settlement for his accountant. Mr Spiers said that he had offered to pay the Accountant on behalf of Mrs Hendry but the accountant had refused insisting that he be paid by Mrs Hendry personally.

Upon my arrival at work I telephoned Mrs Hendry. She appeared very distressed at the situation. Whilst speaking to her I could hear over the telephone the sound of a doorbell. Mrs Hendry went to answer the door and I heard her say "Good morning Doctor, Oh! and Mr Spiers too!"

Mr Spiers came onto the phone and told me of the Doctors concern for the health of Mrs Hendry. He said that he was furious at the attitude of the Accountant and tried to reason with him and also to go above his head, but with no success. He felt that again, payment should be made and the matter taken up at a later date. He said he was not going to let the matter rest there. I told him that I had Mr Warner's authority to forward the money. The money in total £600 was sent to the Springburn Branch of the Trustees Savings Bank.

I now produce TSB withdrawal slip dated 20/01/84 for £600.00.

(Police Item LAS32) and TSB cheque No 503461 for the amount of £600.00 (Police Item LAS33)

At 10.15 the same day I received two phone calls within the space of a few minutes from Doctor Turner. The first was to advise me of Mrs Hendry's condition health wise saying that she was seriously ill and had cancer of the pancreas. On the second occasion she rang back to say that Mrs Hendry should be allowed to travel the journey but it would have to be made by car as Mrs Hendry had suffered a hemorrhage on the flight back from Humberside Airport.

At about 10.30 the same day Mrs Hendry rang and said she had got the Doctor's permission to go to Edinburgh and was being taken there by her son.

I received a further telephone call from Mrs Hendry at 4.50 pm to say that all had been completed satisfactorily and they were on their way back to Glasgow and the amount involved was 11 million pounds and not 9 million.

On Saturday 21st January 198 I received a phone call at home from Mrs Hendry to say that they were about to leave for Edinburgh. There they would pick up a security escort to travel with them, to be responsible for a box containing jewellery, the cheque and numerous documents together with a Rembrandt painting that formed part of the Estate of the late James Campbell and which Mr and Mrs Warner had seen hanging in the bungalow at Mrs Hendry's house on the Isle of Jura. During the telephone conversation Mrs Hendry put the Solicitor Mr Spiers on the phone. I suggested to him that due to the weather conditions, he should travel by the A1 road all the way and that when he was in the Leeds / York area he should phone me and I would drive out to Markham Moor to guide him the rest of the way to Lincoln. I heard no further news until 7.40 pm when I received a phone call from Mr Spiers at my home to say that they had skidded, on a Little Chef car park near Newcastle. His Jaguar car had been damaged and had suffered an oil leak. He said he was getting another car in order to complete their journey. Mr Spiers said that he would telephone me an about one and a half hour's time.

No further calls were received that day.

At 11.50 am on Sunday 22nd January 1984, I was at home when I received a telephone call from Mr Spiers who said that when they had resumed their journey Mrs Hendry had developed a haemorrhage had he had rushed her into a nursing home in Newcastle. Mr Spiers said that he was phoning from Portsmouth where he had been ordered to go by Mrs Hendry to complete some business and had travelled there by leased helicopter.

At 5pm the same day Mr Spiers telephoned again and said he would be returning to Portsmouth very early Monday morning by the same method, having obtained signatures from Mrs Hendry to finalise the business transactions on which he had been sent. He would then go back to Newcastle, pick up Mrs Hendry and travel down by car to Lincoln. I believe it was the same day, that I had the telephone call from Mrs Hendry at the Nursing Home during which she said that Mr Spiers could be contacted at a Fareham telephone number at 6pm. I telephoned this number at 6pm and a man answered. I asked for Mr Spiers he went away and almost immediately Mr Spiers came onto the phone. He told me that expenses had been incurred at the nursing home. The surgeon had accepted Mrs Hendry on a private basis and payment was required prior to her discharge. He asked me to consult with Mr and Mrs Warner to see if £820 could be made available at Fareham Trustees Savings Bank, Portland Chambers Fareham. He wished the money to be collected by his nominee, a "Mrs Kearney". He described her as the lady who had been looking after Mrs Hendry in Glasgow until recently.

On Monday 23rd January 1984, I contacted Mr Warner who agreed that payment should be made. I telephoned the Fareham branch of the T.S.B. and spoke to the manager who agreed to make the advance available. I now produce TSB withdrawal slip for the amount of £820.00 (Police Item LAS34) and TSB cheque No 503465 for the amount of £820.00 (Police Item LAS 35)

At 10.45 the same day Mrs Kearney telephoned me at the bank for the instructions for collecting the money. I informed her means by which the money could be collected and informed her that the amount to be collected was £820. She expressed surprise and said that she had understood the amount to be collected was £2000.

At 11am that day I received confirmation from Fareham Trustees Savings Bank that Mrs Kearney had collected the money.

On Tuesday 24th January 1984, I received a number of calls from both Mrs Hendry and Mrs Warner expressing their distress at Mr Spiers for not having returned to Newcastle.

At 9.45 pm that day I received a telephone call from Mr Spiers, who told me that he had spent the night in a bus station but that Mrs Kearney had collected him and allowed him to clean himself up. He had been unable to return to Newcastle due to lack of funds to pay the helicopter pilot. He said that if £500 could be made available at Fareham Trustees Savings Bank he could guarantee that he would be then able to collect Mrs Hendry from Newcastle.

At 9.15 the following day Mrs Hendry telephoned me and sounded distressed but a little clearer. It was evident that Mr Spiers had telephoned her about the helicopter. Mrs Hendry said that Mrs Kearney had arrived at the phone box to take Mr Spiers for a meal and to tidy up as Mr Spiers was going to try and hitchhike a lift to Newcastle. She also said she was going to sign herself out of the nursing home and get down somehow.

At 9.30 am I telephoned the number that Mr Spiers had given me and found it to be engaged? At 9.33 I tried again. The telephone at the other end rang but no one answered it, at 9.42 the same happened again.

At 9.45 I telephoned Mr Warner and informed him of what had happened and as I was doing this a telephone call from Mr Spiers came in. I took the call and he said that he had been taken to the house of a friend of Mrs Kearney's but would not give the number and said he would ring me again if I wished. Mr Spiers requested that £500 be made available at Fareham and that he could guarantee that the amount would be sufficient to get him back to Newcastle and Mrs Hendry and himself to either Humberside Airport or Wickenby airfield today.

I telephoned Mr Warner who appeared very worried by it all but he agreed that we should do this last thing. At 10.10 hrs the same day I again telephoned the Fareham Branch of the Trustees Savings Bank and requested that the £500 be made available. Sat 10.20 hrs the same day Mr Spiers telephoned me and I advised him that the money would be available to Mrs Kearney for her to collect. Mr Spiers said that he had taken a chance and already asked for a helicopter to be alerted. He categorically assured me that he would keep in touch every step of the way.

The £500 was collected from Fareham T.S.B. I now produce one TSB withdrawal slip dated 24/01/84 for the amount of £500.00 (Police Item LAS 36) and one TSB cheque No503471 dated 24/01/84 for the amount off £500.00 (Police item LAS 37)

At 10.25 the same day Mrs Hendry phoned to say that she had tried to telephone Mr Warner to tell him she was alright but he was not in the office and that would I please let him know. I told her to keep her chin up, everything was alright and we should have her at Dunholme today.

At 2pm Mr Spiers telephoned reception at the bank to say that he was just leaving Southampton.

At 11.40 pm later that day I was at home when I received a telephone call from Mr Spiers, he said that he would be coming down by helicopter on Wednesday with Mrs Hendry and that the details were being worked out and he was trying to arrange it for Wickenby. If that was not possible it would be Humberside Airport. Mr Spiers apologised for not ringing earlier but said he was very tired and had to get some sleep.

At 9am on 25th January 1984 Mr Warner telephoned me saying he was delighted with the news and that I was to inform him as soon as I know the time of the flight in order that he can alert Mrs Warner and doctor Bell (The Warner's local doctor). At 9.25 am I telephoned Wickenby Airfield to enquire as to the state of the roads but there was no reply.

At 11.00am the same day I received a telephone call from a man called Mr Wilson speaking on behalf of Mrs Hendry about arrangements regarding transportation of the cheque. He stated that he was a self-employed security officer and that Mrs Hendry had been flown back to Glasgow for an emergency operation, it was understood for the removal of a blood clot from the area of her spine. She sent a message to Mrs Warner saying that she would ring her as soon as she was out of anesthetic. Mr Wilson asked if I would say where the items held by the security firm would be lodged and that it could be a bank of my choice with safety box facilities and the keys would be forwarded for me to hold.

Later that day I received a telephone call from Mrs Hendry to say that she was just out of anesthetic and despite this she seemed quite lucid and confirmed that she wished items to be lodged at a Glasgow bank of my choice. She said that under no circumstances no one was allowed to open the security box, but I would be given authority to open it to remove whatever was necessary to complete my business transactions.

Shortly after receiving this telephone call I telephoned Mr. Warner at his work but he was unavailable. He telephoned me back and I informed him of the situation. He told me to do whatever was necessary. I telephoned the Trustees Savings Bank in Glasgow and spoke to the assistant manager and asked him about safe box facilities could be made available. He confirmed that they would be and I informed him I would contact him again when more details were known. I was under the impression that at last, things appeared to be moving on.

Mr Warner telephoned to say he had received a call from Mrs Hendry to say that she was signing out of the Nursing Home and returning to her flat as she felt that she could deal with her affairs more efficiently from there.

At 12.35 the same day, I was at the bank I received a call from Mrs Hendry. She told me she was back at her flat. She said she was most distressed, as Mr Spiers had resigned because Mr Warner had said to her Mr Spiers had let her down. She appeared to be tearful and incoherent stating she would ring back at 2.30 pm.

At 1.45 pm, Mr Warner called at the bank, he told me that he feels we should take the bull by the horns and go up to Glasgow and bring Mrs. Hendry to Lincoln if possible. Mr Warner said that he would return to the bank at 2.15 pm when Mrs Hendry telephones.

Mr Warner denied making any remark to Mrs Hendry about Mr Spiers.

I attempted to ring Mr Spiers at his office but he was not there. Since Mrs Hendry did not telephone as arranged I rang her at her flat. She answered the telephone but stated that she was in pain and still suffering from the effects of drugs and the anesthetic. It was difficult to maintain a conversation with her, as she kept moving off the subject being discussed. Later in the day Mrs Warner telephoned to say that she had just had a conversation with Mrs Hendry, things were not much clearer although she got the impression that Mrs Hendry was arranging to transfer funds by another method. They were to try and ring her later in the evening.

At 10.10 am on 26th January 1984 Mrs Hendry telephoned, she said that she felt much better (she seemed more lucid and clear thinking) She said that she had asked Mr Spiers to phone and make arrangements for the cheque to be delivered to me and that Mr Spiers and myself were to be given full authority for the arrangements.

At 10.20 am I telephoned Mrs Warner at the call box and informed her of my conversation. She told me she would ring back which she did at 10.45, when she had spoken to Mrs Hendry and that Mrs Hendry said Mr Spiers would be phoning me during the day and he would have the authority to arrange the transfer of the funds to me.

At 1200 hrs Mrs Warner telephoned me at the bank to say that she had spoken to Mrs Hendry again and also to Doctor Turner who was responsible for the medical supervision. The doctor had confirmed that Mrs Hendry was a very sick lady. Doctor Turner had said that she was starting a holiday the following week and was going to look after Mrs Hendry on a private basis. Mrs Warner had asked Doctor Turner to leave a letter for Mr Spiers asking him to telephone me. At 2.45pm the same day Mr Warner rang to say that he had spoken to Mrs Hendry, she asked him to let me know it could be anytime up to 9pm before Mr Spiers would be able to telephone me.

At 8.08pm that evening whilst at home I received a telephone call from the Solicitor Mr Spiers the telephone sequence went as follows:

Call No 1 "Mr Smith, this is Mr Spiers" click click line lost.

Call No 2 "This is Mr Spiers, I'm back on the job again Mr Smith. This is a very bad line, I shall have to ring you in the morning."

I said, "Mr Spiers we must talk now, this is getting a desperate situation from the Warners point of view."

Spies, "I know it is a desperate situation, it was not helped when a certain person said I could have finished the job when I had wanted. Another thing is that Mrs Hendry's mother has been interfering." click click line lost.

Call No 3 Telephone rang I lifted the receiver there was no answer but a click click line lost.

At 8.35 pm I received another telephone call at my home address from Mr Spiers who said, "Mr Smith, I am very sorry it was a very bad line and I have come to another phone to talk to you."

I said, "Mr Spiers, You and I have co-operated in Mrs Hendry's and the Warners interests. Are you now in a position to honour your obligations to me?"

Spiers, "Yes, Mr Smith, this is what I am ringing about." (At this point there was the sound of a door opening and footsteps approaching)"Mr Smith, someone has come in, and as I cannot talk to you confidentially in front of them I will phone back in ten minutes."

At 8.40 pm the same evening the telephone rang again and I answered it, it was Mr Spiers who commenced trying to justify what he had done and complaining that it was not right he should be criticised for carrying out his client's wishes. I told him that this was not the time for recriminations but that it was time he and I were allowed to do our work professionally. I told him I was prepared to meet him anywhere in an attempt to resolve this matter. I asked if he had to see Mr and Mrs Warner and he said that he had, as he required signatures from them.

I then told Mr Spiers that Mr and Mrs Warner extended the hospitality of their home to him at any time and that they would be only too happy to have him stay for a few days. He said that the offer had already been made and that he had already thanked them for their kindness. I said that I would meet the Glasgow plane at 18.00 hrs tomorrow if he wished. He said that he would visit Mrs Hendry and find out her wishes and then telephone me.

At 4 pm on 26th January, Mr Warner phoned me to say that he had again spoken to Mrs Hendry and Doctor Turner. The most significant thing is that Doctor Turner told him that she was going to attend Mrs Hendry constantly and she was going to accompany her to Lincoln next Tuesday, and she would stay for a few days to settle her in at Mr and Mrs Warner's invitation.

Doctor Turner confirmed that Mr Spiers is going to telephone me that evening which is what happened.

Mr Warner telephoned me to say that Mrs Warner was going to telephone Mrs Hendry at 10.30 pm.

At 11.00 am on 27th January, Mrs Warner phoned to say that she had spoken to Mrs Hendry who was very confused but she got the idea that the cheque was post-dated 3rd February and Mrs Hendry had dared not tell me, she said that Mrs Hendry told her that Mr Spiers would ring me.

At 11.25 am the same day Mrs Hendry telephoned me and she appeared very confused. She said that she had spent a long time on the telephone trying to find out details of the cheque, she said that her mother had been in touch and said that she had not won her case until the court would finally make a ruling on 3rd February. I felt that this was confirming what Mr Warner had said about the cheque. I asked her straight out and she thought that this was right. I got Mrs Hendry to promise as soon as Mr Spiers returned to her flat, she would authorise him to obtain the envelope and see it was delivered to me to hold as security. She promised she would do this and that she would get him to phone me immediately. I also made enquiries to obtain Doctor Turner's telephone number but could not find the right one.

Immediately after this telephone call I happened to pull out the two solicitors' letters that Mr Warner had obtained from Mrs Henry for me to photocopy. One was in the name of a firm of Glasgow solicitors called Ross Harper and Murphy and the other was called Joseph Mellick Solicitors. I placed the letters side by side and it suddenly dawned on me that there existed a similarity in the typing. Upon further examination I realised the phrases "I am" were identical in both letters and appeared to have been typed on the same typewriter. I also noticed that upon closed examination despite looking very official there were spelling mistakes. My worst fears were surfacing.

Mr Warner by this time had arrived at the bank. We both closely examined the letters and came to the conclusion that they had been prepared by the same person. In other words they were forgeries.

Having considered my action from this point on and over lunch, I felt my first priority had to be advising my senior at the bank.

Before I could contact my senior I received a telephone call from "Doctor Turner" who said that she was speaking from Mrs Hendry's flat. She said that she had telephoned to advise me of Mrs Hendry's health, she asked me if I was aware that Mrs Hendry had taken an overdose at the weekend. Whilst on her way down to Humberside Doctor Turner said that she realised that something big was involved, she also said that a Mrs Campbell had phoned three times during the morning but that she had refused her to speak to Mrs Hendry. Mrs Campbell had told Doctor Turner that the call was in connection with a cheque for £25,000, which she was going to give to Mrs Hendry. At this point Mrs Hendry came onto the telephone. She wanted to know what the Doctor and I had been saying. I placated her and said, all I wanted her to do was to authorise Mr Spiers to act directly with myself. Mrs Hendry agreed to do so.

Mrs Hendry was again in command of her faculties and speech this time. She was rather cross and wanted to know what I had said about "conning" (I had referred to this in connection with Mrs Campbell). Mrs Hendry said she would see that I got repaid whatever happened.

At 2.50 pm on 27th January, Mr Spiers telephoned me to say he was on his way to Mrs Hendry's flat. He said he had been given to understand that I wished the cheque to be forwarded by registered post. I said that in the event that he was not coming personally toady, as we tentatively agreed yesterday, then that was what I required. Mr Spiers said he would telephone me from Mrs Hendry's flat in half an hour.

At 3.30 pm the same day I telephoned my senior

and read out a prepared statement.

"This is Leslie Smith manager of Lincoln City Office. I wish to put on record that I have been making advances in the form of overdraft and personal loan facilities to my customers Edward Vincent Warner and Joan Warner of Dunholme Welton, in order that they assist a friend in Glasgow to meet litigation costs in the Probate Court. The amount I have advanced is in excess of my managerial limit the amount is £9,350. It was understood that the money resulting from the litigation would be released in my hands-on 20th January 1984. This money has not been received as of this time today. If nothing positive develops during today and over the weekend then I shall be requesting an interview with you for myself and my customer."

At 4.15.pm that same day Mr Warner came to the bank to find out the latest situation.

At 7.25 pm on 27th January 1984, I was at home when Mr Spiers telephoned me. He said he was calling from Mrs Hendry's flat. He apologised he had not been able to speak before and that he was still unable to as friends of Mrs Hendry's had called to see how she was. He said he would ring back in about an hour.

At 8.25 pm Mr Spiers rang back, he detailed the happenings of Saturday and the reason for the placing of Mrs. Hendry into the Newcastle Nursing Home and he subsequent transfer to Glasgow for the emergency operation (all this had been verified by Doctor Turner, Mr Wilson the security man and by Mrs. Hendry herself.)

Mr Spiers said he had only recently become aware that the cheque was postdated 3rd February. He said I must believe in

him as one professional to another that he did not know last
Saturday when he set out to come Lincoln.

He said he had today obtained the steel box and the
painting and brought them to the flat. He said he had done his
clients bidding at all times at personal risk on more than one
occasion. He felt that he had been wrongly accused of failing
in his duties, and that he was an honorable man who always
completed his duties he had undertaken.

I asked him what was happening concerning the cheque, he
said he would now fetch Mrs. Hendry who would tell me what
was to happen.

Mr. Spiers then called Mrs. Hendry and I heard him say
"I'm on my way now"

I heard her thank him and say "Goodnight."

Mrs. Hendry said that a registered envelope was ready and
tomorrow morning she was going to take the envelope
containing the cheque and take it to the post office herself. She
said she would not trust anyone else to do this. Mrs. Hendry
then went on to say she would telephone me by 11am and tell
me the name of the Post Office and the number of the
registered label. She asked me to make arrangements on
Monday morning with the Trustees Savings Bank Miller Street
Glasgow for them to accept the painting to be held under my
"signature and direction."

I told Mrs. Hendry I had confirmed she was due to fly down
with Doctor Turner on the Tuesday morning flight. She said
she was going to try and make it Monday night and that she
had had a terrible day as the phone had not stopped ringing,
and that all she wanted was to rest.

Mrs. Hendry asked me to contact Mr. and Mrs. Warner and
ask them to be patient, and let he gain her strength to travel
down on Tuesday. My wife had been present by the telephone
and heard parts of the conversation. She then had a word with
Mrs Hendry herself. They exchanged pleasantries and Mrs
Hendry assured my wife that everything would be alright. My
wife made the comment that all would be alright as long as
everything was left to the professionals.

At 11.40 am on 28th January 1984, Mrs Hendry telephoned

me to say Mr Wilson the security officer, had checked at a local post office and any registered mail would not be collected until Monday. I replied that the main post office in Glasgow would be open until teatime and I wanted the cheque sent by registered post from there. Mrs. Hendry said she would get Mr Wilson to take it as due to the doctors' orders she was not allowed out of the flat as she is due to have her stitches out on Monday. She promised she would ring me immediately he returned and give me the registered number of the letter.

I was beginning to have grave doubts regarding this now, as everything done seemed to be with the intention of stalling us. I decided to ring the solicitor whose name was on one of the letters given to us by Mrs Hendry. The solicitors name was Mr Brown and it was my intention to verify that the letter in question did in fact originate from the offices of Ross Harper and Murphy dated 15/1/84. Mr Brown telephoned me back, not being available on my first call. I introduced myself and asked him if he knew of a woman called Barbara Hendry. He told me that she was not a client of the firm but was rather the cause of a complaint by an individual who was a client of the firm. The woman in question lived in the same flats as Barbara Hendry and had lent Mrs Hendry money and consulted a solicitor, as she was unable to recover the loan.

Mrs Hendry was supposed to have an appointment with Mr Brown on Tuesday and I realised this was the day she was supposed to be flying down to Lincolnshire.

Mr Brown also said that bank in Dumbarton had received a suspicious letter on their headed notepaper probably prepared in the same way as the one handed to Mr Warner.

At 2pm the same day my wife and I visited the Warners at their home in Dunholme. I told them of my fears and that I considered that the photocopies in my possession were forgeries. At this stage I said I had to ask them both formally whether they were involved or could be implicated in any form of fraud.

They both replied, "Definitely not."

I noticed that Mr and Mrs Warner did not show any undue

alarm or emotion or disbelief at this revelation (This came over strongly to my wife as well)

It transpired that just before my arrival, the Warner's had spent three quarters of an hour on the telephone with Mrs Hendry. Apparently she was very distressed as she claimed that I had been making enquiries, which were causing ripples as she put it.

She had apparently said, "I don't know what I can do to please that Mr Smith."

The Warners said that they had also spoken to the security guard Mr Wilson who had told them of his attempts to post the registered letter and who said to them, "I have told Mrs Hendry that if what I think is in the envelope is being sent by registered post, that she is mad and she ought to take it with her on the plane on Tuesday."

At this point I told Mr Warner that this was not acceptable to me and I required it to be forwarded as arranged, he agreed to tell Mrs Hendry when he spoke to her later that day.

My wife and I spent a total of three hours with the Warners, at no time would they show me any tangible evidence of any kind to show that this amount of money destined to them did in fact exist.

I noted that at the time both the Warner's were firm in their belief in their friend. It was total and absolute there was no doubt about that.

My wife and I left the Warners house at 5pm with a clear undertaking with them that they would do nothing to alert Mrs Hendry. We would await the promised telephone call advising the name and address of the post office from which the registered letter had been dispatched and the registered label number.

I would then phone the post office and attempt to obtain verification of the acceptance of the registered letter. We would then have to await its arrival if posting is confirmed to see what it contains.

I also around this time due to my increasing suspicions I telephoned the Glasgow Police 'D' Division to ask if they had any knowledge of a "Mr Wilson", a self-employed security guard and ex police officer, believed to be one of six ex policemen carrying out this type of work. I was told that no one present in the information room at that time were aware of any ex officers operating this way within the area, but that this must not be taken as a denial there was any such person.

At 12 noon on 30th January I decided to telephone doctor Bell the Warners Doctor to see if Dr Turner from Glasgow had telephoned about Mrs Hendry's medical condition and to alert him that it was known that Doctor Turner and Mrs Hendry had a flight booked to Humberside 9.20 am Tuesday from Glasgow. The surgery had no knowledge of any travel arrangements regarding Mrs. Hendry travelling down to Lincolnshire I also made a telephone call to the airline and was able to confirm with British Caledonian that the booking still stood and it did.

At 9.20 am on 30th January I rang Mrs Warner at work. She said that she had spoken to Mrs Hendry the previous night, a Sunday, and Mrs Hendry had said that the cheque was being sent off this morning and I would receive details of the post office and receipt number.

At 10am I decided to telephone Joseph Mellicks Solicitors of Glasgow.

I was informed that Mr Spiers had gone out of the office for a while. I asked for Mr Joseph Mellick and was told that he was deceased. I then asked for Mr Sidney Mellick whose initials appeared on the top of the letter. Upon enquiring with Mr Mellick about Mrs Hendry I was informed that he did not have a client of that name. I asked him if Mr Spiers had been out of the country and he informed me that he had not. He also said that the phrase "Probate Court" would not be used to clients in Scotland.

I asked Mr Mellick to respect the confidentially of my enquiry and to make a note of the fact that I had called.

At 10.50am on 30th January, Mrs Hendry telephoned me at the bank. She said that she'd had her stitches removed and was feeling a little distressed because of it. She said that Mr Wilson the security officer had gone to the post office with the letter and she would phone me later upon his return with the name and the registered number.

Mrs Hendry asked me about Mrs Kearney and had been amazed to hear that when I spoke to her on the phone at Fareham that Mrs Kearney thought the amount she should have collected was £2000. I said that the amounts that Mr Warner had authorized were £820 and £500. She said that she had receipts for those amounts that she would see that I received them.

Mrs. Hendry asked why I had been making enquiries at this stage when all had been completed and she felt that I did not trust her. I informed her that my concern was for my customers who had taken on commitments they could not possibly meet and that they were under pressure to repay.

Mrs Hendry replied that this did not matter now as the cheque was on the way to clear all this up. She again promised to let me have the name of the post office and the number of the registered label.

At 11.10 am the same day Mr Warner rang from work to enquire if I had heard anything and to tell me that his wife Joan had received a similar reassuring call from Mrs Hendry saying that all was in order.

Mr. Warner obviously keen to hear good news said that he would ring me again after he left work at 4.15 pm that day.

At 4.50 pm Mr Warner came to see me at the bank after finishing work and asked me if there was any further news. I told him that I had heard nothing further since I last spoke to him.

Mr Warner is a naturally quiet and reserved individual person but on this occasion he was more so. I got the impression that it was just beginning to dawn on Mr Warner that his whole world was going to fall apart, but I was sure that he still thought that his friend would not let him down.

At 9.05 am on 31st January, Mr Warner telephoned me at the bank to see if the cheque had arrived and I informed him that it had not. Mr Warner asked me what would happen from this time forward and I told him that someone from my regional office would probably visit him and take a statement from him. Mr Warner agreed that this was very understandable and necessary. I informed Mr. Warner that unpalatable as it was, they must now face the fact that a very cruel confidence trick had been perpetrated against them.

I told him that it was in his best interests to inform the police of this. Mr Warner said the he and his wife would have to talk the whole matter over and decide between them what action to take.

At 10.40 am the same day, Mr Wilson the security guard telephoned me at the bank. He said that he had rung to apologise that the registered letter had not arrived this morning, he said that he had gone into Glasgow to the Rutherglen Post Office and had unwittingly become the innocent observer of a raid on the post office which had netted the robbers £90,000, and since he was ex police and a witness he had been asked to provide a statement. This process had taken a long time and when he finally got away he realised that the envelope would not be delivered today, He knew that he had let me down and had telephoned to apologise.

Mr Wilson said that he had taken the cheque back to Mrs Hendry and today he had called in to see how she was and found her in an upset state and certainly not well. I said I was sorry to hear this, as it was my understanding that she and Doctor Turner were to fly down to Lincolnshire on the 9.20 flight from Glasgow.

I asked Mr Wilson if he had met Doctor Turner and he said that he had "A most charming lady," he said.

Mr Wilson said that he was no medical man but as a layman it was obvious to him Mrs Hendry would be unable to travel. He said that Mrs Hendry had told him that she had arranged for Mrs Warner to fly up to Glasgow tomorrow and collect the cheque personally.

I said, "That's fine in that case I won't bother anymore."

Mr Wilson apologised again for any inconvenience caused and said that he would have to return to his duties and then rang off.

After putting the phone down, I immediately rang Mrs Warner to see if any such arrangement had been made and she said that it had not.

My wife later informed me that there had in fact been a robbery at Rutherglen Post Office, I think that she had read it in a paper.

At 10.15 pm that evening, Mr Spiers rang me at my home. He said that he had been to see Mrs Hendry who said that she had been told not to ring me anymore, was this correct? I said that it was not correct. I told Mr Spiers that the last communication that I had had with anyone was Mr Wilson and I reiterated the conversation to Mr Spiers in full.

Mr Spiers then said Mrs Hendry wanted to know what arrangements had been made about the security of the painting and I told him it had been left for Mrs Hendry to inform me when Mr Wilson would be able to deliver it to the Trustees Saving Bank, 177 Millar Street Glasgow and that I would make arrangements for its acceptance. Mr Spiers said he understood and would inform Mrs. Hendry tomorrow and she would no doubt telephone me about the matter. Mr Spiers then said goodnight and indicated that he had previously rang at 9pm whilst my wife and myself were out. He apologised for the lateness of the call.

At 10.15 on 2nd February, Mrs Hendry telephoned, She said she had been told not to telephone me by Mr Warner, she understood that Mrs Warner was at this moment travelling up by train to collect the cheque and she could not understand what had gone so wrong. I decided rather than alert her I would play her along by saying there was nothing wrong as I had been out on other business connected with the bank and had not had much contact with Mr and Mrs Warner. I told her that Mr Spiers had telephoned me the previous night and he was going to talk about the security of the picture and depositing it at Trustees Savings Bank Ingram Street. She said she would arrange to have it taken there and would phone and let me have the details.

At 11.05 am I telephoned Mr Warner at his office and he confirmed that Mrs. Warner had gone to Glasgow by train to try and sort the matter out. During the last two days they had spoken to Mrs Hendry on quite a few occasions and were still no nearer an explanation.

Mr. Warner phoned later to say that his wife had arrived in Glasgow but no more than that. He said that he was grateful for the bank's sympathetic action.

Just before lunch the same day Mr Warner came into the bank concerning his wife's account. I indicated the amount of the January salary remaining in each case and said that this was the amount the bank was prepared to make available. He was most happy with this arrangement and withdrew £230 X £5 to meet pressing creditors. I asked him how long Mrs Warner would remain in Glasgow. He said she had asked him if he minded if she stayed up there until Monday. He said he had told his wife, "No, as long as you are going to be alright."

I also asked him what his feelings were on the matter and he said despite what I considered to be irrefutable evidence, he still believed in Mrs Hendry. I asked him to show me one bit of proof and I would willingly admit that I was wrong. Mr Warner said that he hoped he would be able to do this.

At about 3.pm the same day I received a telephone call from Mrs Warner. She said that she was speaking from Mrs Hendry's flat and that Mrs Hendry was very ill. Mrs Warner said she would be staying a few days to look after her. She also maintained that everything is alright and the money is there and that Mrs Hendry cannot understand why I, who had been so kind in assisting her did not now tend believe her.

I asked Mrs Warner if she had met Mr Spiers and who was he.

Mrs Warner replied, "Just a man."

I said that I knew he was a solicitor.

She said," yes."

I said, "But not at Joseph Mellicks."

Mrs Warner said that she didn't know.

I enquired with Mrs Warner when she was going to return. She said she was unsure as she was on leave until the following Monday but could take more leave if necessary. I told Mrs Warner that when she returned she must bring some irrefutable proof of what money is coming to them and the guaranteed date.

Mrs Warner again said that Mrs Hendry was genuinely ill. I asked her if she had spoken to doctor Turner, she said she had and she had confirmed just how ill Mrs Hendry was.

At about 9.15 am on 6th February I was at home and since I had not heard from the Warners decided to ring them. After speaking with Mr Warner I discovered that Mrs Warner was back in Lincoln and it seemed as though I was being blamed for stirring things up with my enquiries and if the bank were patient everything would be all right. I then arranged a meeting the following day with Mr and Mrs Warner at anywhere they chose.

About 15 minutes later and just as I was going to go out, Mr Warner telephoned me back. He said that he had just been speaking with his wife and they had always been open with me, he had decided to acquaint me with the results of his wife's visit to Glasgow. He said that they had been promised full repayment in 48 hours of the amount owing to the bank.

He had spent a lot of time going over figures with someone over the phone that he couldn't name and he had been assured that the money would be forthcoming. Mr Warner said he knew the bank had set its own investigations in motion and he wondered, whilst not wishing to influence the bank in any way, whether this investigation could be indirect rather than direct for 48 hours.

I told him that I had no control whatsoever over what actions the banks inspectors might take.

At 9.45 am the following day Mr Warner phoned me to say he had had no further contact from Glasgow since he had last spoke with me and would call in at the bank during his lunch hour, but regretted that his wife would not be present as she was ill in bed with a heavy cold.

At 12.30 pm the same day I saw Mr Warner at the bank and in the presence of my assistant manager. Mr Warner commenced by saying that Mrs Hendry was ill and distressed because of the enquiries I had made in Glasgow and these had been subject of bad repercussions on her. I could not understand why secrecy was so paramount as we had been told the cheque had been issued on 20th January 1984 and later it was postdated 3rd February 1984. Surely all that was necessary was for the cheque to be delivered into the hands of the bank and all could be settled. Mr Warner could not give an answer to this.

I asked Mr Warner if whether Mrs Warner had met Mr. Spiers, Doctor Turner or Mr. Wilson, he did not answer this but said there was still a lot about his wife's visit that he was still unaware. He repeated his statement of the previous day that he and his wife had been reassured by Mrs Hendry's advisors that the banks and their debts would be settled. Mr Warner again requested that the bank make no direct approach. Throughout the interview I gained the impression that Mr and Mrs Warner still firmly believed in Mrs Hendry and that everything would be all right.

At 12.20 hours on 8th February, Mr Warner called to make a withdrawal of £258 from his wife's account, as she was still in bed ill. Mr Warner still did not have any news from Glasgow but his confidence that the money will arrive was as firm as always.

The next day I telephoned Mr Warner at his office. He told me that he had been in contact with Glasgow the previous night, and that a hiccup had occurred. The money had now been promised for Tuesday next week. I told him that there was delay after delay, which the bank was not able to go along with any further. Mr Warner expressed that if the situation were pushed too much it would blow the whole thing sky high.

Mr and Mrs Warner were still unshaken in their faith in Mrs Hendry and he still maintained that the debts would be paid in full. Mr Warner was asked when he would consider all hope that the money would be forthcoming would be at and end. He thought a little and replied that he considered that the following Friday to be the final day and would not concede before then.

Mr Warner was then asked if he would then be prepared to put the matter in the hands of the police for further investigation. Mr Warner replied that in view of Mrs Warners health he would only do so if medical opinion said that it was in order.

At 10.05 on 16th February since no remittance had been

received during the week or that day I telephoned Mrs Warner at her office and advised her accordingly. She said she was surprised, as it had been promised by this time. Mrs Warner said she would endeavour to find out the latest situation but then she said, " I shall have to wait until she contacts me, she has not been at her flat for the last two days."

I said it was imperative we knew where we stood, and that the bank would like to see her and her husband the following day. She said she would make enquiries and let me know.

At 9.05 am on 17th February, Mr Warner telephoned to enquire if a remittance had been received. I told him that I had had no communication of any kind. I also told him that my Senior and myself would like to see both Mr and Mrs Warner at the bank the same day but he said Mrs Hendry was contacting Mrs Warner today and he wondered whether it would be better to delay the meeting until after then.

Mr Warner then said, "A court decision on the money is being made today."

I said that in that case my senior would want updating as soon as possible.

Mr Warner agreed to come to the bank at 12.20 pm.

At 12.20 that day Mr and Mrs Warner came to the bank as agreed and had an interview with my senior and myself. We were told that Mrs Hendry had been speaking to Mrs Warner today and had been told that a solicitor would be ringing today to confirm that the money was to be sent to clear the bank's debts. The Warner's at this time were still confident that payment was forthcoming, as a result of a court hearing that afternoon at which a ruling was supposed to be given as to whether Mrs Hendry can be considered to have borrowed money against the terms of the will. The Warners at this time had no documentary proof although Mr and Mrs Warner said a letter had been posted from Glasgow, probably a registered one, on Wednesday last, which would set out the whole situation leading up to the court hearing that day.

Mrs Hendry had been asked that I be allowed to see this letter.

Mrs Warner promised to telephone me if the letter was at

home at teatime or if it arrived the following morning.. They also agreed to come to the bank on Monday 20th February 1984.

At 10.05 on 20th February, I was at the bank when I received a telephone call from Mr Spiers. He said he was sorry I had not heard from him for some time but he had to get away for a while, as he had been quite ill after the Newcastle episode. He said "the board" had made enquiries, as a result of a lady claiming Mrs Hendry had borrowed some money from her in October. The result of their enquiries would be known shortly and he - Mr Spiers would personally see I received a letter indicating when the money would be forthcoming, in order that I could show it to my superiors.

I informed Mr Spiers that Mr and Mrs Warner were in a desperate financial plight. He said he knew this and steps had been taken to contact Mr and Mrs Warners other creditors and reassure them. Mr Spiers promised to telephone me tomorrow. He also said Mrs Hendry was staying with one of her sons, "The one who has been in Saudi Arabia."

Apparently the son knew very little about his mother's affairs and she did not wish to enlighten him too much.

At 12.20 pm that day Mr and Mrs Warner arrived at the bank for an interview with my senior and myself. They said that they had not received a letter. It was understood to have been sent the previous Wednesday by ordinary mail. (This was not the first letter to have gone missing and Mr Warner agreed that there had been a number of cases) They had heard nothing concrete over the weekend but had had a number of telephone conversations with Mrs Hendry.

I told Mr and Mrs Warner of the Mr Spiers phone call, and that I did not believe Mr Spiers was bona fide, I would not accept what he had said.

Mr Warner then informed us that they had decided that Mrs Warner should go up to Glasgow again this coming Thursday. The reason she was going alone was the cost of the accommodation. It would be difficult for Mr Warner to stay at Mrs Hendry's flat. My senior told Mr Warner that all the bank was seeking was some form of proof that there was money to cover the debt and an indication of when it would arrive.

Mrs Warner said that she would do her best to provide it upon her return, and Mr Warner promised he would keep the bank advised in the interim.

At 11.25 the same day I was in the boardroom at the bank discussing the matter with my senior when my secretary informed me that Mr Spiers was calling on the phone.

I took the call and my senior listened in to the conversation with me.

The gist of the conversation was that the court decision would be made known on Friday and he (Mr Spiers) would positively guarantee that the cheque would be in the bank's hands by a week on the following Monday, 5th March. I asked what court this was?

Mr Spiers replied, "The High Court in Glasgow."

Mr Spiers said that if no one interfered this would go through and the bank would be paid, he went on to say there must be no enquiries or interference from Mr and Mrs Warner, as Mrs Hendry was not well and added that she was having to look after two grandchildren, as her son was away working in Saudi Arabia, and her daughter was in hospital with Leukemia.

Mr Spiers ended the conversation by reassuring me that the bank would be repaid by a week on the following Monday.

I contacted Mrs Warner to ascertain if she had been to Glasgow and she said the trip had been put off for four or five days.

At 11am on 28th February, I was at the bank when I received a telephone call from Mr Spiers. He apologised for not calling earlier but the Court had been postponed last Friday and the hearing was fixed for that afternoon at 2 pm. He said he was going to forward the court papers to me so I could show them to my superiors. He said that he must go as he had to get ready for the court hearing and said goodbye.

On Sunday 4th March at 5.30 pm I was in Sheffield visiting relatives, when my son rang to say that a man with a Scottish accent had rung my home and had asked to speak to me. I was told that the man would not give his name but that he would ring back.

At 10am on Monday 5th March 1984 I was at the bank, when I received a telephone call from Mr Warner. He asked if I was expecting a letter. I told him that Mr Spiers had said that I would receive one by Thursday before but that it had not arrived. He told me that Mrs Hendry had countermanded Mr Spiers and insisted that the letter was to go direct to Mr and Mrs Warner.

Mr Warner said he now had a letter and had tried to contact me at the bank without success then tried to contact my senior, but had found us both on holiday. Mr Warner said that he would like me to see this letter, but at this stage did not wish the letter to be photocopied. I arranged to see Mr. Warner at the bank at 12.20 in the presence of my assistant manager.

As arranged, Mr. and Mrs. Warner attended the bank and were seen in my office.

Mr. Warner produced a document for my inspection; this was an original and not a copy. It appeared to be a summons taken out by a firm of solicitors called Ross Harper and Murphy on behalf of their client a woman called Margaret Simonette of Red Road Court Springburn Glasgow. The summons was against Barbara Hendry also known as Ferguson for £890. I saw that it was issued by the Sheriffs Court, North Frederick Street Glasgow, reference T1234 134, and was due for a hearing on 20th March 1984 at 11.30 am. The document had two pages and four written sides; it was also perforated down the fold. Page 2 and 3 were returnable to the court with the defendants written response.

Page one of the document in the main was typed on a typewriter with a small dark type, there were two parts in a larger and lighter type. One as I can remember was the addition of the words "including interest" (or some equal phrase) after the amount £890, and down at the bottom was a short sentence indicating a previous hearing on 24th February 1984. Page 2 had two paragraphs, the first referred to the breaking of clause 5 of "James Campbell's will) in that "No money is to be borrowed under the terms of the will." The name Margaret Simonette appeared. There was a complete mis-spelling from that appearing on page 1. As in previous letters the letter 1 (one) had been used and dated. There were also other spelling mistakes. One paragraph also mentioned 9 million pounds and "payment to persons through a bank in Lincolnshire."

I can remember that the amount of £890 was made up of three smaller amounts but I cannot recollect what they were. I pointed this out to Mr. Warner who immediately drew my attention to the fact that in page one against the amount of £890 it said "including interest"

The second paragraph appeared to indicate that the answer to the charge, that money had been borrowed to assist in the obtaining of the inheritance was that it had been borrowed to assist with the payment of medical expenses.

Under the two paragraphs was an oval stamp. I told Mr. and Mrs. Warner that even after seeing this paperwork and having read it I was no happier than I was before. I said I felt that the large type parts of the letter had been prepared on the same typewriter as the Joseph Mellick and the Ross Harper letter. In other words I considered the letter to be a forgery.

Both Mr. and Mrs. Warner were visibly annoyed by my announcement and Mr. Warner said that he believed the letter was genuine. I said the actual document in my opinion was genuine together with the smaller type but the larger and lighter type was the part of the letter that had been falsified.

Mr. Warner said that I had a right to my opinion but he could not share it. He asked me what I would accept as proof. I told him a letter addressed to the bank from the solicitors acting for Mrs. Hendry, whose credentials could be confirmed, acknowledging Mrs. Hendry's debt to the Warner's and indicating Mrs. Hendrys instructions that this money would be sent to the bank for the credit of their account on a certain date.

Mr. Warner said that he would attempt to obtain such a letter. Mr. Warner then asked Mrs. Warner if she had anything to add but she said that she hadn't. Mr. Warner thanked us for our time and left the bank at 12.50pm.

At 14.05pm the same day I was at the bank when I received a telephone call from Mr. Spiers who said that he had received a telephone call from Mrs. Hendry. I was obvious that Mr. and Mrs. Warner had told Mrs. Hendry what we had discussed and that I considered the document to be a forgery. Mr. Spiers was incensed that I had made such an accusation. He said that the document given to Mr. and Mrs. Warner was genuine. I agreed with Mr. Spiers that the document was genuine but that I was also of the opinion that there had been additions made which were not genuine.

I then gave Mr. Spiers a loophole by saying that whether these additions were made after it had left his hands only he would know when the document was returned to him by the Warner's Mr. Spiers said that he was on his way to see Mrs. Hendry and that she was very ill and upset by what had been alleged. He would contact me again after he had visited her.

At 12.34pm on 6th March 1984, I was at home when I received a telephone call from Mr. Spiers, he said that he understood that I required a letter from Mrs. Hendrys solicitors to show to my managers at the bank which would acknowledge her debt to Mr. and Mrs. Warner's and that the letter should show a date on which repayment of the debt was to be made. I told him that this was correct and that it was very urgent. He promised the letter would be with me by the following Monday of the next week at the latest.

Mr. Spiers said that from the previous document I must be aware that Mrs. Simonette was pressing Mrs. Hendry for payment of her debt. He said that the amount borrowed was £200 but that this was typical of the type of people that they had to deal with. He said that he could not understand why Mr. Brown (Presumably of Ross Harper and Murphy and Co) had said that the amount of the estate was only £3 million. I said that I had had no communication with Mr. Brown so I did not know what he meant by this.

Mr. Spiers then requested the address of my superiors, which I gave him, he then said that the letter would be with me as soon as he could arrange it and then rang off.

To date the amount of £13,017 has been credited to the

account of the Warner's by the Trustees Savings Bank by way of loans and overdraft facility. I have made this provision available due to the fact that I was under the impression that through conversations with Mrs. Hendry she had a large amount of funds due to her from a trust fund or inheritance but it has never materialised. Excuses have been made for a long time, which I consider, have been for the purpose of a stalling action. Had I known that this was not true the loan facilities and the overdraft would not have been made available to Mr. and Mrs. Warner. I produce a breakdown of the loans detailing the reasons as to why they were granted.

Throughout my interviews with the Warner's and the telephone calls with Mr. Spiers, Mr. Wilson the security guard, and doctor Turner I have kept a full record by the way of notes which were either written up at the time or very shortly afterwards. These notes are at present in the safe custody of the Trustees Savings Bank at Lincoln and I am prepared to produce them for court purposes if and when required.

The statement was prepared and recorded over a period of three days, as it was obvious I needed some form of evidence to support my suspicions and justify an arrest. There was no doubt that from talking to the bank manager Mr. and Mrs. Warner would not support any prosecution at this stage as they still refused to accept that they were being the victims of a cruel hoax.

Actually I was very impressed with the amount of detail that the manager Mr. Smith had included in his notes. The comprehensive notes made certainly made my understanding of what had gone on a great deal easier but posed more questions than answers at this stage. Who was Mr. Spiers the Solicitor? Who was Doctor Turner and the security guard? a Rembrandt painting? Where does that come in?

After all, in order to make an arrest the investigating officer does not at this point have to prove that the offender is guilty of an offence for the purpose of making an arrest but to show that an offence has been committed and that there are reasonable grounds to suspect the offender of the offence.

The only other issues to consider were, was there enough evidence to justify an arrest which I was satisfied there was, even without the assistance of Joan and Ted Warner and the other problem was the small point that the suspect involved was somewhere in Scotland outside my jurisdiction.

The next step was to submit my file of evidence to Detective Sergeant Norris Upon conducting investigations the investigator will usually have an idea of what is required to be included in a witness statement. For this enquiry I needed to prove that monies had been advanced by false pretences i.e. deception, and that this was corroborated by the manager. This point had been achieved with what I would consider to be additional evidence that I could see would generate further enquiries. For instance, I had made arrangements for the receipts concerning the collection of the money that had been sent to banks in Glasgow and Fareham and had been collected by individuals other than Barbara Hendry. The question I was asking myself was, who were these individuals collecting the money on behalf of Barbara Hendry and what would their story be? I really needed to get my hands on these receipts but would have to wait for the bank to locate them and contact me.

As I was driving back to my base at Market Rasen I was mulling over the evidence thinking about what had happened. Firstly it was becoming obvious that I had found the correct offender in Barbara Hendry, her previous track record certainly "put her in the frame". I could now pursue her since I had got a statement from the bank and that they were willing to support a prosecution.

The bank manager Mr. Smith had spoken to Mr. Spiers, Doctor Turner and the security guard Mr. Wilson on several occasions, all had accents and in the case of Mr. Spiers his accent was described as being a very broad Scottish one.

If Barbara Hendry would not assist during interview I still had to somehow trace the other three individuals involved to obtain their version of events. Also to consider was the fact that the monies sent by the TSB at Lincoln to destinations for collection such as Fareham and other banks in Glasgow had been collected by persons other that Barbara Hendry. I had the names of Cairney and McPhee as being the persons collecting the monies, but who were they?

As I pulled into Market Rasen police station I remembered that during my interview with the bank manager he had told me that he rang Mr. Wilson the security guard on a Glasgow telephone number and spoke to him and upon asking he had given me the number. I rushed to my office hurriedly sorted through my paperwork and there before me was a Glasgow phone number with the name Wilson written next to it.

I sat down and dialled the number. After a couple of rings a man with a Scottish accent answered it.

"Mr. Wilson, security." said the voice.

"Hello." I said making out I had not heard his greeting.

"Wilson, security." said the voice in an official manner.

"Oh I'm terribly sorry." I replied, "I seem to have the wrong number." and put the phone down.

I sat back in my chair and thought to myself, are all these other people involved or what? If the security guard was in on the fraud then he certainly seems to be up front about it.

A few days later and in my absence I returned to work after a couple of days off to find some paperwork on my desk. Upon looking at the front sheet, I immediately recognised the very distinctive and neat writing to be that of Detective Sergeant Norris. My first thought was "That didn't take long."

The report on the front went as follows:

Kim,

It looks as though we have got a substantial deception here you had better get packed you're off to Glasgow!

I will make enquiries about getting magistrates warrant for her arrest will speak to you later. Please read the attached

Norman.

Upon turning the page Norman had attached a report in support of an application to a court for the purpose of obtaining a warrant for the arrest of Barbara Hendry.

Norman had written:.............

Barbara Elizabeth HENDRY is an evil woman who is bleeding every last penny out of Edward Vincent WARNER and Joan WARNER. This unfortunate couple have been completely deceived by HENDRY and even now will not accept the true situation. They are therefore unwilling to make a compliant to the Police or cooperate in any way. This has made the obtaining of evidence in this matter extremely difficult.

Whilst HENDRY is at large it is my belief that she will continue to fraudulently obtain money from the WARNERS. Therefore for the protection of the WARNERS and in the interest of preventing crime I suggest that we proceed against HENDRY.

Whilst on the not unreasonable assumption that HENDRYS story of being a beneficiary is entirely false, I suggest that we apply for warrants for her arrest as follows;-

1. For That You in the County of Lincoln on or about 23rd December, 1983, dishonestly obtained for Edward Vincent WARNER and Joan Warner a pecuniary advantage, namely being allowed by the Trustees Savings Bank (England and Wales) to borrow by way of overdraft, by deception, that is to say by falsely representing that you required the sum of £485 to settle outstanding final accounts owed to four solicitors.

Contrary to Section 16(1) Theft Act 1968

The evidence to support this allegation will be provided by Leslie Alan SMITH (see page 7 of his statement of evidence) and an officer of the Trustees Savings Bank, Springburn Branch Glasgow. (see receipt for £485 signed by HENDRY on 23rd December 1983)

2. For That You at Welton in the County of Lincoln on or

about 27th December, 1983, dishonestly obtained for Edward Vincent WARNER and Joan WARNER a pecuniary advantage namely, being allowed by the Trustees Savings Bank (England and Wales) to borrow by way of overdraft by deception, that is to say by falsely representing that you required £531 to discharge an account owed to a solicitor.

<u>Contrary to Section 16(1) of the Theft Act 1968</u>

The evidence to support this allegation will be provided by Leslie Alan SMITH (see page 8 and 9 of his statement of evidence) and an officer of the Trustees Savings Bank, Dennistoun Duke Street Glasgow. (See receipt for £600 signed by HENDRY on 28th December 1983).

3. <u>For That You</u> in the County of Lincoln on or about 16th January 1984, used a copy letter dated 15.1.84 purporting to have been written by Messrs Ross Harper and Murphy and a copy of a letter dated 15.1.84 purporting to have been written by Messrs, Joseph MELLICK which were and you knew or believed to be, false instruments with the intention of inducing somebody to accept them as copies of genuine instruments and by reason of so accepting them to do or not to do some act to that person's or another's prejudice

<u>Contrary to Section 4 Forgery and Counterfeiting Act 1981</u>

The evidence to support this allegation will be provided by Leslie Alan SMITH (see pages 11 and 12 of his statement) and by Messrs. Ross, Harper and Murphy, Joseph MELLICK (see their letters dated 29th February 1984 and 20th February, 1984, respectively addressed to the Trustees Savings Bank)

I suggest that Detective Constables BOOTH and McGARRAGH (who have conducted all enquiries so far into this matter)

Be allowed to travel to Glasgow after obtaining the warrant for HENDRYS arrest. They will then be in a position to obtain the necessary evidence from Glasgow branches of the Trustees Savings Bank and the solicitors whose headed notepaper has been used. They can arrest HENDRY and bring her back to Lincoln.

Detective Constable BOOTH is of the opinion that once HENDRY has been arrested and we can demonstrate to the WARNERS that they have been the victims of fraud; they will then cooperate with us.

In any event, I believe that we have a good chance of securing convictions against HENDRY for the offences suggested above and I therefore recommend this line of action.

Detective Sergeant NORRIS

2

This is a most serious offence, although the WARNERS still do not accept that they have been deceived we have other evidence and must act.

I believe officers should travel to Glasgow in possession of a warrant to arrest HENDRY. They can conduct the necessary enquiries in Glasgow to complete the file prior to the arrest. A Policewoman will be required for escort duties.

Signed
Detective Inspector.

3.

Before we take out an arrest warrant we will need evidence of ID. Please have nin- hydrin test carried out.

Obtain statement from Hull.

Statements will be required from Scotland from Banks and solicitors, we will get them ourselves.

Detective Inspector for action as discussed.

Detective Chief Inspector.

Having read the attached report all was looking very promising. As expected, it was very well supported by the

Detective Sergeant and the Detective Inspector, but as usual the Detective Chief Inspector always had to put his two penneth into the mix. He had suggested Nin Hydrin, which is basically the fingerprint process that is used to obtain any fingerprints from paper, and to point out that we would require statements from the banks. Pretty basic stuff really but one had to really act with surprise at this suggestion when confronted by the boss as if no one had previously considered it! That together with his style of handwriting, which was basically unreadable made any discussion or dialogue with him very difficult indeed!

It became common knowledge that I had been given permission to travel to Scotland to make an arrest and to conduct what could be lengthy enquiries. In the event I soon found that the non-believers who had previously scoffed at my enquiry suddenly had relatives in Scotland or knew the area obviously wanting to take advantage and have a few days away. In one case a detective made an approach asking to travel with me stating that his help would be invaluable because he "spoke the language!

A few days later I was called to see the Detective Chief Inspector with regards to my visit to Scotland.

"You will need to take a policewoman with you Booth," he said.

"Yes sir I realise that." I replied.

"Don't waste too much time up there I want you back down here as soon as you can we're very busy as you know."

"Yes I also realise that as well Sir, but I'm not in Lincoln CID any more I'm at Rasen."

"That's beside the point," he said. "Anyway I have found you a Policewoman to take with you and its Policewoman O'Connor." I always remember her as having a very healthy appetite for a good helping of food in those days, and could she eat!. I have often since wondered how on earth having such an appetite she could maintain such a slim figure, but she did. I did not know her well at that time, but can recollect previously seeing one of her statements that she had recorded from a rape victim and recollect it as being amongst one of the best statements I had ever read, that is "best" due to its content involving important descriptions of the offender together with details of the offence and all very accurate and chronologically detailed. I knew that she was well up to the task in hand.

I also needed a fellow detective to accompany me to Scotland and despite several offers decided to take my colleague who also worked out of the city in the rural and at that time on an area adjacent to mine. His name was detective constable Bob McGarragh a tall slim individual who possessed a rapier like sense of wit and who on occasions has verbally demolished occupational adversaries willing to verbally "have a go at the police" We settled on a date for our venture into Scotland and the only thing left to do was to make a few phone calls to make arrangements with our Scottish colleagues.

I had telephoned Glasgow CID on several occasions asking for assistance but never really got what I considered to be a helpful response. When they received my telephone calls it would be at least a couple of days before any reply was obtained and even then I had to chase them up. I had previously asked for enquiries to be made about the security guard Mr Wilson but just got a "Don't know him," response. In reality a comparison between working in a city the size of Lincoln and Glasgow could not realistically be made, as they were different worlds apart. I was early in my CID career and had not had much experience at that stage of working in larger cities so it was going to be an interesting exercise, anyway crime was the same all over the country, or was it? I would soon find out.

At the start of April I received a telephone call from the Trustees Savings Bank to inform me that they had managed to locate the receipts with regards to the collection of monies from various banks in the UK so I made the arrangements to attend Lincoln Police Station on 4th April to interview a member of staff from the bank and record a statement.

Statement of   David Reginald Clay   Bank Inspector
C/o Trustees Savings Bank Lincoln

I am employed by Trustees Savings Bank (England and Wales) in the capacity of Inspector, I work from the bank's premises situated in Lincoln.

The Trustee Savings Bank of England and Wales is a TSB within the meaning of the Trustees Savings Bank Act 1981, and as such its rules are certified by the Chief Registrar of Friendly Societies.

As a result of information received I contacted the Springburn Branch of the Trustees Savings Bank,, 567 Springburn Road, Glasgow, The Trustee Savings Bank, 424 Duke Street, Glasgow and the Trustee Savings Bank Portland Chambers, West Street, Fareham, Hants and requested the forward withdrawal receipts issued by them and acknowledged by Mr. L. Smith, the Lincoln Trustees Savings Bank Manager, Bank Street Branch. The exhibits were posted at my request to myself from the respective banks and I hand them to Detective Constable Booth of the Lincolnshire Police.

Mr. Clay during the recording of his statement produced all the compliment slips and receipts signed by the individuals at the respective banks for the collection of the monies sent by Ted and Joan Warner at the request of Hendry. Police Items DSC 1 to DSC 16.

I now had the original withdrawal slips in my possession together with the Letters of Authority for P. Phee and C. Cairney to collect the monies sent from TSB Lincoln to the respective banks. It would be interesting to see what P. Phee and C. Cairney had to say about the reasons why they collected the money and what they had done with it? Both would be seen in due course either in the capacity of witness or defendant! Firstly though before anything else the slips would be submitted for fingerprint testing to see if any of the suspect's fingerprints were on any of the slips. Long shot again or what? Only time will tell.

Chapter Eight: Travel north for arrests

A warrant for the arrest of Barbara Hendry had been secured from a local magistrate, it was placed on our file ready for the trip up north.

On 17th April 1984 detective constable McGarragh, policewoman O'Connor and myself travelled up to Glasgow discussing the case along the way. We had been booked into a hotel for overnight accommodation as is the norm. It was best to start early the next morning and call at the flat of Barbara Hendry firstly to catch her by surprise and also to find her there before she left to go out.

We arrived in Glasgow just after 2pm and went into the CID office at Clydebank. I did wonder what type of reception we were going to receive.

We were first introduced to the detective sergeant that was covering the area. He apologised that they were a little busy but he was aware that we were arriving from Lincolnshire and that he was aware of what it was all about.

"You will need a search warrant, I shall get that arranged for you as soon as I can," he said. "If it's alright with you we will execute the warrants tomorrow morning and see what we get.

He went on to explain that there was a "turf war" going on between rivals that were in dispute over the areas for the selling of ice cream in parts of Glasgow. There had previously been some very serious assaults and on one occasion an individual had been shot. What had happened the previous night was that the dispute had again escalated and that one of the ice cream sellers had been asleep in his flat when tyres had been placed outside the door of his flat and set on fire. In the flat were a large number of people staying there and a number of them had died in the fire that followed and others had been taken to hospital. Officers from the same CID office were dealing with a violent rape that had been committed overnight and things were obviously very busy. Whilst this was all being explained to us a uniformed police constable entered the CID office looking rather dishevelled. I saw that his uniform was in disarray and his flat cap was on the side of his head, he also appeared in a state of shock.

He relayed the story that he had been on routing enquiries to the flats at Red Road Court in Glasgow, arrived at the location and just after stepping out of the car a paving slab had been dropped from 13 floors above onto the roof of his patrol car going straight through the car roof through the car and onto the tarmac.

I was beginning to find all this a little hard to take in and came to the conclusion that the Glasgow CID were very busy after all, and I had distinctly got the wrong impression.

The detective sergeant looked at the constable and told him to get himself sorted out.

He turned to me and said, "Red Road Court that's where we are going tomorrow and where Hendry lives."

"Right," I replied, "Is it always as busy as this? I asked.

"We do tend to get busy now and again," which I took in the tone as being an understatement.

It was at this point a male obviously another detective entered the CID office.

"Sarge," he said, "I've just come from the hospital and another one has died." The detective sergeant had a very resolved but disappointed expression on his face.

"Don't worry," he said turning to me and my colleagues "we will get there tomorrow when we've got this lot sorted out."

After what I had seen I didn't really mind how long we had to wait and if this was a snapshot of a CID career in a large city then I will never again question my existence in good old Market Rasen, there's a lot to be said for living there I thought. The locals don't know how good they've got it!

"Well if it's ok I will go and find a bank I will need some money," I said.

"Well don't take that shiny new briefcase with you." he said looking at my briefcase! "Or you will get mugged round here!"

(I had taken my new black briefcase with me to create a good, efficient impression and in an attempt to look the commensurate professional detective!)

"I'd better use my handcuffs and lock it to my wrist then." I said.

The detective sergeant replied in a serious and rather matter of fact manner. "We had one of those last week" he said. "A security guard was robbed with the money in a briefcase chained to his arm."

"What happened?" I asked.

"He got his hand chopped off at the wrist." he replied. "The villain cut it off with an axe and ran off with the briefcase."

I then decided that at this point the bank could wait until I am out with the obviously more experienced and street-wise members of the Glasgow CID! But then I can live with that.

***

That evening we were taken out for a drink and then taken to our hotel the arrangement having been made for an early start the following morning when the local CID would collect us from our hotel and take us to the Red Road Court area of Glasgow.

It was all coming together really well. We were in Glasgow about to confront a woman who I was satisfied was the person who had perpetrated the deception on Joan and Ted Warner over a number of years. Silently in my mind and after arriving at my hotel room I mulled over the available evidence in my head to confirm to myself that the woman I was about to confront was the actual offender. I was still sure in my mind that I was onto the right person.

Having made previous enquiries about our suspect and her previous activities I thought it reasonable to assume that any offence would not be readily admitted and had brought with me from Lincolnshire copies of the two letters produced by Mr. Warner at the request of the bank manager Mr. Smith. Both letters purported to have originated at solicitors' offices in Glasgow. Both firms of solicitors were highly regarded and respected firms and I knew from making previous telephone enquiries that every assistance would be given.

Off I went across Glasgow to visit Ross Harper and Murphy and Joseph Mellicks Solicitors. The purpose of the visits was to establish if as thought the letters produced by Barbara Hendry to Joan and Ted Warner and the to the bank manager were, as suspected to be forgeries. It was established that both letters were false in their entirety and although the solicitors in question had no knowledge regarding the content of the letters they did however acknowledge that the letterheads in question were the type that were either in use at their firms or had been in use. With regards to an invoice with the number of 10901, the letter had been sent from the solicitor's office but with a different content. It was later found that civil action had been taken against Barbara Hendry concerning a debt involving non-payment to a local landlord called Van Daal.

It was obvious that the letter had been altered and a new content inserted without the knowledge of any of the solicitors involved.

The evidence obtained confirmed my suspicions and would serve as good evidence for the purpose of interview and the preparation of any subsequent court case.

Bearing in mind how active the solicitor Mr. Spiers had been I had decided to trace him and established that there was only one possibility within the Glasgow area. Mr. Spiers had allegedly spoken to Mr. Smith the bank manager on numerous occasions and had actually spoken to staff in the housing department at West Lindsey District Council on behalf of Joan and Ted Warner and their pending eviction, with the intention of getting their eviction date deferred. I eventually ended up at Hope Street Glasgow and the offices of Joseph Mellicks Solicitors where I saw Mr. Spiers a Solicitor.

Malcolm Spiers   Solicitor
I am a junior partner in a firm of solicitors called Joseph Mellick.

On Tuesday, 17th April 1984, I was shown by Detective Constable Booth of the Lincolnshire Police a letter purporting to have originated from this office. (Police Item LAS28).

Upon examination it can be seen that it is a photostat copy of a letter displaying the heading of Joseph Mellick (Solicitors and Notaries Public) 160 HOPE street Glasgow, dated 15th January 1984.

Having read the content of the letter, I can say that I have no knowledge of it and that such a letter being utterly ungrammatical and nonsensical not to mention mis-spelt would not have been issued by this law firm. There would not be any hand writing on a letter dispatched by us except for a signature from a member of the firm. The document shown to myself is false in its entirety and has not been dispatched from this office.

I would like to add that the letter shown to me is on paper with a letterhead that has not been used by our firm since the death of our senior partner Joseph Mellick on 29th September 1983.

I produce a letterhead used by our firm prior to 29th September 1983 (Police Item MS 1) and a Joseph Mellick Solicitors letterhead used by our firm since 29th September 1983 and is still in use. (Police item MS 2)

Mr. Spiers also stated he did not have any knowledge of a Bank Manager called Mr. Smith at Lincoln and had not spoken to anyone by that name or Donald Hendry or Barbara Hendry or Morrison or Bain

The visits to the solicitors were important and really needed doing before any searches or arrests were made. Now the evidence had been obtained we were ready to go. It had been proved that the real Mr. Spiers was not involved and someone had, for the purposes of the fraud assumed his identity and that the letters produced to the bank manager and Joan and Ted were forgeries. All we had to do now was to trace the bogus solicitor!

***

The following morning we were all up bright and early and in time for the local CID to come and collect us. The local detective sergeant was a very experienced and likeable individual who in my view had "earned his spurs" in a very difficult and challenging environment. He was very helpful and supportive and had a very good grasp of what we were attempting to achieve.

We departed from our hotel at about 8am on Wednesday 18th April 1984 and were driven through various areas of Glasgow. The area that we were going to was on the outskirts of the very notorious Gorbals district an area that I had heard of but never actually visited.

We finally arrived at our destination. The area comprised of three very large tower blocks very close to each other and by looking at the windows I could see tv aerials sticking out together with washing lines and windows that have been previously broken and either boarded up or covered in what appeared to be polythene.

After getting out of our vehicle one of the officers said, "That's where the Police car had the paving slab dropped upon its roof". He pointed to the entrance obviously in the direction of where we were going. Upon entering the building I discreetly looked upwards towards the roof of the towering block just to make sure that there was not another paving slab making its way downwards towards us.

We entered a dimly lit area and were confronted with an array of doors and two lifts in front of us that had obviously seen better days. We were at the point of walking towards the lifts when out of a ground floor door came a male aged about 50 years. I saw that he was wearing what appeared to be some sort of uniform consisting of a blue shirt and dark trousers.

"Ay can I help you?" He asked.

"Ay you can," replied the detective, "And who might you be? He asked the man in the uniform.

"My name is Wilson, Percy Wilson, I'm the security here," he replied.

Upon hearing this I took a silent gasp this is "Wilson security" I thought, the security guard who is supposed to be looking after the Rembrandt painting it is obviously the man who the bank manager Mr Smith has been talking to? Could I be hearing things?

"Say that again," I asked, pretending that I had not heard.

"I'm Wilson security "he said, "I look after the flats."

This confirmed to me that we were on the right track.

"We will come and see you later," I said and we all went into a lift that had a distinct smell of disinfectant about it and I pressed the button to the 12th floor of the block.

"Did you hear what he said?" Detective Constable McGarragh asked.

"Yes I did," I replied, "we can sort him out later, he's not going anywhere."

The lift ascended and we arrived at the twelfth floor, the doors opened and we were confronted with further doors that were obviously the entrance to a number of flats on that floor.

Upon being about to knock on the door it opened and a man came out nodded and went on his way leaving the door ajar. Not being individuals who would miss an opportunity we all went in. Sat in the chair in the lounge was a rather portly rotund woman with light graying blondish hair. When asked her name she replied, "Barbara BAIN."

Detective Sergeant Livingstone who explained that we had a search warrant to search the premises spoke to the woman.

"What's this all about?" she asked.

The woman was allowed to read the warrant to search the premises.

Dc McGarragh replied, "You are not obliged to say anything unless you wish to do so but what you say may be put into writing and given in evidence. We have reason to suspect that you have committed criminal deceptions and we intend to search for any documentary evidence to support this. Where are your papers?"

The woman replied, "I don't have any."

Dc McGarragh, "Have you a typewriter?"

Hendry replied, "It's upstairs."

McGarragh, "Is there an upstairs?"

Hendry replied, "In another flat."

At this point the detective sergeant cautioned her and told her that she was under arrest.

A search of the premises was conducted and the following items were found and seized;

An Access recovery letter from off the mantelpiece in

the lounge. Exhibit 1). This was a debt recovery letter for the amount ££1068.00 in the name of Malone C/o D Hendrie

Two handwritten cards from within a handbag in the lounge.

Exhibits 2 & 3). These two handwritten cards, The first card had the address of Joan and Ted Warner and also West Lindsey District Council the area in which they lived together with the council phone number and also details of a credit company and two account numbers. The second card had the address of the TSB in Lincoln together with the bank account details and account numbers of both Joan and Ted Warner at TSB Lincoln.

A handwritten document from freezer box in master bedroom Exhibit 4 Document outlined hand written details of Argyll family:

Wed 8th May 1963 Divorce Duke 4 years

Daughter Francis Duchess of Rutland Belvoir Castle

Son Brian Sweeney London House Upper Grosvenor Street.

Barbara Hutton - Mother Edna Woolworth Hutton.

Miss Margaret Wigham 1930 Debutant aged 17.

Prince Aly Khan

1931 Lieutenant Commander Pearson Glen Kidson.

1932 Engagement to Charles Sweeney.

Feb 21st 933 April confirming pregnancy

May 30th Miscarriage.

January 1934 8 months pregnant Still born baby girl.

June 19th 1937 Francis Helen

April 5th 1940 Brian Charles

A handwritten card from within a cooler box in the master bedroom. (Exhibit 5). Handwritten directions from a cooler box in the master bedroom giving detailed directions from Welton Lincolnshire (The home address of Joan and Ted) to Patterdale

Typed account from within a cooler box in the master bedroom. (Exhibit 6) The account was indicating expenditure of Robert Ferguson over three days being 18/01/84, 19/01/84, 20/01/84, and 21/01/84. It outlined expenses for petrol, speakers for car, repairs to car Robert pocket money, Robert tiles, Robert adhesive etc a total of £1883.00.

A vehicle carrier document from within a cooler box in the master bedroom (Exhibit 7). This document was for the hire of a motor car the driving licence produced was in the name of Cairney but hired in the name B Hendry. The hire period being from 21st January to 24th January 1984.

A credit payment demand from within cooler box in the master bedroom. (Exhibit 8). This item was a final payment request for the amount of £287.23.

A vehicle repair document (Exhibit 9) This item was an invoice for the repair of a Jaguar motor car Registered No PSU 256P. The invoice is in the name of Mrs. Ferguson and a Mr. Spiers dated 24th January 1984 for the amount of £117.50 paid cash. The repair took place in Birmingham.

Typewriter from the top of the cooler box (Exhibit 10). Chances are that this would have been used to type some of the forged letters. Exhibit 10

A painting from spare bedroom on top of the wardrobe (Exhibit 11). The painting appeared to be a "Rembrandt" look alike. Was this the mysterious Rembrandt? Chances are it was.

The search provided evidence linking Barbara Hendry to both Joan and Ted Warner and showed details of their bank account. What would prove to be of further use in the investigation was the hand written paperwork that gave a brief history of the life of the Duchess of Argyll outlining important dates? Was this a form of aide-memoir that was to be used during conversations either face to face or on the telephone? And of course the "Rembrandt" painting. All in all I was satisfied with the search results and considered it to have been well worth doing! At the conclusion of the search Barbara Hendry was arrested, taken to the police station at Baird Street and placed in a cell.

In the meantime it was established that the male person leaving the flat at the time of our arrival was allegedly the husband of Barbara Hendry, Donald Hendry.

At 12.10pm the same day Donald Hendry attended the police station where his wife was being held voluntarily, he was seen in an interview room at Baird Street Police station Glasgow. He was interviewed regarding any possibility of his involvement in any offences of Criminal Deception.

Dc McGarragh, "You are not obliged to say anything unless you wish to do so, but whatever you say may be given in evidence. Do you understand?

Hendry, "Yes Sir."

Mc Garragh, "As you know we have arrested Barbara in respect of criminal deception. I would like to know of your involvement?"

Hendry, "None Sir. I've had nothing from her."

McGarragh, "Has she ever told you that she is the illegitimate daughter of the Duchess of Argyll?"

Hendry, "Aye she has, the Countessa De Leone."

McGarragh, "Did you believe that?"

Hendry, "That's what she told me. I wanted to believe it. If it was a lie from me it was a lie to me. I love her I wanted to believe it."

McGarragh, "Have you ever made any phone calls about this?"

Hendry, "I won't lie to you, Aye I have."

P.W. O'Connor, "Can you remember who you said you were?"

Hendry, "No I can't, it was a solicitor from Harpers."

P.W O'Connor, "Who did you speak to?"

Hendry, "Mr. Smith at the Trustees Savings Bank in Lincoln."

O'Connor, "And what did you say to him?"

Hendry, "She was supposed to be ill in hospital somewhere, I can't remember where exactly, somewhere near Sunderland. There was money coming from Switzerland but she needed the money for the hospital."

O'Connor, "Did you speak to Mr. Smith more than once?"

Hendry, "Yes twice I think."

O'Connor, "And why did you do that?"

Hendry, "She asked me to, it was to get money for her. She always said "I'm keeping you" but she didn't. All the money went to her and her family."

O'Connor, "How did you know what to say?"

Hendry, "I didn't it was all written down for me. I didn't want to do it but she said about the inheritance."

McGarragh, "Who did you take her mother to be."

Hendry "The Duchess of Argyll."

McGarragh, "Did you believe it?"

Hendry, "I wanted to."

McGarragh, "Who was Granny Bain?"

Hendry, "Banette said it was her step mum."

McGarragh, "Who is Banette?"

Hendry, "That's a name for Barbara, it's Swiss. Her real name is the Countessa De Leonie."

McGarragh, "How long have you known her as that?"

Hendry, "As long as I have known her. My family believed her but have turned against me."

McGarragh, "How did you come to know her?"

Hendry, "My ex-wife went to prison for drunken driving and when she came out of Gateside prison she brought Banette with her."

Mc Garragh, "So you have believed the story from then?"

Hendry, "I wanted to, I had to believe it."

McGarragh, "How did you know about the relationship with the Duchess of Argyll, what did she tell you?"

Hendry, "It was Granny Bain or her husband were related to the Duchess of Argyll."

O'Connor, "Did Granny Bain have any other children?"

Hendry, "Yes Lily, she looks just like Banette."

O'Connor, "What was her relationship to Barbara?"

Hendry, "She told me they were half-sisters, same mother different fathers."

O'Connor, "When you phoned Mr. Smith the second time what did you say?"

Hendry, "Just different things, it was all written down."

O'Connor, "Was it the truth?"

Hendry, "It was waiting for the money from Switzerland."

McGarragh, "Was there money in Switzerland?"

Hendry, "I don't know she told me she was coming into money when she was   54."

McGarragh, "She is 54 now isn't she?"

Hendry, "Aye she is but was coming into money."

O'Connor, "How much did she say? Was it thousands or millions?"

Hendry, "I don't know, but it was a lot of money. She told me her Granny had a house in Lucerne."

O'Connor, "Have you or Barbara ever spoken to, or had contact with the Duchess of Argyll?"

"Hendry," Banette phoned London once and said it was her mother."

McGarragh, "Tell me about the phone calls that you have made to Mr. Smith the bank manager."

Hendry, "I felt terrible about that. There was once he phoned back and said that he had phoned Harpers and said that the person he spoke to was different, with a different voice, I told him that there were two men with the same name."

McGarragh, "Was the name Spiers?"

Hendry, "That's the man, Spiers. You see it was all written down for me. It was difficult to remember."

McGarragh, "Did you realise that what you were doing was wrong?"

Hendry, "Yes I did. I didn't want to do it. She said it was only until her inheritance came through. I used to have three whiskeys before I could do it, then if he asked me any questions I couldn't answer him."

McGarragh, "Were you frightened?"

Hendry, "I didn't want to do it."

McGarragh, "Was that because you didn't believe Barbara?"

Hendry, "I didn't know what to believe, she told me it was alright and that her mother would pay us. I had to believe her I'm just an ordinary workingman. I honestly didn't know what to believe. I know I was wrong to phone Mr. Smith, will you apologise for me?"

At 12.15 pm the same day the interview was concluded.

Outside the interview room Donald Hendry approached and asked, "What happens now?"

Bearing in mind that he had admitted his involvement but

we were at that time unable to arrest him in Scotland for an offence that he had committed in England without an arrest warrant. At the time of obtaining the arrest warrant for his wife Barbara we were unaware of his involvement.

"You will look after her?" He asked.

"Yes," I replied. "She will be returning to Lincoln with us to be further interviewed."

"Can I come and visit her?" he asked.

"Of course," I replied.

He thought for a minute and then asked, "You will feed her won't you?"

"Of course we will," remembering that there were fish and chip wrappers in the bin at the flat "We have some of the best fish and chips in the country in Lincoln, if you like we will get her some of those for her supper."

"If I travel down will I be able to see her maybe I could give her the fish and chips?" he asked.

"Of course you can" came the reply and he was provided with the address of Lincoln Police Station. At this point I had played light of it and Donald Hendry thought his part was all over having been interviewed. I might not have had at that time the power to arrest him in Scotland and my intention was to get him south of the border where I certainly did have the power to arrest him and if he showed up in Lincoln he certainly would be arrested. Let's see if he turns up I thought to myself.

After releasing Donald Hendry our attention turned to his wife Barbara who was in custody.

After sorting out the relevant paperwork we decided to take Barbara Hendry down to Lincolnshire to interview her regarding the allegations of criminal deception.

The journey was to take several hours and it was decided that no conversation would take place regarding the offences without her solicitor being present. This is normal procedure as often is the case allegations are made that the defendant was put under pressure to answer questions without a solicitor being present. What was evident during the journey was that she was an accomplished whinger. She had complained earlier that she was feeling unwell so we decided to have her seen by a Doctor to certify her fitness to travel.

On route she wanted to use the toilet and we made a stop at the "Police approved" Little Chef. Policewoman O'Connor enquired if she should accompany the prisoner to the toilet at which I had said there was no need. This perplexed the young Police Woman as it went against all her recent training. What I did not disclose is that upon entry to the car park of the Little Chef, I had seen the size of the toilet window and having met Barbara Hendry and taking into consideration her stature was quietly confident that there was no way she would be able to squeeze through the toilet window and escape, even if she had wanted to!

We continued our journey down to Lincolnshire and lodged Barbara Hendry overnight at Lincoln Police Station ready for interview the following morning. I was pleased at the end of the journey to really have a break from the whinging and moaning of one Barbara Hendry.

Chapter Nine: The interview

At 09.40 am on Thursday 19th April 1984 in the company of Detective Constable McGarragh, I attended an interview room at Lincoln Police Station where I saw Barbara Hendry of Red Road Court Springburn Glasgow. Barbara Hendry had at this time elected to be interviewed without a solicitor being present.

Detective Constable Booth, "I must inform you that you are not obliged to say anything unless you wish to do so, but what you say may be put into writing and given in evidence. Do you understand?"

Hendry replied, "Yes."

Booth, "What we want to talk you about is your involvement with Edward and Joan Warner of Welton near Lincoln, Do you know them?"

Hendry, "yes of course I do, they're my good friends and I won't have anything said against them."

Booth, "What we want to talk to you about is the money they have loaned you."

Hendry, "Yes they have, but I'll pay them back, they were helping me out."

Booth, "How did you meet them?"

Hendry, "It was about seven or so years ago, I met them in Scotland but I've done nothing wrong."

Booth, "For what purpose have you had this money?"

Hendry, "It doesn't matter; I don't want to talk about it."

Booth, "What I want to do is to find out what has been happening. If there is nothing wrong then fair enough but I want you to tell me how much you have had and where it has gone."

Hendry, "Don't ask me that. I don't want to talk about it. I don't want anyone to know."

Booth, "We have been making enquiries about it for a while and I want you to tell me."

Hendry, "Who's told you? Was it Joan or Ted because they

wouldn't say anything?"

Booth, "Why bring Joan and Ted into it?"

Hendry, "I had a phone call the other day everything was alright then."

Booth, "How long have you been taking money from the Warners?"

Hendry, "Taking? Taking? Don't say that, it wasn't like that they were helping me out."

Booth, "Helping you do what exactly?"

Hendry, "I don't want to go through it, it's embarrassing."

Booth, "You accept then that Mr. and Mrs. Warner have been sending you money then?"

Hendry, "Yes I do."

Booth, "And that it has been sent direct and arrangements have been made through the Trustees Savings Bank?"

Hendry, "Yes, that Mr. Smith, he's a liar, he been boasting to all the girls in the office."

Booth, "Tell me about it."

Hendry, "I don't want to."

Booth, "How much do you think that the Warner's have sent you?"

Hendry, "I don't know but that Mr. Smith has been taking two thirds of their income from them, He's a greedy man!"

McGarragh, "Is that in respect of the money they have loaned you?"

Hendry, "Don't say it like that, it makes me sound wicked."

(It was at this point I thought to myself "Now that's an understatement!")

McGarragh, "Have you collected money from the Springburn Branch of the Trustees Savings Bank?"

Hendry, "Yes I have."

McGarragh, "Have you been to any other branches in Glasgow to collect money sent to you by the Warner's?"

Hendry, "Yes I have but do we have to go all through this?"

McGarragh, "Yes we do but we must ask you the questions."

Hendry, "I understand but I have done nothing wrong."

McGarragh, "Have you ever claimed to be the illegitimate

daughter of the Duchess of Argyll to the Warner's or Mr. Smith at the Trustees Savings Bank?"

Hendry, "That's a lie, why do you have to bring all that up?"

McGarragh, "That is part of the allegation."

Hendry, "Joan and Ted wouldn't say anything like that, they're my friends."

McGarragh, "Have you ever told any of those people that you are due an inheritance or legacy from the Duchess of Argyll's estate valued at a million pounds?"

Hendry, "It's lies."

McGarragh, " Have you ever prepared any document claiming this is so and sent them to either the Warner's or Mr. Smith?"

Hendry, "No I haven't."

McGarragh, "Think carefully on this, have you ever sent a document purporting to have come from the bank of Kantonal in Switzerland to the Warner's or Mr. Smith?"

Hendry, "Why is everyone doing this to me?"

Booth, "Are these allegations not true?"

Hendry, "Joan and Ted are my friends."

Booth, "Are these allegations true or not?"

Hendry, "What will happen to me?"

Booth, "I cannot answer that question because it is not a decision I will make. I suggest that you answer the questions truthfully."

Hendry, "It's not true. That Mr. Smith he's a greedy man, I don't like the way he treats Joan and Ted."

McGarragh, " I put it to you that you claimed the money you obtained from Joan and Ted was for legal fees to release an inheritance due to you from the Duchess of Argyll."

Hendry, "That was Donny, He's got a big mouth, he told everyone about it."

McGarragh, "How did he find out about it?"

Hendry, "It doesn't matter."

Booth, "Somebody must have told him about it?"

Hendry, "It just got out of hand, it snowballed. You must think I'm very wicked?" (I thought yes I do actually!)

Booth, "I think that a great deal of thought has gone into this."

Hendry, "It's not like you think. It's just got out of hand."

McGarragh, "Let's go over this again. Are you related in any way to the Duchess of Argyll?"

Hendry, "No I did a terrible thing."

McGarragh, "Are you due any inheritance from her?"

Hendry, "No."

Booth, "Have you obtained money from the Warner's by claiming that you are due such an inheritance from her?"

Hendry, "Yes."

Booth, "Have you used the money for any legal fees?"

Hendry, "No, only to pay some fines."

Booth, "So it is true to say what you have had was not put to the purpose that you claimed?"

Hendry, "That's correct. Do I have to go through it all?"

Booth, "So in effect you deceived Joan and Ted?"

Hendry, "Don't say that."

Booth, "That is what happened isn't it?"

Hendry, "Yes."

Booth, "Where has all the money gone?"

Hendry, "I have nothing."

BOOTH, "During the time the money has been sent to you, a man called Mr. Spiers has been involved. Who is he?"

Hendry, "He's a solicitor."

Booth, "Are you sure it was Mr. Spiers?"

Hendry, "Yes."

Booth, I have seen Mr. Spiers who you claim it was and I am satisfied that he is not involved."

Hendry, "Donny made me do it."

Booth, "What are you saying?"

Hendry, "Donny rang up Mr. Smith and he said he was Mr. Spiers a solicitor."

Booth, " Mr. Smith at the Trustees Saving Bank was given two letters, one from Joseph Mellicks solicitors and one from another firm called Ross Harpers and Murphy, where did they come from?"

Hendry, "I gave them to Joan and Ted and they gave them

to Mr. Smith."

Booth, "Where did you get them from?"

Hendry, "I don't want to talk about it."

Booth, "Tell me about it then."

Hendry, "I typed them because Mr. Smith was pressurising Joan and Ted and they kept asking me to do something."

Booth, "So you have been stalling Joan and Ted because at the end of it there is no inheritance or legacy and it was all lies?"

Hendry, "Don't say that it all sound so terrible."

Booth, "Well that is what has happened, isn't it?"

Hendry, "Yes."

Booth, "So it is true to say that you have been pretending to be the illegitimate daughter of the Duchess of Argyll?"

Hendry, "Yes it's got out of hand. I'll pay Joan and Ted back."

McGarrgah," How can you do that? You have already said that you have no money?"

Hendry, "I will pay them back, I have an inheritance due to me. It's Uncle Jimmy's will."

McGarragh, "How much do you expect to get from that?"

Hendry, "I don't know."

McGarragh, "Who is the solicitor?"

Hendry, "It was McTaggart but he tried to get money from me so I put it in the hands of the Law Society."

McGarragh, "Who is dealing with it now?"

Hendry, "The Law Society."

McGarragh, "Surely they only investigate solicitors, they wouldn't pursue your claim, they would appoint somebody to deal with it. So who is dealing with it now?"

Hendry, "I don't know I've lost touch with it all."

McGarragh, "How long has the estate been in question?"

Hendry, "Eight years."

McGarragh, "Have you got documentary evidence to support this?"

Hendry, "No none, I've got his will."

McGarragh, "Where is it now?"

Hendry, "In the sideboard."

McGarragh, "Are you sure? I searched that."

Hendry, "That's where it should be."

McGarragh, "Well if you have a will at home you should know how much there is?"

Hendry, "I don't."

Booth, "I have a receipt written on Trustees Savings Bank paper."

Hendry looked at it and nodded.

Booth, "What can you tell me about it?"

Hendry, "Yes I signed it."

Booth, "Did you get £600.00 on this occasion?"

Hendry, "Yes."

Booth, "I have another receipt written on Trustees Savings Bank paper dated the 13th December 1983, do you recognise it?"

Hendry, "Yes."

Booth, "Did you sign it?"

Hendry, "Yes that's my signature."

Booth, "So on that date you got £862.00 from the Springburn Branch of the Trustees Savings Bank then?"

Hendry, "Yes, but do I have to go through all of these?"

Booth, "Yes you do."

Booth, " I have another receipt written on Trustees Savings Bank paper with no date on it, Do you recognise it?"

Hendry, "I wouldn't remember dates it's my signature."

Booth, "I have another receipt again written on Trustees Savings Bank paper dated 21st December 1983 for £630.00. Do you recognise it?"

Hendry, "Yes I signed that at the bank."

Booth, "So you received the £630.00?"

Hendry, "Yes but don't go through them all."

Booth, "I want to show you another receipt on Trustees Savings Bank paper for £ 485.00 dated 23rd December 1983."

Hendry, "Yes I remember that because it was a couple of days before Christmas."

Booth, "So you got the £485.00 on this occasion?"

Hendry, "Yes."

Booth, "I want to show you a letter of authority authorizing a Patrick Phee of Flat 5-1 Red Road Court to collect £800.00 from the Springburn Trustees Savings Bank."

Item shown to Hendry.

Booth, "Is that your writing?"

Hendry, "Yes I wrote that."

Booth, "Why?"

Hendry, "I was ill that day and Mr. Phee went and collected the money. "

Booth, "Did he give you the £800.00?"

Hendry, "Yes."

Booth, "I have another here which is a receipt signed by Mr. Phee dated 12th January 1984 when he collected £850.00 (shown receipt)

Hendry, "I haven't seen that before."

Booth, "You wouldn't have, but did Mr. Phee give you the £850.00?"

Hendry, "Yes."

Booth, "I want you to look at another receipt written on Trustees Savings Bank paper dated 13th January 1984."

(Shown receipt)

Hendry, "Yes that's another one Mr. Phee collected."

Booth, "Did you get the £300.00?"

Hendry, "Yes, he always gave me the money he collected."

Booth, "What did you tell him?"

Hendry, "I told him my mother was sending it to me."

Booth, "I have another receipt written on Trustees Savings Bank paper dated the 19th January 1984 for £ 1,500.00."

Hendry, "£1,500.00?"

Booth, "Yes."

(Shown receipt)

Hendry, "Yes, That's my signature, I had the £1,500.00"

Booth, "I want you to look at another receipt written on Trustees Savings Bank paper dated the 20th January 1984 for £600.00."

(Shown receipt)

Hendry, "Yes I went to the bank and signed that."

Booth, "So I take it you got the £600.00?"

Hendry, "Yes but do I have to go through all these?"

Booth, "Yes we do. "

Hendry, "How much is that, it all sounds terrible doesn't it?"

At this point I got my calculator out (I had a good idea that it would come to this and that at some point I would be asked this question)

Booth, "I make that £60,037.00 so far."

Booth, "I want to show you another letter of authority authorising Christine Cairney to collect £820.00 dated 23rd January 1984."

(Shown receipt)

Booth, "Do you recognise this?"

Hendry, "Yes."

Booth, "Is that your writing?"

Hendry, "Yes."

Booth, "Who is Christine Cairney?"

Hendry, "It's a friend of mine from Petersfield."

Booth, "Did she get the money from the bank?"

Hendry, "Yes."

Booth, "Did she give it to you?"

Hendry, "Yes she did."

Booth, "Did you make arrangements for a password to be used?"

Hendry, "Yes, CAMPBELL."

Booth, "For your information is this the slip that she signed?"

(Shown slip)

Hendry, "Yes, I see."

Booth, "I have another slip here dated 24th January 1984 for £500.00 that Christine Cairney collected."

Hendry, "Yes, that's at Fareham."

(Shown receipt)

Booth, "Did you collect these on the same day?"

Hendry, "No that one (Pointing to 23rd January slip) was on a Monday and the other one was on a Tuesday."

At this point I checked my diary and said "That's correct, Did Mrs. Cairney give you all the money she had collected for you?"

Hendry, "Yes."

Booth, "I have three others left which were collected at a different bank. "

Hendry, "Yes Dennistoun."

Booth, "So that's all the banks?"

Hendry, "Yes, Fareham, Springburn and Dennistoun."

Booth, "I want to show you another slip dated the 22nd December 1983 for £260.00."

(Shown slip)

Hendry, "Yes, that's my signature, I remember that one."

Booth, "These last three are for £260.00, £600.00 and £450.00 do they all bear your signature?"

Hendry, "Yes."

Booth, "And you have had the money?"

Hendry, "Yes."

Booth, "So it is correct to say that despite the fact that you haven't collected all the money, the money you haven't collected has still been given to you?"

Hendry, "Yes, that's right."

Booth, "Tell me what have you done with all the money?"

Hendry, "I don't know, I've nothing to show for it."

Booth, "Where did you stay when you were allegedly ill in Fareham?"

Hendry, "My sons."

Booth, "Tell me about the telephone calls form Fareham to Mr. Smith at the bank?"

Hendry, "Donny made those, I told him to tell Mr. Smith I had been taken ill, I was stalling him, trying to put him off."

Both, "How did you get down to Fareham?"

Hendry, "Robert my son took us in his car. There was me Robert, Donny and Christine Cairney, Roberts's girlfriend. Robert and his girlfriend and Christine stayed in the hotel."

Booth, "Who paid for the hotel?"

Hendry, "I did."

Booth, "Out of the Warner's money?"

Hendry, "Yes, Don't say that they were my only friends. It sounds horrible doesn't it?

Booth, "Mmmm, I have here a type of legal bill addressed

to yourself indicating you have expenses of £775.00, Do you recognise this?"

At this point Hendry was shown a copy of a legal bill given by the Warner's to Mr. Smith at the bank.

Hendry, "Yes, I typed that."

Booth, "What did you type it on?"

Hendry, "The typewriter you've got. I had fees to pay so I altered it."

Booth, "Who did you give it to?"

Hendry, "Joan and Ted."

Booth, "So it's a forgery then?"

Hendry, "Don't say that please it sounds bad."

Booth, "Well it is, so you had fees to pay and you forged a letter purporting it to have come from a solicitor?"

Hendry, "Yes I did."

Booth, "You see you have used an old letter as I have traced the numbers 10901 to a legal bill that you have previously received."

Hendry, "Yes that's right I used an old letter."

On the old bill you used was the name Robert Van Daal, do you know him?"

Hendry, "Yes."

Booth, "Who is he?"

Hendry, I'm not going to say, I don't want to."

At this point I showed Hendry an invoice in her name with the address of Burnside Bungalow Keills Bridge Isle of Jura Argyllshire.

Mrs. B Hendry v Robert Van Daal invoice number 10901

Hendry, "Yes, that's the one, Robert was going to move to a house at Bridge of Weir. Van Daal was the landlord and I had to stand as guarantor. Robert didn't pay his rent and we were served papers for it and that was one of them."

Booth, "I have here two letters, one on the official paper of Ross Harper and Murphy and the other on the official paper of Joseph Mellicks both reputable lawyers in the Glasgow area."

Hendry was shown the letters."

Hendry, "Yes, I remember those. I typed them and gave them to Joan and Ted and they took them to the bank where

Mr. Smith copied them and I remember Joan was cross."

Booth, "Did you type those letters out?"

Hendry, "Yes I did."

Booth, "So you have brought in the name of the Kantonal Bank in Zurich?"

Hendry, "Yes."

Booth, "Mr. Spiers rang up Mr. Smith at the Trustees Savings Bank in Lincoln and told him about a bank in Zurich."

Hendry, "That's the same one, it was Donny ringing up to stall Mr. Smith."

I then read out to Hendry a portion of the statement made by the Bank manager Mr. Smith outlining what "Mr. Spiers" had said in conversation.

Hendry, "Yes that was Donny."

Booth, "Later Mr. Smith was told by "Mr. Spiers" that you were too ill to travel, what about that?"

Hendry, "I wasn't very ill at all, but I didn't want to go and see Mr. Smith it was all closing in."

Booth, "I thought that you were supposed to have cancer of the pancreas?"

Hendry, "Yes I wasn't very well."

Booth, "And what about the haemorrhage you had on the plane then?"

Hendry, "I had a nose bleed."

Booth, "Was that when you flew down to Humberside?"

Hendry, "Yes."

Booth, "And when Mr. Smith picked you up in the car?"

Hendry, "That's when he gave me the flowers."

Booth, "When you were in the car you had a letter with you?"

Hendry, "Yes that was for Joan."

Booth, "And you read it out while you were in the back of the car, didn't you?"

Hendry, "Yes."

Booth, "What did it say?"

Hendry, "I can't remember exactly but there was something like "it's nasty isn't it". I remember that."

At this point Hendry was shown the letter produced by Mr.

Smith.

Booth, "It says here "nasty to say the least". Is this the one?"

Hendry, "Mmmm. It was for Joan. How did you get it?"

Booth, "So you typed the letter?"

Hendry, "Yes. "

Booth, "So it's a forgery then?"

Hendry, "Yes."

Both, "There is some mention of a Security Guard called "Wilson" who was going to bring down some jewellery and a Rembrandt to Lincoln. Does he exist?"

Hendry, "Yes it's Randolf, you met him yesterday."

McGarragh, "But he is a night watchman at the flats. Does he have a security business?"

Hendry, "No."

McGarragh, "So that's a lie as well?"

Hendry, "Yes."

McGarragh, "But he has rang and spoke to Mr. Smith at the Trustees Savings Bank in Lincoln."

HENDRY, "Yes but he didn't know anything about it I told him what to say."

Booth, "Can you remember telephoning Mr. Smith at the bank in Lincoln?"

Hendry, "Yes."

Booth, "Can you remember what was said?"

Hendry, "Yes it was about wanting some more money to settle an account."

Booth, "Yes, What was mentioned was that the extra expenses had been incurred and £ £485.00 was wanted to give to four solicitors. Can you remember that?"

Hendry, "Yes."

Booth, "Did you tell Mr. Smith that?"

Hendry, "Yes."

Booth, "Was it true?"

Hendry, "You know it wasn't true."

Booth, "So you were lying?"

Hendry, "Yes, but don't say it like that."

Booth, "But that is what it was, wasn't it?"

Hendry, "Yes."

Booth, "There is some mention of a Rembrandt painting."

Hendry, "Yes, that's the one that was in Uncle Jimmy's will."

Booth, "Where did you get it from?"

Hendry, "I bought it."

Booth, "Did you tell Mr. and Mrs. Warner it was a Rembrandt?"

Hendry, "Yes, I told them it was part of the inheritance."

Booth, "Uncle Jimmy's?"

Hendry, "No."

Booth, "So you told them it was part of the inheritance from the Duchess of Argyll?"

Hendry, "Yes."

Booth, "Is it a Rembrandt?"

Hendry, "No, it's a good copy."

Booth, "Mr. Smith says that when some of the money was sent to Fareham Trustees Savings Bank, he was told that you were in a nursing home in Newcastle. Is this correct?"

Hendry, "No I wasn't but Donny told him that I was."

Booth, "Did you tell Donny to tell Mr. Smith that?"

Hendry, "No."

Booth, "When did you start accepting money from Mr. and Mrs. Warner?"

Hendry, "A number of years ago."

Booth, "Have you had money sent to you by the Inland Telegraph Service?"

Hendry, "Yes I collected it from Post Offices."

Booth, "I have a number of receipts here what were sent to you on Jura from Mrs. Evelyn Warner at Hull."

Hendry, "Yes, that's Ted's sister-in-law."

At this point Hendry was shown a number of Post Office receipts.

Booth, "Have you had this money?"

Hendry, "Yes it sounds bad doesn't it?"

Booth, "Where is the money."

Hendry, "It's gone, I haven't got anything."

Booth, "We have further enquiries to make and will see you

again later."

At 12.20 hrs the same day the interview was concluded and Barbara Hendry was placed in the cells.

As is the norm after an interview we held a debrief to see where we were with the enquiry. Donald Hendry had admitted playing the part of Mr. Spiers the solicitor and his wife Barbara had admitted receiving the money from Joan and Ted Warner by deception. It all appeared a bit too easy at this stage.

The deception had been going on for a number of years and in excess of £60,000 had been obtained by false pretences. We needed to trace the "Doctor" that had spoken to the bank manager over the phone to outline how ill at one stage Barbara Hendry was, together with other individuals who had collected money from various post offices.

Also under consideration was the recovery of any funds but looking at where Hendry was living, together with her lifestyle this remained unlikely. Also at the back of my mind I knew that at some time in the near future I would need to visit Joan and Ted Warner and inform them of the progress we had made in the enquiry. The bottom line being that they had been the victims of a cruel and elaborate deception over a number of years with no likelihood of recovering their money. It was going to be a difficult situation, which would require careful handling I did not really relish the prospect but it had to be done. The bright side of the enquiry was that I was confident the deception had finally been brought to an end but now the real work was about to start.

***

At 1530 hours the same day in the company of Detective Constable McGarragh I attended an interview room at Lincoln Police Station where I again saw Barbara Hendry.

McGarragh, "You are not obliged to say anything unless you wish to do so but what you say may be put into writing and given in evidence. Do you understand?"

Hendry, "Yes."

I then read a page of the bank manager's statement to

Hendry and said to her, "Do you remember about wanting £485.00 to pay the final account for four solicitors?"

Hendry, "Yes, I recollect something regarding four solicitors."

Booth, "Did you get the money?"

Hendry, "Yes, I collected it from the bank."

At this point Hendry was shown another receipt.

Hendry, "Yes that's my signature?"

At this point I read another extract from the statement of the Bank Manager and asked, "Can you remember saying that one of the solicitors involved considered himself as the most senior and wanted £531.00 and that you had taken £120.00 to his home?"

Hendry, "Yes I did."

Booth, "…and you obviously informed Mr. Warner you had gone to the Island of Lewis to consult with a "Gentleman of Law".

Hendry, "Yes I remember that."

Booth, "Did you tell Mr. Warner that?"

Hendry, "Yes I did."

Booth, "Did you go to the Island of Lewis and contact a "Gentleman of Law?"

Hendry, "Yes I did. "

Booth, "Who was that?"

Hendry, "My ex-husband, he was a policeman."

At this point Hendry was shown another receipt on Trustees Savings Bank paper.

Booth, "Do you recognise this?"

Hendry, "Yes, I collected that from Dennistoun."

Booth, "In effect you have made arrangements with Mr. and Mrs. Warner to have this £600.00 made available and collected it?"

Hendry, "Yes."

Booth, "When the circumstances surrounding the reason why you wanted it were false."

Hendry, "Yes they were."

Booth, "So this £600.00 was in respect of the payment you wanted for a solicitor that didn't exist?"

Hendry, "That's right."

Booth, "But really you wanted £531.00 and got £600.00?"

Hendry, "Does it matter? I had the money."

Booth, "There is mention of you going to a bank in Glasgow with a solicitor called Legget, Who is he?"

Hendry, "It was my Uncle Jimmy's solicitor on the business and taxation side."

Booth, "Did you go to the bank with him?"

Hendry, "No."

Booth, "But you collected the money on the strength of it, didn't you?"

Hendry, "Yes."

Booth, "It has been mentioned that while the jewellery, the cheque and the Rembrandt were on the way down from Scotland there was a robbery at a Post Office."

Hendry, "Yes there was one but it was a bit of luck really because it helped stall Mr. Smith, we said that it had held things up."

Booth, "Several references have been made that you needed to travel by ambulance. Were any such arrangements made?"

Hendry, "No, it was all part of the story."

Booth, "Were you ill at all?"

Hendry, "I was poorly."

Booth, "Did you need to travel by ambulance?"

Hendry, "No."

Booth, "Have you got cancer of the Pancreas?"

Hendry, "No."

McGarragh, "So in effect what you have done over the last 7 years is dishonestly misled the Warner's and Mr. Smith into believing that you are related to the Duchess of Argyll and due an inheritance of seven million pounds."

Hendry, "Yes, it just got out of hand."

McGarragh, "Furthermore, you have dishonestly obtained money making those people believe you needed money to pursue your legal claims to an inheritance that didn't exist."

Hendry, "It sounds terrible, I had to keep lying to cover it all up. It got out of hand, it snowballed, I couldn't face them all.

McGarragh, "Do you want to make a written statement?"

Hendry, "Oh no, I couldn't. I don't want to go through that all again."

At 16.30 hours the same day the interview was concluded and I formally charged Barbara Hendry with three offences of Criminal Deception, to which she replied, "Yes that's it, that's what I did."

Later at 1845 hours in the company of Detective Constable McGarragh I attended the foyer at Lincoln Police station Lincoln Police Station where I saw Donald Hendry.

Booth, "Thank you for coming down from Scotland you obviously know that we need to speak to you.

Hendry, "Aye I do, how is Banette is she alright?"

Booth, "Yes she is."

McGarragh, "You are not obliged to say anything unless you wish to do so but what you say may be put into writing and given in evidence. We have made further enquiries into the matter we discussed yesterday and I am arresting you on suspicion of committing Criminal Deception. Do you understand?"

Hendry, "Yes but, but."

Booth, "No buts, you know what this is all about."

Hendry was taken to an interview room at Lincoln Police Station where he was interviewed in the company of the Duty Solicitor.

Hendry, "Yes, I would like to tell you all about it. I couldn't sleep last night, I was so worried,"

McGarragh, "Tell us about your part in the deceptions and the actions of Barbara towards the Warner's."

Hendry, "I told you I made all those phone calls, I didn't want to do it, but I thought it would be alright and the money was on its way."

McGarragh, "Did you believe that she was the illegitimate daughter of the Duchess of Argyll?"

Hendry, "Aye, she told me she was the Countessa De Leone, that's her other title and I believed her. I even had a phone call from her mother, at least that's who she said she was asking how much I wanted, she said I wasn't good enough for her and offered me money."

McGarragh, "Do you know who made the phone call?"

Hendry, "No, she offered me £5000 or £10,000 but I wouldn't take it I didn't' want the money."

McGarragh, "Are you telling us that throughout your life with Barbara you genuinely believed all of this?"

Hendry, "Yes I did. In fact she came with me to meet my parents and she said she was the Countessa De Leone and she rang up the jewellers, Thompson's in Aberfeldy, they came round to bring a couple of trays of rings to look at to see if she wanted to buy some but she sent them back. Barbara told me the man to contact was Lord Wheatley who would verify who she was. She said all sorts of things. She told my mum she was going to take me to Switzerland and make me a Baron. In fact she borrowed £500 from my family to pay her tax. She also had some rings from McGowan's in Edinburgh. My parents were impressed, they'd never seen anything like it."

Booth, "When did all this start?"

Hendry, "Barbara was working in a hotel and came home one day and said that she was bringing some people home for tea. It was Joan and Ted."

Booth, "Did you now that Barbara was borrowing money from Joan and Ted?"

Hendry, "I didn't until recently because Barbara would have all this money and I asked her where it was coming from and she said her "Mummy" the Duchess was sending it to her."

Booth, "How long has it all been going on?"

Hendry, "I don't know, I'm beginning to wonder but we've known Joan and Ted years, but just a minute, who are these people then that I was supposed to have met? her mother the Duchess? I don't know."

Booth, "What can you tell me about Mr. Spiers?"

Hendry, "Oh yes that was me."

Booth, "Tell me about it."

Hendry, "Barbara was getting money sent to her from the Warner's, She told me that she wanted me to ring up a Mr. Smith, he's a nice man at the Trustees Savings Bank at Lincoln to tell him various things to stall him."

Booth, "What did you tell him?"

Hendry, "Lots of things. Barbara had it written on the card what I had to say. But I couldn't do it anymore."

Booth, "So you pretended to be a Mr. Spiers a solicitor to assist Barbara to get monies released?"

Hendry, "Yes, I'm sorry."

Booth, "What you said did you know it wasn't true?"

Hendry, "Of course I did. I had to have a whiskey before I would say it though."

Booth, "What about legal documents like this?" Hendry was shown the two legal letters provided by Barbara Hendry to give to Joan and Ted to be shown Mr. Smith the bank manager. (Police Item LAS 28)

Hendry, "Yes I've seen them before because Barbara typed them and I went down to the library and copied them for her."

Booth, "What typewriter did she use?"

Hendry, "She's clever, she used the one in our flat but she also used another in the office at the flats because she said it wouldn't be right to do them all on the same typewriter."

Booth, "So she typed quite a few letters then?"

Hendry, "Yes, she used to type them in bed first thing in the morning because she said her brain was more alert."

Booth, "Where are all the letters?"

Hendry, "Barbara was mad one day because Joan and Ted had been to the bank and seen Mr. Smith and let him photostat some of the letters, then Joan and Ted went to see him again and he told them that he thought the letters were forgeries."

Booth, "What did Barbara do?"

Hendry, "She got rid of them all, three bags there were."

Booth, "Can you remember how many times Barbara has been to the bank or the Post Office to collect money?"

Hendry, "I can't remember but it's a lot, she never let me go because she didn't want me to sign anything."

Booth, "Why was that?"

Hendry, " Because she had told Joan and Ted that we had separated but we hadn't really, in fact when Joan came up to Glasgow I wasn't supposed to be there and Barbara told Joan that I was just visiting. She told Joan and Ted that I had cancer once but I didn't."

Booth, "What do you know about what Barbara had told Joan and Ted?"

Hendry, "She told them that she would give them a lot of money and buy them a BMW and a hotel for their daughter."

Booth, "Who else have you telephoned?"

Hendry, "I phoned a number in London and I phoned the housing department in Lincoln and told them that the money was on its way."

Booth, "Tell me about that?"

Hendry, "Joan and Ted had told Barbara that they were behind with the rent and Barbara got me to telephone the housing department to tell them that the money was on the way. I told them that I was a Clerk of the Court in Scotland."

McGarragh, "Do you mean to tell me that Barbara knew that the Warner's were behind with the rent and still pressed them to send money to her?"

Hendry, "Yes, she had a registered envelope come for her the day before she was arrested. I don't know how much was in it because she never told me but she brought herself two pairs of sunglasses, £59 they cost."

McGarragh, "So Barbara knew that the Warner's were getting short of money?"

Hendry, "Yes in fact I can remember Mr. Smith telling me what a desperate financial plight the Warner's were in and I told Barbara and she said "That's a lie." You see Mr. Smith was a nice man but Barbara said he was greedy and a liar but she told me that when she went down to meet him he gave he a bouquet of flowers."

Booth, "I know about that."

McGarragh, "What do you know about Mr. Wilson's part in all this?"

Hendry, "He was the same as me I think, he believed her. He made a couple of phone calls reading out what she had written down."

McGarragh, "But she borrowed his typewriter?"

Hendry, "Yes, I had to fetch it for her he didn't know what it was for."

Booth, "How many times did you ring Mr. Smith posing as Mr. Spiers?"

Hendry, "Quite a few."

Booth, "Where did you phone from?"

Hendry, "The flat or a hotel and I phoned a couple of times when we were down in Fareham to see Barbara's son. I phoned from Stubbington."

Booth, "What did Barbara tell you when she was getting the money and it was mounting up?"

Hendry, "She said "Don't worry I will get a personal cheque from Mummy and square up Joan and Ted." It's terrible when you think about it. She told Mr. Smith she was going to buy a hotel in Portsmouth and make him a Director."

Booth, "What did Barbara say about telling people that she was the illegitimate daughter of the Duchess of Argyll?"

Hendry, "She told me that if the police ever asked me that I was to deny it and say that I didn't know what they were on about, but I'm pleased it's all coming out now. She told the Warner's that I was in debt to my ex-wife but it's all lies. Do you know that she even stopped my family seeing me in hospital?"

Booth, "What else happened?"

Hendry, "She used to telephone Mr. Smith to delay things but I don't know what would have happened in the end."

Booth, "Where has all the money gone?"

Hendry, "I don't know, she never gave me any of it. She used to give a lot to Sonny."

Both, "Who is that?"

Hendry, "That's her son Robert. She brought him two Jaguars because he was going to start a business."

Booth, "You see Donny, although you accept your part in this by posing as Mr. Spiers there are other people involved like Mr. Wilson the security guard at the flats."

Hendry, "I see, Yes."

Booth, "Who is Doctor Turner?"

Hendry, "I think a woman called Beth Skillern was her."

Booth, "Who is she?"

Hendry, "She lives in the flats, she phoned once but Barbara would tell such stories that they didn't think that they were doing any wrong."

Booth, "Does Doctor Turner really exist?"

Hendry, "Yes there is a Doctor Turner."

Booth, "Where can I find Beth Skillern?"

Hendry, "She lives at the flats in fact," he paused a minute and then said, " Her telephone number is 041 *** **** "

Booth, "What else?"

Hendry, "Barbara brought Robert clothes and all sorts."

Booth, "What else have you Photostatted for Barbara?"

Hendry, "I Photostatted a birth certificate for her once, I got four copies but I didn't really read them. I just gave them to her. I think that she sent one to Joan and Ted."

Booth, "Yes but what happened to the other three?"

Hendry, "I don't know what Barbara has done with them."

Booth, "Telephone calls have been made to Mr. Smith at the Trustees Savings Bank from all over the country."

Hendry, "Yes I made them but I told Barbara that I wasn't going to make any more."

Booth, "Have you stayed in any hotels with Barbara?"

Hendry, "Yes quite a few."

Booth, "Where are they and what are are they called?"

Hendry "Let me think. There was the Royal Hotel in Glasgow, the Bucannon Hotel opposite Queen Street Station in Glasgow, the hotel in Rutherglen and the Pine Trees Hotel in Glasgow."

Booth, "What happened at the hotels?"

Hendry," What do you mean?"

Booth, "Who did Barbara say that she was?"

Hendry, "I can't remember really but she used to give out £5 and £10 tips, the staff loved it."

McGarragh, "Did you go with Barbara to collect any money from the Post Offices?"

Hendry, "I know she went to them regular, but she didn't tell me about it."

McGarragh, "Because the Warner's, that's Joan and Ted, and his sister-in-law Evelyn, had been sending money up to Post Offices in Scotland for a long time.

Hendry, "Where does Ted's sister-in-law live?"

Booth, "Hull."

Hendry, "I've been there."

Booth, "What have you heard Barbara tell the Warner's?"

Hendry, "She said that she had a big fund coming. I believed it as well."

Booth, "But you still rang Mr. Smith at the bank and pretended to be Mr. Spiers the solicitor."

Hendry, "Yes it was wrong, I shouldn't have done it."

Booth, "And there are the forged letters."

Hendry, "Yes, I know. I've seen her cutting the letters up with a razor blade and sticking them together again and typing on them to make new letters."

Booth, "How often?"

Hendry, "I've only seen it a couple of times."

Booth, "Have you made any other phone calls and pretended to be anybody else?"

Hendry, "No Sir, no I haven't that was enough."

Booth, "Do you obviously realise what you were doing was wrong?"

Hendry, "Yes, I do."

Booth, "And by making these calls you have assisted Barbara in her story and made Mr. Smith of the Trustees Savings Bank release more money?"

Hendry, "Yes, I realise that."

Booth, "Have you ever been to any Post Offices to collect money for Barbara?"

Hendry, "Yes a while ago but not recently."

Booth, "The Bank Manager, Mr. Smith says that a Mr. Spiers phoned him to say that he was flying to Zurich."

Hendry, "Yes, I remember that, it was me."

Booth, "Can you remember saying that seven hundred and fifty five thousand pounds was to be sent to the Warner's?"

Hendry, "Yes, Barbara told me to say that."

Booth, "Did you ring Mr. Smith saying that you were in Zurich?"

Hendry, "Yes I did."

Booth, "…and you assured him that you would return with

the money?"

Hendry, "Yes I did."

Booth, "Can you remember ringing Mr. Smith at the Trustees Savings Bank and telling him that you had been to the Probate Court and that you required £1500 extra?"

Hendry, "Yes I did and Mr. Smith made arrangements to have the money sent to Scotland."

Booth, "Who collected it?"

Hendry, "Barbara did."

Booth, "Did you tell Mr. Smith that Mrs. Hendry was too ill to   travel?"

Hendry, "Yes I did."

Booth, "Was she?"

Hendry, "No."

Booth, "How about £600 for an account? Did you tell Mr. Smith that you had to have the £600.00?"

Hendry, "Yes I did and he sent it again."

Booth, "Did you also tell Mr. Smith that the car had skidded on a Little Chef car park and had an oil leak?"

Hendry, "Yes but that did happen but were on our way to Ronald's in Fareham."

Booth, "Who is that?"

Hendry, "Barbara's son."

Booth, "You also told Mr. Smith that Mrs. Hendry has had a hemorrhage and had been rushed into a Newcastle nursing home, was that correct?"

Hendry, "No it was a lie. Barbara told me what to say."

Booth, "Did you mention traveling by helicopter?"

Hendry, "Yes, but I didn't go on one."

Booth, "Was there extra money wanted due to expenses at the Nursing home?"

Hendry, "Yes I rang Mr. Smith and told him I needed more money to pay the costs and he sent some up, £800 I think."

Booth, "What about the bus station?"

Hendry, "Yeah, I told him that I had spent the night in one I think I told him I wanted some more money and he sent it to Fareham."

Booth, "Did you ever ring Mr. Smith at home?"

Hendry, "Yes, a few times. I felt sorry for that man but I only told him what Barbara told me to, don't misunderstand me I knew it was wrong."

Booth, "So what you have done is told stories to Mr. Smith in an effort to get him to release more funds for false purposes which he has done?"

Hendry, "That's right, I feel sorry for Joan and Ted and Mr. Smith know I shouldn't have done it but Barbara said she would square it all up in the end."

Booth, "We have further enquiries to make and we will see you later."

At 19.45 hours the same day Hendry was handed to the custodian and replaced in his cell.

At 12.35 hours on Friday 20th April 1984 in the company of Detective Constable McGarragh I attended an interview room at Lincoln Police Station where I again saw Donald Francis Hendry.

Booth, "I must inform you that you are not obliged to say anything unless you wish to do so, but what you say may be put into writing and given in evidence. Do you understand?"

Hendry, "Yes I do."

Booth, "Since we last saw you we have made further enquiries and we have now established that a very large sum of money has been sent to you and Barbara from the Warner's."

Hendry, "Yes, I told you that they had been sending money."

Booth, "That's right but I'm talking about thousands somewhere between thirty and fifty thousand pounds."

Hendry, "I knew it was a lot but not that much."

Booth, "Where has all the money gone?"

Hendry, "I haven't had much of it, she bought me a suite and I stayed in the hotels with her but I don't know where it has all gone."

Booth, "What has she spent it on?"

Hendry, "Well she bought her son Robert the Jaguars but they're not new ones and there is the furniture in the flat.
She bought that but where the rest has gone I don't know."

Booth, "Can you remember copying the birth certificates?"

Hendry, "Yes."

Booth, "Did you read them?"

Hendry, "No, I just went to Denistoun library, photostatted them and gave them to her. I didn't read them."

Booth, "I have seen the copy that was sent to Joan and Ted Warner and it clearly implies that Barbara was related to the Duchess of Argyll."

Hendry, "Yes, that's what I said she was saying; she told people she was the Countess De Leonie

McGarragh, " Can you see what has been happening that this has all been one big deception on the Warner's and they have been used and taken for all their money."

Hendry, "I know it's terrible. I don't know why I did ring Mr. Smith saying I was Mr. Spiers but Barbara wrote down what I had to say and she'd give me a whiskey and I'd read it. She's very persuasive you know."

At this point we had a general conversation with regards to Hendry's background and at 13.10 the interview was concluded.

At 14.20 hours the same day and at the request of Donald Hendry I again attended an interview room where we saw Donald Hendry. I reminded him that he was still under caution and he said, "Since I last saw you I have been thinking about where all the money has gone. You see as I said we stayed in the hotels and Barbara was buying things for the flat and clothes for Robert."

McGarragh, "What did Robert think?"

Hendry, "I don't know."

McGarragh, "Can you remember where else the money has gone?"

Hendry, "You see we had to move from Jura when the bills started mounting up, I can remember one month the phone bill was £178 then it all started again on Jura and we had to move again."

McGarragh, "So you accept that by ringing up Mr. Smith and posing as Mr. Spiers you did wrong?"

Hendry, "Yes."

McGarragh, "How many times?"

Hendry, "A few,, five or six."

McGarragh, "And it was to arrange money to be sent to Glasgow and Fareham each time?"

Hendry, "Yes."

McGarragh, "Do you want to make a written statement about it?"

Hendry, "Yes."

McGarragh, "Do you want to write it or shall I?"

Hendry, "You can."

At 14.30 hours the same day Detective Constable McGarragh wrote Hendry's details at the top of a voluntary statement form and then the preamble, which he read over and signed. Hendry then dictated his statement, which was written down.

VOLUNTARY STATEMENT

NAME   Donald Francis Hendry Occupation Unemployed

ADDRESS Flat 12/1 10 Red Road Court Springburn Glasgow

I Donald Francis Hendry wish to make a statement. I want someone to write down what I say. I have been told that I need not say anything unless I wish to do so and that whatever I say may be given in evidence. Signed D Hendry I've lived with Barbara Hendry for ten or eleven years. My ex-wife met her in Gateshead prison and invited her up for a holiday. I got divorced and made my home with Barbara. She told me that she was the illegitimate daughter of the Duchess of Argyll, the Countessa De Leonie. She told me not to tell anybody about it but she told a lot of people about it. I believed her wholeheartedly because I had a phone call from a lady who said she was the Duchess of Argyll. I called her Mrs. Campbell, she asked me how much money I wanted to leave her daughter, £5000 or £10,000 was mentioned. I said I didn't want the inheritance, I was there because I loved Barbara. During this time she was getting money from Joan saying it was to pay off legal debts, but it was for debts for the house. She was giving money to her family making out she had a lot of money. She was saying she had a lot of money in the building society that Joan's daughter worked at. She made out to the Warners that her lawyers had had me put into a psychiatric prison because I had threatened to expose her. All this was a load of rubbish and I didn't know anything about it until Joan came up to see Barbara. I knew something of what was going on but from Christmas things went quiet. She would close the door on me. I wasn't allowed to hear the phone calls. There was money going into banks at Duke Street and Springburn. I questioned her where the money was coming from; she said it was coming from her mother. The first two or three times I believed her, then I said that the money was coming from Joan then she admitted it. Then Barbara said that Joan was getting loans from Mr Smith at the bank, but she would be alright because of her big legacy coming from Switzerland. Then she had to get some letters typed to send to the bank for Mr Smith and Joan. I took the letters. I photocopied some letters but I didn't know what they were about she told me not to look. Mostly she used the old typewriter in the flat, sometimes she used the one in the flat's

147

office, the housing office "So they won't say it was the same typewriter" she said. She was cutting up solicitor's letters and sellotaping them together. I had to photocopy the letters and take them back to her. When she started doing this I started to get a bit doubtful. She said, "It will be alright Donny, It's just to stall them till I get my inheritance" and " my mum is going to send Joan and Ted a cheque" The last letter I sent, Joan telephoned Barbara and said that Mr Smith had seen it and said it was a forgery. Barbara started tearing up all the papers, legal documents and letters. She put them in a bag and got rid of them. She told me that if the police asked about the Duchess of Argyll that I knew nothing. On about five or six occasions Barbara asked me to make phone calls. It was all written out to tell me what to say. I didn't want to do it. We always had a row about it I know I was wrong doing it but as she said "It was to get Joan and Ted off the hook until the inheritance came through". I phoned Mr Smith twice from Stubbington, I told him I was Mr Spiers. I can't remember what I said it was all written down. It was to do with paying court bills. I think one was to do with the bank of Kantonel. I told him once I was ringing from Zurich. I rang Mr Smith at home twice and told him what Barbara had told me to say. The only reason I pretended to be Mr Spiers, the solicitor, was because Barbara told me it was to keep Mr Smith off Joan and Teds back. Each time it was to have money paid to Barbara from Joan and Teds account, except the last time when I told her I wasn't going to ask for any more money. I made a phone call to London and to the council it was all to do with Joan and Teds debt. I told them I was the Clerk of the Court and gave them the message she had written down. I had to say that Mr and Mrs Warner were in the position because they were beneficiaries of a will and the money would be paid by the 16th or 17th of the month. I can't be sure what month it was. I phoned these places twice. I know that I was wrong to make the phone calls but I did genuinely believe that there was a big inheritance due. It was a lie from me, it was a lie to me. I am very sorry for the trouble I have caused all those people and would like to apologise most sincerely. If there anything I can possibly do to make up for it I will.

Signed D Hendry

I have read the above statement and have been told that I can correct alter or add anything I wish. This statement is true I have made it of my own free will.

Signed D Hendry

At 16.30 the same day the statement and the interview was concluded.

At 19.45 hours the same day I formally cautioned and charged Donald Hendry with one offence of criminal deception to which he made no reply. Both were replaced in their cells and stayed in police custody overnight.

Silently I breathed a sigh of relief. We had obviously got the right people and that Donny had admitted his part. After talking to him it was obvious to me that I had not met "the brains behind the job" but he had to accept his part in the deception as after all he had posed as the solicitor Mr Speirs and had even telephoned the local housing authority posing as a "Clerk of the Court" in a calculated attempt to stop Joan and Ted being evicted as they had got behind in paying their rent. I really saw this as a very cynical ploy.

It had been decided that because of the seriousness of the offence and the relationship between Hendry and Joan and Ted that a special court would be convened and an application would be made for both to be remanded in custody at a local prison. Both appeared at Court the following day and a successful remand hearing took place. Both were remanded in custody and taken away to appear at court at a later date. The application was obviously contested but dismissed.

It was at this point when both Barbara and Donald Hendry had admitted the offences of Criminal Deception and had been charged I decided that since I was absolutely certain that a scam had been practiced I would visit Joan and Ted and break the bad news. I wanted to be beyond doubt in my mind that I got to the bottom of the problem and had established just exactly had been going on.

In my quieter moments, not that there had been many in the

last 24 hours, I was becoming to be very suspicious how easy it had all been dealt with. Barbara Hendry had made some admissions but declined to make a statement and her husband had admitted his part and made a written statement.

Upon seeing Joan and Ted I still had some unanswered questions that I knew I was going to be asked. I had more or less found out who had been playing the various parts in the deception such as Mr. Spiers and the Security Guard but this had not been fully resolved as they had not been all traced and interviewed.

I left Lincoln Police Station and drove towards Dunholme not really sure what I was going to say to Joan and Ted but satisfied that whatever form it took it would no doubt be a devastating blow for them.

Here I was about to tell a very trusting and honest couple that their " friend " of seven years was nothing more than a calculating and ruthless fraudster and that all the money that had been sent to the Hendry's had been lost and no doubt frittered away.

I duly arrived at the house early evening and walked up the path and knocked on the door. As usual the door was answered by Ted who gave me a look in the eye that made me think that he knew what was coming, either that or I was imagining that to make the task easier for myself.

I was invited into the lounge and sat down in the chair. Both sat as usual in a very clean neat but sparsely furnished lounge, but the atmosphere had changed. They said that since my last visit a few days before neither had slept. The matter had been discussed at length and after listening to another request for money to assist with "expenses" from Barbara Hendry a couple of days before, they realised that something was wrong they had decided to stall Barbara not really because they were suspicious, but that together with the fact they did not have any further avenues available where they could borrow further money and assist their "friend". Joan had pressed Barbara during a telephone call as to when it would all be finalised but received another reason why the settlement of the inheritance had been delayed. Barbara had asked if something was wrong but Joan had put her mind at rest saying that "she was feeling a bit under the weather that's all."

After this further delay and the further request for money both Joan and Ted thought enough was enough whilst still hoping that it was all a mistake and that the inheritance was genuine. They had remembered our previous conversation and that they had virtually promised me that they would not send any further money to Barbara but had been faced with a conflict as if they declined to send any further money according to Barbara all would be lost. Eventually they decided that they could not raise any further money from anywhere else.

It was a strange situation whereby both Joan and Ted although very good listeners just continued talking about the weather and all sorts of issues, anything but what I was there for and I could not basically get a word in. I later came to the conclusion that this was some sort of reaction to their predicament and that they did not really want to hear the obvious bad news that I was the bearer of. I just decided to sit and listen.

During our conversation it was revealed that Joan and Ted had seriously "gone without" to assist Barbara with funds regarding the settlement of her inheritance. The family car due to the expense was hardly being used except for special occasions eventually being sold and that both had to either catch the bus to work or rely on lifts from work colleagues. Both Joan and Ted had for a number of years gone without their annual holiday and the money put by for such events had been sent to Barbara. Ted stated that between Joan and him due to the shortage of money they had, on occasions made a tin of corned beef last for three meals., They had even in an attempt to save money had their telephone disconnected and all telephone conversations with Barbara Hendry had taken place at the phone box in their village at pre-arranged times irrespective of the weather. Both Joan and Ted were very proud people who would not even entertain the prospect of contacting relatives or even closer family regarding their own dire financial needs. But in order to help a dear friend they were prepared to approach friends and relatives to borrow money, later finance companies and finally the bank. They were both distraught at the thought of being victims of a deception. This revelation did not surprise me, as they were on the verge of admitting that they in fact had been victims of a grand deception over a number of years. Their good nature had been taken advantage of and left them in a financial position, from which in my view, they were unlikely ever to recover from, which in the event turned out to be true.

In the end I had to confront Joan and Ted with the fact that Barbara Hendry and her partner Donnie had both been arrested, Barbara in Glasgow and brought down to Lincoln, and Donny in Lincoln when he arrived to visit Barbara. I informed them that the flat in Glasgow had been searched and that a number of items had been found which corroborated the fact that we had "got the right" people. Furthermore they had both been interviewed and admitted their part in the deception that had run over a number of years.

"Where is she now?" asked Ted.

I told them that both had been arrested and interviewed and were in the cells at Lincoln Police station and would be going to court the following morning.

Upon being told the facts both Joan and Ted went silent and looked at each other. Over the years I have been in a number of different situations and been the bearer of bad news from victims of traffic accidents to murder victims and whilst this situation did not rate as high on the scale of some of the previous situations, I have rarely felt as sorry for a couple as I did at that time for Joan and Ted. Upon looking at their faces I could see that both of them were devastated by the news. The fact that they had been deceived out of a large amount of money and that they have been left in serious debt levelled with the fact that their trust in Barbara and Donny over a period of years had been totally abused. I actually witnessed Ted slump down into the chair and looked perplexed, he was obviously at a loss to understand what had gone wrong.

The first thing Ted said, in response to the news was "How's Barbara?" then realising what he had said shook his head and went silent. Joan in contrast was stuck for words.

I decided that the first step would be to record a statement of complaint from either Joan or Ted. Ted made the decision for me in stating he was prepared to make a statement and appear in court if necessary. Now was not the time to "Rake it all up" and decided to leave both Joan and Ted to talk together and would call again later.

Chapter Ten: The story unfolds

I attended their house a couple of nights later sat down and discussed the scenario from beginning to end over a period of four or so hours. The couple were extremely disappointed about what had transpired, secretly hoping that a telephone call would be received at the phone box down the road stating the inheritance had been resolved.

Before actually settling down and writing a word Ted said to me, "Since it has gone this way, I think we had better tell you it all."

He left the room and returned with an old rather battered looking suitcase which when he opened it I saw contained a large quantity of neatly bound letters and other documents.

"We have saved all the letters and the other documents you had better have a look at them."

Upon looking through the documents they had retained I found that there were in excess of 100 letters from Barbara Hendry together with a quantity of legal documents from various solicitors, Trust deeds a copy of a birth certificate and a rather elaborate looking will written neatly on A3 paper, and in longhand. The writing appeared to be in old script. The will was titled "The will of Barbara De Leonie Burnside Bungalow Isle of Jura.' I also saw that the will had also been witnessed by two individuals one being called P Bryson Stoeness of Halling road Dunoon giving his occupation as a Surgeon and the other a James McGrouther of Castlegreen Street Dumbarton his occupation being given as a Solicitor. Upon reading the will, which was on the correct form and gave details of how any inheritance received should be divided up naming a number of beneficiaries including Joan and Ted Warner. To the untrained eye it looked an authentic document and had obviously taken a lot of time and care to prepare, but in due course it will be further examined and the witnesses to the document if they existed will certainly need to be traced. Also typed on the front of the will was the words "ORIGINAL

WILL COPY WITH TILSON & CO SOLICITORS
GLASGOW" this would be easily enough to prove or
disprove…. all in due course I thought to myself.

The first task was to place all the letters and documents in
chronological order so the story was in sequence and accurate.
The sorting out of the documents took the remainder of the
evening being ably assisted by Joan and Ted who often broke
off the task to explain the circumstances behind many of the
documents.

Both Joan and Ted relayed the story from the start. How
they had first met Barbara and how she had confided in them
that she was the illegitimate daughter of the Duchess of
Argyll. They had been shown birth certificates that verified
her claim, in particular the birth certificate showed her place of
birth as Oceanside New York. There had been a plethora of
letters from various firms of Solicitors and Trust documents
and what puzzled them both was that they had spoken to a
security guard called Mr Wilson whose responsibility was to
guard the Rembrandt painting that they had seen on a visit to
Barbara's cottage. They had also spoken to Dr Turner a doctor
from Glasgow who had been treating Barbara on a private
basis and had also spoken to the bank manager Mr Smith.
Then there had been the solicitor Mr Spiers who had been
pursuing the inheritance in Switzerland and had spoken to the
bank manager on a number of occasions! There were so many
questions to be answered. They had been hoping that I was
wrong despite the evidence building up. After a long evening
it was time to go and to actually let it all sink and put pen to
paper at our next appointment. I thought that there would be a
few letters but not as many as they had in their possession. I
realised that recording a statement would be no small task as it
would be necessary to go through all the letters and exhibit
them in any witness statement that was to be recorded. As in a
majority of fraud cases it can be a laborious task because
during the recording of any statement the statement taker has
to keep in mind the offence that is to be proved. In this case
the offence would be forgery and deception so what had to be
shown in support of any charges is that the victims were

deceived and lied to and this is where the letters and other correspondence come into play. As it happens I was ready for this part of the enquiry and looked forward to seeing just what lies had been told and the depths the deception actually went to.

I left Joan and Ted's house later that evening and it is not very often that I have felt as sorry for two individuals as I did that night. It was obvious to me that they had total trust in Barbara Hendry and that trust had been betrayed on a grand scale. What I also found of surprise is that the fraud had been carried out over the period of a number of years from 1976 to 1983 in total nearly 7 years! I was astounded at the amount of paperwork that they possessed. I had previously wondered how this type of fraud would be carried out and how the deception could have continued for such a long period of time but having seen the paperwork including solicitors letters on headed notepaper together with a number of writs and summons's it was obvious that a lot of work had gone into this offence. I felt that the honesty together with the trusting nature of Joan and Ted had been seriously taken advantage of and I was able to console myself with the fact that my persistence had no doubt brought it to an end although deep down I knew to the lack of finance the whole saga would be coming to an end sooner or later. It was also obvious that Barbara Hendry was not too concerned as long as she was still being sent money from a couple who could not afford it. Thinking it through, my resolve hardened further, no matter how long it took and how much work was to be involved this woman needed to be stopped and brought to justice.

As corny as it seems detectives do encountered cases that they feel so strongly about that they will follow leads to the end of the earth to finalise an enquiry and I was satisfied that this was going to be mine - for the time being anyway, whatever it takes.

Over the following three weeks I sat down at the home of Joan and Ted in the evening and after they had finished work and compiled a witness statement of exactly what had happened. Rarely had I encountered a situation where an offender had so literally taken advantage of their victims and taken it to such an extreme lengths.

Both Joan and Ted had on such a grand scale "gone without" to assist Barbara Hendry in the belief that they were helping a friend financially. I genuinely believed that the helping out by Joan and Ted was not a matter of making a profit for them but sincerely helping a person they honestly considered to be a friend only to have been taken advantage of. (certain readers will no doubt view this with a certain amount of cynicism, but take it from me as the investigator who got to know both Joan and Ted extremely well this was certainly not the case.)

The actual taking of the statement included recording and exhibiting a large number of letters and Inland Telegraph Service receipts, which totalled around £60,000 (approx quarter of a million pounds today) over a period of years, money that had been sent at Barbara's request to her at various locations in and around the UK. I was surprised by the amount of paperwork in their possession. The paperwork explained numerous delays that had occurred; various expenses that needed paying and most were on the headed notepaper of solicitors. In all there were over 100 letters produced to me by Ted, I could not wait to read them all, identify the lies that had been told and "nail the offender". I was satisfied that Barbara Hendry would not be expecting Joan and Ted to have retained all this paperwork as on occasions she had sent legal paperwork to Joan and Ted with the express request that it was "read and sent back by return of mail" obviously the intention was to leave Joan and Ted with very little paperwork at all in case the police became involved. This conduct is typical behavior by the way of good housekeeping by a fraudster.

I began by arranging the letters in some sort of chronological order and it started to tell a story. I formed that impression that to someone whose dealings with the legal system were limited, that the letters received would be considered genuine. Upon closer examination and bearing in mind the observation made by the representative from the

Trustees Savings Bank I did not share the opinion that all were typed on the same typewriter but some probably were. I would have to bear this in mind, as there was always the possibility that there were other typewriters used by Barbara Hendry that I would need to obtain for forensic examination at a later date. This would be another point to bear in mind later in the investigation, but for now the priority was to record a witness statement from Ted and put the investigation on an official footing which took around two weeks to record.

I knew that the investigation would be intact as applications to remand both Barbara Hendry and Donny Hendry in custody had been made and were successful. I quietly hoped that Barbara Hendry would be finding her prison food acceptable! Both Joan and Ted would arrive home from work, have tea and then at an arranged time I would call around to the house and continue the statement where we had previously finished.

On one occasion I was offered a bite to eat but then realised that I was being literally offered the last egg in the house, which was going to be cooked as scramble egg for me. Both Joan and Ted were such proud people and the further I probed into the circumstances surrounding the situation the more I realised how breathtaking the cheek of the offence was turning out to be.

What I also found of surprise was the total faith that Joan and Ted had in Barbara Hendry believing that the inheritance existed and that all would be finally sorted out after the various legal problems had been resolved.

I was intrigued to find out that both Joan and Ted had spoken to other individuals that had reassured them all was in order.

The Security Guard had told Ted that the "Rembrandt" painting existed and during one telephone call made remarked "Yes, it's here I'm looking at it now, it's being well looked after!"

On another occasion during which Barbara Hendry had been described as being "too ill" to travel, Joan had spoken to a "nurse" that confirmed the version of events to her, and as for "Mr. Spiers" the solicitor who had made numerous phone calls to Mr. Smith at the bank neither Joan nor Ted had spoken to him. I soon concluded that the reason was that in the event that either Joan or Ted did speak to Mr. Spiers they would recognise the strong Scottish accent as that of one Donnie Hendry the partner of Barbara and the "scam" would be compromised. It never fails to amaze me how low some people would stoop.

STATEMENT of   Edward Vincent WARNER   63years
Tech Clerk

I live at the above address with my wife Joan and have done so for 29 years. We have two children who are both married and have left home.

I am employed by Ruston Gas Turbines in Lincoln in the capacity of Technical Clerk and I have worked for the company for 19 years. My wife Joan is employed as a Clerk in the Social Services department in Lincoln.

In 1976 my wife and myself went on holiday to Scotland, we had occasion to stay at the Station Hotel in Aberfeldy.

During the stay my wife and myself got talking to and became friendly with a woman who gave her name as Barbara Hendry who was working at the hotel as a waitress. She told us that she earned 30 pence and hour and she was in the process of saving up for a TV set. We actually got talking to Barbara while she served us and we exchanged pleasantries at meal times during our stay at the hotel.

During the first week I think it was a Thursday, Barbara invited Joan and myself around to her house for a cup of tea. We decided that since Barbara was pleasant we should go, and early that evening a man who Barbara introduced as Donnie came to the hotel to pick Barbara up after work and all four of us walked down the road to her house, it wasn't very far. We all went into the house and had a cup of tea and generally chatted.

We talked about all sorts really and I can remember talking about the copper stills in the distillery across the road from their cottage. It was whilst we were at the cottage that Barbara talked about a man called "Uncle Jimmy" who lived at the cottage with them. Barbara said that Jimmy was upstairs and that she had to do some business for "Uncle Jimmy".

Barbara also said that she had a lovely ring but was unable to show it to us because Uncle Jimmy was asleep and it was in his bedroom. It was whilst Joan and myself were at Barbara on the first occasion that a young man came into the house and Barbara introduced him to us as her son Robert and said that he had just popped in to get something to eat and to borrow some money from her. I was not sure whether he lived there or not but Barbara said that he was also working at the Station Hotel.

I can remember Barbara mentioned that the following day she had some business to attend to and Joan suggested that we take her in the car, but I dismissed the idea since we were on our holidays. We continued talking in general and eventually made our way back to the hotel.

The following day, a Friday, we again saw Barbara at the hotel and we made arrangements to go out that evening for a drink. That evening Joan and myself went with Donny and Barbara to a small public house just outside Aberfeldy. During the visit we again chatted about things in general, such as clothes, the weather, Scotland, things like that and after about half an hour we all went back to Barbara's cottage where we continued chatting, in fact Barbara gave Joan a cape and skirt.

It was during the visit I can remember Barbara in conversation saying that her mother, she always referred to her as her "Mummy was purchasing a hotel in Oban" and suggested that Joan and I must go to the opening in the New Year.

The phrase "Mummy was used on such regular basis that Joan and myself often speculated as to who "Mummy" actually was and concluded that she must have been some society figure. I happened to mention that I liked Rhodedendrums and with that Donny went into the garden and pulled one up and gave it to me. I planted it in our garden when we got home.

We again saw Barbara the following morning when she served us our breakfast at the hotel and later again in the morning when she and Donny came to see us off when we left for home.

Upon leaving, Barbara asked us to write to her when I arrived home which I did a few weeks later. A few months after arriving home we received a letter from Barbara saying her "Mummy" would be opening the new wing at an old people's home. In the early days speculation about "Mummy" was rife.

I produce a letter sent to my wife and I from Barbara Hendry dated 2nd November 1976

During the following year Barbara and ourselves exchanged letters on a regular basis. She informed us that she was in poor health and that she and Donny were going to move to the Island of Jura to live. She sent a letter with a map attached showing us how to get there.

The correspondence continued and on 15th December that year another letter arrived. The letter stated that if Joan and myself let Barbara and Donny know when we were going to take our annual holidays then they would between themselves arrange theirs at the same time.

Barbara would continue to stay in touch with us by ringing Joan at work and tell her what was happening.

Sometime around Christmas 1976, Barbara said that her Uncle Jimmy had died and left her all of his money. She implied at a later date the amount that she had been left was around thirty five thousand pounds but stated that she did not want the money to change her style of living as she was happy being housewife.

In a letter sent to Joan and I by Barbara after Uncle Jimmy's death Barbara mentioned that she had to fly to Edinburgh to sort out his estate. She said that if we ever needed to contact her then we were to reverse the charges, which we occasionally did.

By this time Joan and myself were still wondering who

Barbara's mummy was as she would make reference to her on a regular basis which would lead us to think about who she was with regards to "society".

I can remember Barbara saying things like "mummy" has given her £1000 pounds to go shopping with at Christmas. "Mummy was in business" and that she "had an office".

During February 1977 Barbara again wrote a letter in which she stated that she wanted Joan and me to visit her again. There was a lot of chitchat in the letter but she also mentioned that she was related to Lady Lithgow and Lord Astor, also that she had known them since she was a child. She further stated that she would introduce them to us when we visited her but due to numerous reasons this event did not happen.

Barbara would continue to keep in touch with Joan and myself on a regular basis.

Barbara would continue to refer to "Mummy" as being in business and having an office but did not elaborate on these points.

February to July 1977 went by and the contact between Barbara and us continued as she had by this time had a telephone installed at her house on Jura. Joan and I had by this time loaned Barbara about £500 but I cannot recollect the reason why we leant it to her. I think that one installment of £100 was sent to Barbara as she said she wanted it so she could arrange bail for Donny as he had been arrested because he had not paid the maintenance to his former wife. I can remember Barbara saying that the police who had arrested him came in a motor launch but I cannot remember anymore than that. The distinct impression given was that "Mummy" didn't approve of Donny as he did not really fit in and was not of a like background.

On 16th July 1977 another letter arrived. Barbara said in it that she shortly expected to receive a bequest from the estate of her deceased uncle James Campbell. I took this to be the person who had been previously living with her called Uncle Jimmy but who had recently died. Barbara said that the matter would take several months to finalise.

A CRUEL DECEPTION

In August 1977, Joan and I went on holiday to the Island of Jura. We met Barbara and Donny in West Loch Tarbert. On the Sunday night Barbara booked us into the Tarbert Hotel where she and Donny had been staying. They met us at the front door and booked us in at reception. We stayed one night and Barbara paid for the hotel and the following day we all went to Jura. I can remember Barbara receiving a telephone call, which she took in private in her room. She didn't tell us straight away what it was about but said later that it was somebody wanting money in connection with the estate that was due to her. I took this to mean Uncle Jimmy's will.

One evening whilst we were all sat in the house on Jura, Barbara was sat there when she mentioned that she had vandals in the house previously. She said, "It's a good job they didn't damage that!" and she pointed to a painting hung on a wall in the room. I saw that the painting depicted an old man and it appeared to be very old.

Barbara said that it was a Rembrandt and that it had been framed in a certain way so that the signature could not be seen. She went on to say that it was the only painting that the insurance company had allowed Uncle Jimmy to keep in his possession. Barbara told Joan and me that the painting was very old and very valuable.

Sometime during the holiday Barbara said that she had to take care of some business and Joan and I went with her to Beaumore on the Island of Islay to meet a man called Mr. McTaggert. Barbara told Joan that he was a solicitor involved in the will of Uncle Jimmy. Barbara introduced us to him and Joan accompanied Barbara into his office.

One day we went out for a drive to the north of the island and Barbara pointed to a white Range Rover, she told us that it was Lady Astor who was sitting in it. I had no reason to disbelieve what I was being told and to this day still do not know if it was true.

During the stay I can remember a couple came to the house and Barbara said that they had brought a car and charged it to Barbara's account. I don't know the full details but things became a little heated during it. I can remember Donny or

163

Barbara saying the man held a position at the Distillery on the island. When the couple had gone Barbara showed us the bill and became quite indignant about it.

Upon leaving and going home it was whilst en route we stopped at Talbert to telephone. We asked how things were and to let us know that they we were alright. Donny told us that Barbara had taken an overdose and was being flown to Loch Gilphead, he said that Barbara had done it because that she was upset we were going and that she couldn't pay us the money that she owed us. We were very upset at this and couldn't fully understand it, in fact we considered turning back and going to see her but we carried on home because we couldn't get any information from Donny and we didn't know where it was that she had been taken.

We arrived home and were in touch immediately and for a day or two Donny appeared to be on his own.

A few days later Barbara was out of hospital and we contacted each other, we didn't mention the overdose, as Barbara didn't want us to know about it.

We kept in touch over the next few months during which I told Barbara that Joan was ill and the next thing I knew was a telegram arrived. The telegram read

"Joan Sorry to hear you're ill. Get well soon. Everything perfect here. See you soon Banette "

Just before Christmas 1977 another telegram arrived saying that Barbara was still ill and that she was tending to her affairs with the assistance of "Alexi", of whom I had never heard of but assumed it was somebody connected with "Mummy." "Alexi" signed the telegram.

One night, whilst telephoning Barbara we spoke to this Alexi, She said she thought it was nice of us to help Barbara. Joan and I still did not know who she was but one day Barbara said Alexi used to be her secretary but we never actually met her.

During the time we had known Barbara up to Christmas 1977 we sent her various amounts of money a total of £950 to help her out. Either Joan or I would go to the Post Office at

Lincoln and send it by British Money Order and we kept all the receipts, which I am able to produce.

After Christmas 1977 and during the next few months or so, Joan and I would keep in touch with Barbara by telephone. Barbara would either ring us at the telephone box at Dunholme or would ring Joan at work. On occasions when Barbara could not contact Joan she would ring me at work.

Around 31ˢᵗ May 1978, another letter arrived from Barbara on Jura. It said that she was in contact with a Miss Sinclair who worked for a solicitor called McTaggert who was dealing with Uncle Jimmy's estate and that she had to sign further papers in order to release the money due to her. I am able to produce the letter, which she sent.

No further monies were sent to Barbara around this period but we stayed in regular contact with her.

Barbara kept asking us to go on holiday with her up to Jura but for some reason we didn't go and I cannot exactly remember why, but we continued exchange letters. During telephone calls Barbara would say that she was still trying to get the will of Uncle Jimmy resolved but was having difficulty in doing so. The reason for the difficulty was that her mother (Barbara had told my wife on an earlier date that she was the illegitimate daughter of Margaret the Duchess of Argyll) was a trustee in the estate of the late James Campbell and that the Duchess was trying to stop the money being released but did not elaborate on the reason why.

A few weeks later another letter arrived in which we were informed that Barbara was again ill. She told us that she was suffering from fluid on the knee together with poor eyesight and loss of balance. We felt very sorry for her and were aghast at the amount of bad luck from which she was suffering; everything appeared to be against her.

On 6ᵗʰ August 1978 another letter arrived from Barbara in which she appeared to be very upset. She outlined the cause of her upset as being attributed to a letter she had in turn received from our son. The circumstances were that he had written to her as he was very unhappy with our relationship with Barbara, in fact he stated that he did not believe her and the stories she was telling us. We had told him that the money we were sending Barbara was to assist her with her mounting legal costs and he was aware that the money had not yet been paid back. The whole matter had upset our son who had decided to make his feelings known to Barbara, which he did. Both Joan and myself were also upset with our son, as we firmly believed in what we were doing and had full trust in Barbara.

The money sent to Barbara up to this point was sent for various reasons, which I can remember. Most of it was in connection with her mounting legal bills incurred by her attempting to release the will, infact at one point we paid one or two of her electricity bills due to the fact that her finances were so tight to help her out.

On 26th February 1979 another letter arrived in which Barbara mentioned "your ring". The circumstances were that she had told Joan that she had a valuable ring and said that it was an opal surrounded by diamonds, the ring was supposed to have been part of Uncle Jimmy's estate and she would give it to Joan, but when we ever saw her she always had some reason for not having it in her possession whenever we met.

Barbara and ourselves continued to stay in touch by telephone. The next letter arrived around 27th March in which Barbara stated that things were coming together well, but she did not appear to be very friendly with the solicitor Mr McTaggert, however, Barbara did say she was dealing with a Miss Sinclair at the same firm of solicitors. Barbara also said that she was shortly going "to sign". We took this to mean the release of her inheritance and the sorting out of the will was not too far away. Letter attached to this letter was another letter from Miss Sinclair at McTaggerts solicitors.

Enclosed within the letter was a letter on official headed notepaper from Mactaggart and Co Solicitors P.O. Box No 1 72/74 Main Street Largs KA30 8AL Ayreshire dated 14th March.

Dear Mrs Hendry
  James Campbell's Executory

We shall be obliged if you will please call at our Bowmore office to sign the account of Charge and Discharge of James Campbell's Executory at your earliest convenience

Yours truly
p.p. MACTAGGERT &CO
Signed
A Sinclair

I think around this period Barbara was on the telephone and we would usually ring her at her neighbour's house whose name was Nancy. Both Joan and I were under the impression that the whole thing was not very far from being sorted out. Joan and I sent Barbara and Donny a box of Thornton's toffee and in the next letter around April Barbara mentions this together with the fact that Donny was ill.

Barbara also said in the letter that she was going to give our daughter a crystal decanter when our daughter got married, she said her "Mummy" and we both took this to be the Duchess again had bought her it.

It was around August 1979, that the whole situation began to worry my wife Joan and she started to lose some weight. I think that Joan was worried about us getting our money back and I later found out that whilst I had been in bed one night Joan got up and wrote a letter to Barbara outlining her concerns. Shortly afterwards a reply came back through the post from Barbara expressing her dismay

Barbara was very reassuring in telling us not to worry and that the money we had lent her would all be paid back in full when the will was sorted out. She said that Donny had been off work sick and that her electricity had been cut off and we both got the impression that she was very short of money and began to feel very sorry for her.

We obviously considered Barbara a good friend and so much so that we had invited her to the forthcoming wedding of our daughter. Accommodation would not have been a problem as we were quite prepared to squeeze her in at our house on during the week of the wedding.

Barbara had indicated to us that the solicitor working for her on the release of the will was dragging it out and she had told us that she had made a complaint to the Law Society who was looking into it for her. Barbara had also told us that despite being ill she still wanted to attend the wedding. Barbara made a point of mentioning that she was still very worried about paying back the money that she owed us.

Around 31ˢᵗ August 1979 we received another letter from Barbara which outlined things we had talked about on the telephone and in this letter Barbara asked if Joan could make her a dress. Attached to the letter was another letter from solicitors called Anderson Banks & Company of Argyll. I came to the conclusion that these were the people looking into Mr Taggert's affairs as a result of the complaint made by Barbara.

At sometime around this period, Barbara sent Joan and I a Royal Bank of Scotland receipt dated 3ʳᵈ April 1979. The receipt indicated that £7340.00 had been paid into an account. I cannot remember the reason for the receipt but we both thought that Barbara had got some of her money through.

We continued to keep in touch with Barbara by telephone as usual and Barbara wrote another letter in which she again spoke about the Law Society and travelling to bring the ring and crystal for us to Lincoln, in fact she mentioned how sad she was about Lord Mountbatten getting killed.

Both Joan and I would occasionally send gifts back to Barbara and Donny Joan sent Barbara a cape, skirt and a jumper, which Barbara wanted to use to attend some type "function"

All the money my wife Joan and myself could raise went to Barbara and since our daughter's wedding was fast approaching we found that we needed money for ourselves, things became more and more difficult and we decided that we desperately needed money to make our daughter's wedding day special. Around 26ᵗʰ September 1979 after having discussed it between ourselves Joan and I went to a local loan company called Mercantile Credit and took a loan out for £700, with £187 interest. The payments were 24 months of £41 per month.

During the regular telephone calls between Barbara and us Barbara constantly mentioned how she was looking forward to coming to our daughter's wedding.

The expected expenditure for the wedding came to more than we had anticipated and just prior to the occasion Joan and I borrowed £400 from our friends to send to Barbara on Jura. In addition we also sent some of our own money. Barbara told us that we would have it returned in time for the wedding but it did not appear for various reasons given by Barbara. We were most disappointed as we needed the money but this was tempered by the fact that we were helping a friend in need.

On 19th October 1979, another letter arrived from Barbara in which she refers to the estate again and having very little money. Barbara again mentioned having to go to court which we took to be in connection with her inheritance and she enclosed some legal papers to look at which we did. Barbara asked that after having read them that we send them back to her, (Yet again the fraudster is requesting papers to be returned so they cannot be produced in evidence) which we did, but I cannot recollect what the papers said.

I think that it was about this time that we sent Barbara some more money at her request I cannot recollect just how much it was, the reason being that she had told us that due to the expense she was incurring in connection with her legal bills both she and Donny had very little money. She went on to explain that all of Donny's wages were having to be paid into the court, leaving them very little or nothing to live on.

Our daughter's wedding came and went and Barbara failed to attend. She had given various reasons why she was unable to come and neither the crystal decanter nor the ring Barbara had promised to send had failed to materialise by this time. I thought that one of the reasons why she did not attend was because of the expense together with the court appearances *that she was having to attend We continued to keep in touch more by telephone rather than by letter.*

Barbara wrote again and informed us that she was ill and that Donny had injured himself by falling down the stairs. She did however appear to be upbeat about the inheritance and gave us the impression that things were starting to be sorted out and that we would soon be able to get our money back.

Barbara also told us that because of her financial situation she was in danger of being evicted from her house and she would soon have nowhere to live, but told us not to worry about her as things as she would soon be paying us back what was owed. This partly put our minds at rest.

In a letter Barbara said that she had remembered something called a "Forward Trust" that she was entitled to. She explained that she was going to get a quarterly allowance of £525 from her grandmother's estate. Barbara also mentioned having an argument with the solicitors dealing with Uncle Jimmy's estate but I cannot remember the exact details.

Around 23ʳᵈ February 1980 a parcel arrived, the parcel contained a quantity of material for Joan to make Barbara a skirt together with a cheque for £11.00 which was to be payment for the lining and making the skirt which Joan did and sent it up to Barbara.

During July another letter arrived enclosing some legal document explaining she was having trouble getting the will released. Around the same time another legal type letter arrived but I cannot remember the details of it because Barbara was always insistent that after reading any legal letters they should always be sent back to her. (Here again this is typical fraudster behavior asking the victim to return paperwork with the intention of making any subsequent investigation more difficult.) I can recollect that one letter explained that whole matter would soon be concluded and that the money would be released. This gave both Joan and myself a degree of comfort as although we have never had a large amount of dealings with solicitors and the like or legal documents all we read sent by Barbara did tend to indicate things were in hand and it would soon be all resolved.

Barbara went on to say in one of her letters that she was having to sell all her furniture to assist with her legal expenses and we both formed the impression that she was really struggling financially. She claimed that her solicitor Mr. McTaggert was overcharging and that he was one of the reasons why things were being held up.

The telephone contact continued and during a conversation Barbara remarked that Donnie was receiving radium treatment for an illness, it was coming to a point in the Warner household where there was speculation as to whether there would ever be an end to the continual run of bad luck that was being suffered by Barbara and Donnie. Barbara also sought to re-assure us that the amount owing would soon be repaid in full.

Between Joan and myself and having never even met the solicitor McTaggert we both became to dislike him often discussing between ourselves just how a man in the position of a solicitor could behave like that and seem to be able to get away with it.

Another letter arrived in July that year that we found very upsetting as in the letter Barbara outlined how Donny had been diagnosed with cancer and had been receiving radium treatment. Barbara also mentioned that the cheque would be on its way soon.

Both Joan and I discussed Barbara's predicament and decided to send her some money, which we could hardly afford to help her out. I cannot remember how much it was on this occasion but we sent it by the Inland Telegraph Service to Jura for her to collect.

Barbara and ourselves still kept on touch on a regular basis. Around 25th August another letter arrived from Barbara in which she again refers to her "Mummy" and also reiterated the facts about Mr. McTaggert holding up the will and his involvement with the Law Society. Barbara again told us how desperate she was and having very little food in the house to eat. She said that Mr.McTaggert had "Done her out of £12,306".

The telephone calls between Barbara and ourselves continued and around 1st September 1980 we sent another amount of money to Barbara but I cannot recollect how much but it was to assist her with her legal expenses incurred whilst attempting to get the inheritance released.

On a day shortly after we had sent the money requested another letter arrived. In the letter and in it Barbara says that she was on her way to the Post Office to see if our registered letter had arrived, she mentions that she was going to move to another address but didn't want anyone to know where because of not wanting Donny's ex-wife to trace her. Barbara again mentioned the Lawyer's dealing with the estate and this led Joan and me to believe that the legal proceedings were still underway in an attempt to release the money and the will.

Barbara again wrote to us on 3rd September 1980. In this letter Barbara told us that she needed more money to pay for something called "Queens Counsel". We both understood that this was something to do with all the legal proceedings in trying to get the wills and the inheritance sorted out. Not only that, we thought that Barbara had incurred extra expenses by trying to make a claim against the solicitor Mr. McTaggert who we understood from Barbara had acted incompetently. Barbara said things would not be progressing any further until more money had been paid.

Barbara in this letter told us how to go about getting a further loan from a company to send to her to assist with her legal bills, she told us to tell the company which we applied to that, the amount was for a holiday or for central heating or something like that and that she thought that we would get any amount requested as we were both in steady employment.

Both Joan and myself discussed the prospect of getting further into debt and the fact that we would not be telling the truth but whatever we intended to borrow we always intended to pay it back in full. We decided that we had to go ahead with it as we were obviously helping a friend in need who was always going to pay us back in full and with interest but the interest was not a factor that assisted us in making any decisions.

Having discussed this over the phone with Barbara who in hindsight obviously sensed our reluctance she told us that she would be sending us some money to pay us back on a regular basis from Donnie's wages but it did not materialise.

Barbara said that she realised it would be difficult for us to get any further loans but reassured us that any money she sent to us would of course be used for the purpose of the legal expenses and releasing the wills.

Around 10th September 1980 another letter arrived from Barbara. In the letter she told us how desperate things were getting. She said that she needed £481.00 for the Queens Counsel and that the solicitor Mr. McTaggert was holding onto the cheque. The full details we did not understand but Barbara sent us a solicitor's letter which explained the situation. We did not fully understand it but we had to read it and send it back to her again which we did. I cannot remember exactly what it said but recollect that it was something to do with the wills.

Barbara wanted a further £481.00 sent to her to speed things up,

Shortly after receiving another letter Joan and I sat down and discussed it between ourselves if we should help Barbara. We decided that we would as things were getting desperate at our house as well and we were hoping that our money would be returned. If we decided not to assist at this late stage we could not risk both our own money and money that friends had lent us not being returned. We decided to help Barbara out again.

We went to a company called Mercantile Credit based in Lincoln and re-negotiated out existing loan and obtained a further £500.00. Fortunately we were not questioned as to why the money was wanted and we had decided between ourselves that if the reason was explored as to why we wanted further money that I was to do the talking despite not being too happy about it.

A few days after obtaining the loan Joan and myself drove up to Kennercraig and met Barbara and Donny and picked them up to take them to Oban, as Barbara had told us the

£500 had to be paid to a firm of Solicitors called Anderson and Banks. We gave Barbara the £500 (We always gave her a little more to help her out) and we went to Oban. We stayed at a hotel for two nights and we all paid our own accommodation. I think the hotel was called the Place Hotel. We did not go with Barbara to the solicitor's but she returned and told us that she had paid the money and the solicitor had given her £70.00 expenses. That evening Barbara brought us a meal. I remember that Joan and I had gammon.

We all had a drive around for a while and Joan and I returned home. We had gone equipped to sleep in the car if necessary to save any additional expense. Upon arriving home there was a telephone call from Barbara to inform us that her electricity supply had been "cut off" and she desperately needed to pay her bill. Barbara seemed to be very upset and that her financial problems were mounting up. We rose to £80 needed for the bill and sent it by the Inland Telegraph Service to Jura.

Around 30th September 1980 another letter arrived from Barbara in which she talked about things in general.

Another letter arrived on 7th October 1980 and in it Barbara again talked about the legal proceedings. She told us that she had to appear in court as a witness, which we took to be about the will again. We had sent her some flowers and she acknowledged the receipt of them, orchids they were. Barbara also enclosed in the letter what she called a "warrant" but we didn't fully understand it but as always she requested that we read it and return it, which we did.

On 8th October 1980 another letter arrived. Barbara thanked us for the parcels which we sent, I cannot remember exactly what the parcels were but it would most probably been toffee. Barbara mentioned the court case again and that a solicitor called Mr. Thornton had been to see her. (Upon reflection although not realised at the time "Thornton" seems a very apt name!) Barbara went on to say that the solicitor Mr. McTaggert had been fined. We took this to have been imposed by the Scottish Law Society for his alleged incompetence in dealing with the estate. She also said that she

174

was having to sell a lot of her possessions such as her TV, lawnmower etc, to meet her expenses. Barbara said she would be flying down soon to see us.

On 14th October 1980, Joan and myself sent Barbara £180 to her at Craighouse, Isle of Jura. The money was sent to her in two lots, one of £80 and the other of £100. I cannot recollect the exact reason why the money was sent but I can say that it was definitely in connection with her having to pay further legal fees.

On 17th October 1980 a further £50 was sent to Barbara to assist her.

It was around this time due to our financial commitments that we couldn't fulfill all the requests for money that Barbara was making to us and Joan any myself approached my brother Laurence and his wife to assist us, which they did. We told them basically what it was about and they sent the money to Barbara on Jura. I do not know exactly how much Laurence and his wife sent Barbara but it was in the region of Four thousand pounds. Both Joan and myself had agreed that whatever was sent we would between ourselves pay it back.

Around 28th October 1980, another letter arrived from Barbara and in it she thanked us for the money sent to her by my brother-in-Law Laurence and his wife. Barbara also enclosed a receipt for the amount of £257 in acknowledgement.

Sometime in November 1980 we received another letter from Barbara in which she again talks about the will and saying that as soon as she signs and her signature is proved to be authentic it will speed things up. Barbara told us that she was leaving the Island of Jura and that she wanted to use our address for correspondence such as the shares bond and the like to be delivered to

On 6th November 1980, Joan and I sent Barbara Hendry £150 to Craighouse by the inland Telegraph Service. Shortly afterwards Barbara spoke to us on the telephone and said that she wanted more money to meet the mounting legal fees and Joan and I borrowed the money from another friend.

I think it was around 20th December 1980 Joan and I went up in our car to go to Helensborough where we stayed overnight in a hotel. The following day we drove to the Kennercraig ferry terminal to meet Barbara and Donny who arrived at 11.30am. We picked them up and went on to an address. I don't know exactly where we went but we were introduced to a woman who was referred to as "Nana Bain". Barbara said it was a woman with whom she had spent a lot of time with when she was young. It was at this time Barbara said that she had received a message from Nana Bain to say that "Mummy", who we took to be the Duchess of Argyll had told her (Barbara) to catch a plane to London to go and see her. After the visit we went to Glasgow where we stayed the night somewhere near Queens Park. The following morning Barbara and Donny went into Glasgow to take care of some business, which we again took to be in connection with the will.

Donny later returned alone and we went and collected Barbara. We all left Glasgow and called at a place called Patterdale to meet Barbara's Aunt Joan and Uncle Fred. Both Joan and Fred had been mentioned in conversation previously and we understood that Joan was supposed to be "Mummy's" cousin.

After calling at Patterdale Barbara, Donny and ourselves returned to Dunholme where they both stayed with us over Christmas 1980/1. Upon our arrival home there was a telegram that had been delivered to our house for Barbara. I did not read the telegram but she told us that it congratulated her on getting things "sorted out". We again took this to be in connection with the will although she did not tell us whom the telegram was from.

Over the Christmas period Barbara told us just how complicated the will was and how expensive the legal process in connection with it was turning out to be. Barbara said that she needed a further £400 to meet the mounting legal expenses and Joan borrowed it from a friend and gave it to Barbara before she returned. Barbara even wrote out a receipt for the money and gave it to Joan. One day over the Christmas period all four of us went into Lincoln, as Barbara wanted to do some shopping. Barbara used an account card I think that it was in the name of House of Fraser, which she used in Binns in Lincoln. Barbara spent around a thousand pounds. She brought me some gloves and Joan a nightdress and crystal vase. I still have the receipts that Barbara left at our house.

Barbara said that she had to get back to Scotland to see "Mummy" and the Board of Trustees in connection with the will. The whole visit to our house lasted over three days. We took her back up north and dropped her off at her son's house in Rotherham. Barbara continued to keep in touch by telephone and on 30th December 1980 Joan and I sent Barbara £200 by the Inland Telegraph Service which she said she wanted sending to the Hope Street Post Office in Glasgow and which she collected. I cannot remember the exact reason why she urgently wanted the money but again it was in connection with legal expenses that she had incurred.

On 12th January 1981 another envelope arrived at our house. I noticed that the postmark was Craighouse Island of Jura. There was no letter inside just a newspaper cutting, which outlined the rising costs of legal fees. Barbara had told us that she was going to send it because we had previously made mention of how much the legal fees were costing as between us neither Joan and myself had any idea of how much these things could cost.

A CRUEL PRICE RISE
You can't shop around when you
want a family will administered
……..not even if it's just to hear
that grandma has left you her old
armchair.
You have to get a lawyer.
and just like house conveyancing, a
job normally done by the office clerk

177

> **- the sorting out of family affairs is a**
> **dripping roast for the solicitors,**
> **because they all charge the same.**
> **Incredibly, the Law Society has just**
> **decreed increases of up to sixty- one**
> **per cent in fees for lawyers handling**
> **estates.**
> **No wonder the Scottish Consumer**
> **Council has demanded the setting up of**
> **an independent body to fix legal**
> **charges.**
> **When local authority lawyers are**
> **Being asked to accept SIX per cent**
> **rises…it's diabolical their private**
> **practice colleagues can command**
> **ten times as much.**

The article appeared to reinforce a lot of what Barbara had told us.

Barbara and us kept in touch over the telephone as usual although the letters were less frequent; she still kept making requests for various amounts of money because the legal fees were mounting up. We still kept sending Barbara the amounts requested at this point and later because she always told us that it was all so close to being sorted out and we had sent her such a large amount of money that we felt finalisation was not too far away.

During the month of January 1981 we sent Barbara a total amount of one thousand and seventy five pounds mostly borrowed from friends obviously on the understanding that it would be repaid with interest when the inheritance was settled but all our friends declined the offer of interest to be paid.

On the telephone one day Barbara told us the she needed further money urgently to help with the winding up of the estate. She said she wanted the sum of £750, which we obviously did not have, but we told her that we would get it for her if possible. In the event Joan went and saw a friend of hers and was able to obtain the £750 but it would take some time.

Barbara came down to Lincoln on 3rd February 1981 with a man called Duncan Henderson. They both arrived in a black Mercedes car. Barbara said (in confidence) that Duncan was the Duke of Argyll's chauffeur and she said that "Lauren", that's the present Duke used the car for business purposes.

The following day Joan went into Lincoln and obtained the £750 from her friend and gave it to Barbara who wrote out a receipt and gave it to Joan

Barbara and Duncan stayed the night at our house and left the following morning to travel back to Scotland.

On 13th February another short letter arrived from Barbara who stated that she was penniless but she was going to sort it all out when the inheritance was settled, she stated that she would pay for me to fulfil my lifetime's ambition to return to Canada.

I was very touched by this but did not consider it a reality and all our assistance provided to Barbara was not for personal gain.

Barbara again contacted us and requested further money and on 14th February 1981 we sent her £550 up to her in Scotland.

On 19th February 1981 my wife and I sent two further payments of £100 to Barbara.

On 13th March and at the request of Barbara, Joan and I sent a payment of £200 to Barbara at Craighouse by the Inland Telegraph Service.

Another letter arrived from Barbara on 18th April 1981 in which she said that she had made arrangements and would send us some receipts that we would be able to take to our bank in Lincoln and that the bank would give us the money that would solve our problems. We would be able to pay our loans off and give all our friends from whom we had borrowed money from their money back. We checked our post for a couple of days but nothing came.

On 24th April and at the request of Barbara during a telephone call we sent Barbara four more payments in total of £380, which were sent at her request to Rutherglen Post Office in Scotland.

On 28th April 1981 three more payments in total of £280 were also sent to Barbara in Scotland.

During April or early May 1981, Barbara came down to our house with her son Robert and Donny in Robert's car. The reason for the visit was that Barbara said that she had some business to attend to. She said that she had to go to the National Westminster Bank in Lincoln to make arrangements because she had some money to be paid into the Lincoln branch. The money was going to be paid in on her behalf from an account in Switzerland.

I went to the bank with Barbara but since it was a confidential matter I waited outside. When she came out she showed to me a piece of paper, which I recognised as a paying- in slip. I looked at it and saw that it said the amount of £47,000 on it but I think that I gave it back to her shortly after seeing it.

Barbara, Donny and Robert stayed two nights then left and went back to Scotland I cannot remember the exact date.

On 18th May Barbara asked for some more money but this time it was only £45, which we sent to her up at Craighouse. On this occasion we did not need to borrow any money from friends, as we were both working and such a small amount was affordable from our very limited budget.

On 23rd May 1981, another letter arrived from Barbara and in it she talked about collecting her birth certificate and other papers from the Royal Bank, as they had to be taken to Zurich by Courier the letter was written on the paper of the Royal Hotel in Glasgow.

During 1981 a large number of payments were sent to Barbara Hendry at various locations in Scotland for her to collect. These payments were again sent to help fund her legal battle in attempting to get her inheritance released. As we continued to make payments to Barbara more legal obstacles would surface that had to be overcome with financial assistance from ourselves.

On 8th June 1981 a further £400 was sent to Barbara Hendry at Craighouse via the Inland Telegraph Service. I cannot exactly remember the reason why we sent it but it was obviously again in connection with her mounting legal expenses.

On 1ˢᵗ July 1981 a further £53 was sent to Barbara Hendry on Craighouse by the same method.

On 16ᵗʰ June 1981 three further payments in total of £300 were sent to Barbara at her request. On this occasion she requested that it be sent to a Post Office in Glasgow. I assumed that this was because sending it to a Post Office in Glasgow would be easier as some of the solicitors involved in the legal case were based in Glasgow.

On 24ᵗʰ July a further £200 was sent to Barbara at Craighouse on the Isle of Jura.

On 7ᵗʰ August 1981 on single payment of £40 was sent to Barbara again at her request. The amount was sent to Craighouse on the Isle of Jura and collected from a local Post Office.

Both Joan and I were being told on a regular basis that the inheritance would soon be concluded but in the meantime there were still expenses that Barbara needed assistance with. We again discussed the matter between ourselves and concluded that we had come so far down the financial route that refusing to assist Barbara any further could result in a fall out and we could not risk the possibility we would not get our money back. We had by now borrowed money to help Barbara from our relatives, friends and loan companies we were committed financially.

On 13ᵗʰ August and again at Barbara's request we sent a further £100 pounds.

On 24ᵗʰ August 1981 nine further payments in total of £850 we sent to Barbara again by using the Inland Telegraph Service. The money was sent on Barbara's instruction to the Post Office located at Hope Street in Glasgow. I still have the receipts, which I can produce if necessary.

On 29ᵗʰ September 1981, my wife sent four further payments in total of £365 to Barbara Hendry. This again was at Barbara's request. The money was sent to Bridge of Weir in Scotland.

On 2ⁿᵈ October 1981 we sent another £100 to Barbara. On this occasion she requested that we send it to Hope Street Post Orifice in Glasgow, which we did.

On 29ᵗʰ December 1981 we sent a further amount of £48 to Barbara Hendry by ourselves at her request to Craighouse.

Around 15ᵗʰ September 1981 I travelled up to Scotland to take Barbara some money. I think that the amount was around £680. I cannot exactly remember but I borrowed £380 from my brother and his wife. I met Barbara and her son Robert at Abingdon in the car park of a Little Chef and handed the money over. Barbara told me that she urgently needed the money to cover further expenses that she had incurred in trying to get the inheritance released but I distinctly remember that she needed the money very urgently so I drove up in the car and took it to her.

It was during 1981 because of all the money both Joan and I were sending Barbara that our finances became very tight indeed and I approached my brother and his wife to see if they could assist Joan and I in providing Barbara with the money that she required. We did not tell that the full reasons why we needed the money but they decided to help us out which they did.

Altogether we borrowed about £4000 from my brother and his wife. Sometimes they gave the money to me and other times they posted the money to Scotland to locations that Barbara had told me that it wanted sending to for her to collect.

After arriving back at home a day or so after the 17ᵗʰ September 1981 a "Thank you" card arrived from Barbara in which she thanked me for taking the money to her up in Scotland.

Throughout 1982 very little correspondences came to us from Barbara but she mostly kept in contact by telephone. We did send her further payments that she requested in connection with her legal fees incurred in attempting to release her inheritance.

On 26ᵗʰ January 1982 the amount of £90 was sent to Barbara at her request. It was again sent by the Post Office Inland Telegraph Service for her to collect from Craighouse.

On 10th February 1982, another payment of £70 was sent to Barbara to help her with her expenses it was sent for collection on the Island of Jura.

On 25th February 1982, the amount of £73 was sent to Barbara by ourselves for her to collect on the Isle of Jura.

On 10th March 1982 another payment of £100 was sent to Barbara but on this occasion she telephoned us and asked us to send the money to a Post Office located at George Square Glasgow for collection.

On 2nd April 1982 another payment of £100 was sent to Barbara, which she collected from Craighouse.

One day during the same month but I cannot remember the exact date another letter arrived and in it Barbara says that she is sorry for the way that Joan was feeling the way she was. The reason for this was that Joan had written a letter to Barbara asking when everything was going to be finally sorted out. I can remember that Joan was not feeling very well and the whole situation was beginning to get her down. In the letter we received from Barbara she inferred that it would not be long before it was all sorted out.

On 9th June 1982 another payment was sent to Barbara. The amount was £50 and again it was sent at Barbara's request to D Hendry at Craighouse Isle of Jura.

On 28th May 1982, a letter arrived which we took to have come from Barbara, in fact shortly after we received it Barbara rang us by contacting our next door neighbour and enquired as to whether we had received it. Upon opening the letter we saw that it appeared to be some kind of writ and on the reverse we saw that it mentioned the name of James Campbell together with references to his "Estate" which Barbara had told us was part of her legacy. In the writ it said that the sum of £5000 had to be paid to the firm of Universal Stores who were holding some shares from the estate. Barbara told us that this money had to be paid or it would hold things up even more. We didn't want this to happen as we were getting rather desperate and could not afford to wait much longer for the inheritance to be settled and for us to get our

183

money back. Barbara reassured that it would all soon be resolved.

On 28ᵗʰ May 1982 two further payments of £115 were sent to Barbara at Craighouse in accordance with her request.

Shortly afterwards and a few days later a letter arrived from Barbara to Joan reassuring her it would soon be concluded.

On 17ᵗʰ June 1982 another letter arrived from Barbara and when I opened it I saw that it appeared to be a will. Upon closer examination I could see it was the will of Barbara Hendry.

Barbara had previously told both Joan and myself that when her inheritance was finally settled that she would repay us in full. She also said that if anything happened to her she had "taken care" of the situation by having her will made over to the both of us. We both read the will and saw that it said Barbara was due to an inheritance somewhere in the region of six million, five hundred and seventy five thousand pounds and that she was going to leave me £150,000 our daughter £50,000 and my brother and his wife, fifty thousand pounds. I also noticed that Barbara had signed the will in the name of Barbara De Leonie or Hendry. I can recollect that Barbara had mentioned the name Leonie on occasions in the past when we had visited her in Scotland.

Upon reading the will I saw that it appeared to have been very professionally prepared and the amounts involved bearing in mind our pervious conversations did not really come as a surprise. Barbara had previously told us that she would pay us back in full together with interest, which we declined, but to see it all professionally written down suggested to us both that all was in order. I could also see that a solicitor had witnessed the will.

Upon seeing the will written down and being told that matters would soon be coming to a close both Joan and myself seemed reassured and I was of the impression I was worrying about nothing and that our friendship and with Barbara was not misguided.

On 1st July 1982 at Barbara's request we sent £100 to her in Glasgow.

On 17th July we sent a further £100 to Barbara by the Inland Telegraph Service for her to collect.

On 29th July 1982 again at Barbara's request we sent a further £350 to her. On this occasion she wanted the amount sending to a Post Office in Glasgow. She had previously explained the reason why she wanted this amount which would have been in connection with her legal expenses but I cannot recollect the details. On 30th July 1982 an urgent matter surfaced in connection with the inheritance and Barbara contacted us to explain that legal fees had to be paid otherwise things would be held up further. As a result of our conversation I was able to borrow the required amount and on almost the same day the amount of £585 was sent to Barbara via the Inland Telegraph Service for her to collect at Craighouse.

On 4th August we again sent Barbara at her request the amount of £300 for her to collect from Craighouse.

During August and September a total of £2100 was sent to Barbara to assist her with her legal fees.

Sometime during September a bunch of flowers arrived at our house sent by Interflora. Contained within the flowers was a card, which thanked us for all our help that we had given to Barbara. It was from a person whose name was "Lake Falconer McGrouther" We had both heard this name before and took it to be the Solicitor that was helping Barbara finalise her inheritance.

"A small token of our gratitude in appreciation for what you and your husband have done for Barbara and I. Without you she would not have pulled through

Your dearest Servant"

Lake Falconer McGrouther.

During 1982, many other things happened but unfortunately I cannot recollect all the details. I can recollect that Mr McGrouther who was the solicitor acting for Barbara Hendry was supposed to have gone to Zurich to tie up all the "loose ends" at a bank called the Kentonal Bank. This was what Barbara had previously told us was the name of the bank dealing with the inheritance. Barbara said it was imperative that Mr. McGrouther lived there for a period of time, as there were a lot of details that needed sorting out.

During 1982, the telephone calls between Barbara and us increased and she was on the phone on a regular basis. She kept wanting more money to be sent for various reasons all seemed to consist of different financial obstacles that needed to be overcome and all in connection with the release of her inheritance that again could only be resolved with financial assistance from my wife and myself.

Since we had sent a large amount of money that we had borrowed from friends and relatives we had to again return to the various finance companies that we had previously either approached or taken loans with. The companies involved i.e Lombard North Central and Mercantile Credit would extend our loans and provide us with cheques for the amounts required. These cheques we would pay into our bank, wait twenty fours hours or so, then cash the cheque and send the money to Barbara at various destinations throughout Scotland by registered post.

I cannot provide exact details of all the amounts sent at this time but it will be reflected in the details of the loans from the respective companies. I think it was about October 1982, that the Post Office Inland Telegraph Service ceased to operate and we had to send the amounts of money to Barbara by registered post.

I am able to produce a Lloyds Bank Credit Slip dated 20th September 1982, for £100 and a Midland Bank Paying In slip dated 19th September 1982 for £500. This would be another £500 cheque from a loan company that we paid through our daughter's bank account at the Midland Bank.

These payments continued through 1983 and were being sent to Barbara by ourselves. Sometimes it would be sent to her in the name of Barbara Ferguson. I cannot give exact amounts of what was sent to her but I have retained all of the Certificates of Posting throughout this period.

During the early part of 1983 the telephone calls form Barbara and ourselves continued but the letters ceased. I was aware that on one of Barbara's visits down to Lincoln she went to the National Westminster Bank and opened a bank account in her name but used our address. The account soon became overdrawn and I received several letters from the National Westminster Bank asking for the outstanding balance to be settled. I went to the bank and made arrangements so that I could pay it off. The amount owed was around £100 and at this time our finances were very tight indeed but they agreed to let me pay it off at £5 per week. The bank gave me a paying-in book, which I still have in my possession.

Sometime during 1983 I think it was in the early stages Joan and I received a bouquet of flowers together with a card. The card thanked us again for "Looking after Barbara" and saying that the estate would soon be finalised. It was signed "Mr.McGrouther" who we knew as Barbara's solicitor.

There was a period of three days but I cannot remember exactly when but Barbara told us that she would not be contactable because she would be traveling to Zurich to sort out the estate. For three days there were no telephone calls or letters, or indeed any requests for money. Upon her return Barbara telephoned us saying that she had been in Zurich and everything had gone well and the estate would soon be sorted out.

There were a number of payments during 1981 1982 and 1983 that were sent to Barbara Hendry that I cannot remember why they were sent but the reasons would definitely be to do with the releasing of the estate.

Either Joan or I would pay a cheque into the bank to get it cleared and then quickly sent the cash to Barbara Hendry.

During the second half of 1983, both Joan and I were getting rather concerned about the whole situation and wanted it to come to a satisfactory conclusion. We had asked Barbara on a number of occasions when it would be settled and she kept telling us that it wasn't very far away but the legal obstacles kept coming and holding things up. We had to continue to find more money to assist her as financially we had passed the point of no return.

Sometime in June 1983 a legal type letter arrived at our house from Barbara and much to our relief it also indicated that the end was near. It said the funds had been moved to our account in fact into Joan's name and it mentioned a sum of six million pounds. We had to sign this letter and provide specimens of our signatures and send it back "return of post" to Barbara but I Photostatted it before I sent it back. (Letter to be sent back again)!

In July 1983 another letter arrived at our address from Barbara. It was a legal type letter in which it showed that the Royal Bank of Scotland was demanding £426 from her urgently and that the amount involved had to be sent by return of post and by registered letter. We again raised the amount and sent it to Barbara.

Sometime around 21st October 1983 another letter arrived from Barbara and upon opening it I could see that it was a legal bill for the amount of £775.05. Barbara had told us previously all about her legal charges and she told us that when this legal bill had been paid it would open the door for the release of the inheritance. I saw that the letterhead was from a firm of solicitors called Ross Harper and Murphy in Scotland and it looked very official.

As a result of this letter Joan and myself went down to our bank, the Trustees Savings Bank in Lincoln and saw the manager Mr Smith. We told him that we required a short term loan which we obtained to the value of £700 and £50 of this was to be the first payment. A few days later as a result of a request from the bank manager we returned to the bank to show the manager the legal bill as he had requested that we provide him with some documentary proof.

We raised the difference in the amount and sent it to Barbara by registered post to her new address at a block of flats in Red Road Court Glasgow.

At the end of October 1983 or early November another legal type letter arrived at our address from Barbara Hendry. Upon opening it I saw that it was written on Bank of Scotland notepaper and it said that £500 had to be paid. It was a loan of £500 that the bank had made to Miss Emily Astor. I did not know Emily Astor but I knew that the name Astor was connected to the Argyll family so I assumed that it was in connection with Barbara's inheritance.

I went to see Mr. Smith at the bank and showed him the letter. I informed him that wanted to increase my loan to cover the £500. Mr. Smith advanced the amount to my bank account and I wrote a cheque and withdrew the cash. The cash was sent to Barbara Hendry on 8ᵗʰ November 1983.

Also during November two further legal letters arrived at our house, one was from A.R. Murray Sheriff's Officers of Glasgow. It said in the letter that the settlement of the estate had been delayed by an oversight of a legal technical detail and that the £500 mentioned previously should be paid. It was addressed to Mrs. Hendry and it inferred that all financial assets were being transferred to a third person in England, which we took to be ourselves. The letter also said that legal action would be taken against anyone who divulges the persons concerned to be ourselves. It was all to be kept very secret. Another letter came at the same time, it was also on headed note paper being the note paper of another firm of solicitor's called Murdoch Jackson of Glasgow. In the letter it mentioned the name of a solicitor called McGrouther who I recognised as being the solicitor who had gone to Zurich in connection with the inheritance. The letter mentioned that

Mr. McGrouther was still in Zurich and that more money was required as "the Family" were behind it all which I took to mean they were being obstructive "especially the Duchess".

We also received a legal letter from Barbara that she said she had received from a firm of solicitors called Cochran, Dickie and Mackenzie of Paisley Renfrewshire. The letter said that a further £483 had to be paid for work done on the estate by another Trustee who wanted payment for his work. Barbara asked if I could help her. I again went down to see my Bank Manager Mr. Smith and explained the situation to him. I also took the letter with me as I suspected that he would want to see it before advancing me any finance. As I expected, and after

189

outlining my situation, the Bank Manager asked to see the letter. I showed it to him and after reading it he agreed to extend my loan to include the £483. I immediately sent the money to Barbara when I returned home.

Towards the end of November I received another legal letter from Barbara Hendry. The letter said that Barbara's divorce she had previously gone through but was not absolute but before any monies could be released and put in our names the divorce had to be declared absolute or her husband who was her next of kin could make a claim on the estate. The letter stated that for the divorce to be sorted out the sum of £775 had to be paid.

I talked the matter over with Joan and we decided that because we had come so far we had to see it through. The amount of money that we were raising and sending to Barbara would all have to be paid back and it was becoming an increasing worry. Joan had not actually said as much to myself but she was worried just in case the inheritance remained unresolved we would be left with the mounting debt.

The same thought had crossed my mind but I had not mentioned it to Joan, as I did not want to worry her further.

I went down to the Trustees Savings Bank and again saw the manager Mr. Smith and I told him about the additional money requested and the reason for it. I had told Mr. Smith that I would be traveling to Glasgow to take the money myself.

Mr Smith advanced me the money I wanted, it was £775 plus £75 for my personal expenses £850 in all. I had intended to travel up and take the money myself but upon speaking to Barbara she told me that the amount had risen to £800 so that meant that I could not afford to go so I sent Barbara the whole £850.

In late November 1983 Barbara sent Joan and I some form of slip that we had to sign and send back to her. I saw that the slip had the name "Bank of Kantonel Zurich" on it. The reason that Barbara gave us for signing it was that the money was going to be put in our names and the people at the bank had to have in their possession specimens of our signatures.

Before I returned the slip I photocopied it, which I now produce.

Just after sending Barbara Hendry the £850 she telephoned and she said that "Marty" a solicitor supposed to be linked to McGrouther had been involved in a car accident and suffered a heart attack, hit a lamp post and died. He had the £775 on him. The accident resulted in "Marty" not making the court, which had been cancelled, and another court date fixed with a new solicitor, which had resulted in extra expenditure of £550. Barbara asked if we could assist in paying this amount to the new court.

I went to see Mr. Smith the bank manager at the Trustees Savings bank and told him of the extra expense and the reasons for it. He advanced the additional amount of £550 adding it to my loan. Upon returning home I posted the £550 to Barbara. On this occasion Barbara wanted the money sending to Springburn Post Office in Glasgow.

At about the same time I again went to the Trustees Savings Bank and saw Mr. Smith the manger. I told him the circumstances around Barbara's divorce proceedings had that since it had not been settled a further £600 had to be paid into the Court that was dealing with it. I cannot remember all the details but explained it as I knew it to him. I asked him if £600 could be made available to me, which he did.

Mr Smith made arrangements for the £600 to be sent to the Trustees Savings Bank in Springburn for Barbara to collect. Barbara told us later on the telephone that she had received the money but I don't know if she collected it herself because I understand that on some occasions other people collected it for her.

Shortly afterwards Barbara Hendry and ourselves again spoke on the telephone and she told us that the Judge in connection with the hearing on the new court date hadn't turned up and that he had been traced to Aviemore. Barbara told us that the Judge would not proceed with sitting on the case until another fee of £512 had been paid. I went to see the bank Manager Mr Smith about the extra expense and asked him to make the £512 available, which he did together with

£50 expenses. I signed a release form at the bank and the money was sent to a bank in Scotland. I do not know who actually collected it but I know that Barbara received it.

The telephone calls between Barbara and ourselves continued and she told us that she had been presented with an ultimatum that action was going to be brought against her for arrears of rent from a flat that was rented from her daughter who was living in the flat that belonged to Barbara's mother, the Duchess. We gained the impression that Barbara's daughter was demanding the money and had to have it by 12 O 'clock on a certain day or she would be in trouble.

I went to see the bank manager Mr. Smith at the Trustees Savings Bank and explained the position to him. He advanced the money to me by way of increasing my loan facility and sent it through the Trustees Savings Bank system to Glasgow.

I can also remember at about this time additional expenses were incurred regarding the inheritance and either Joan or I went to see the Bank Manager obtained the required amount and sent it to Barbara. I cannot remember the reason or the exact amount sent to her.

On one occasion Mr. Smith the Bank Manager rang me at work which he had never done before to inform me that he had received a telephone call from Barbara Hendry who told him that the final conclusion of the estate was near and she required a further £400 or so to settle the account of four solicitors. She had said it was very urgent. I told Mr. Smith that I agreed the amount should be made available to her.

It was by this time getting very close to Christmas 1983, and Barbara rang us up at the phone box near our address (this was by prior arrangement as due to our mounting debts our phone had been disconnected to save money) She told us that she had been to Edinburgh to see four lawyers to collect some documents from each one. The first two had co-operated alright, the third was not very helpful and she went to see the fourth at his office but she didn't see him. I understand that this fourth one was messing Barbara about and she ended up seeing him at his home address but he refused to help her until he returned to his office and during office hours. I remember

Barbara telling us she had been very badly treated by him had that he had "shown her the door".

Barbara went on to say that she had a very long walk under stormy conditions back to the hospital presumably in Glasgow and ended up having treatment, she later said that the fourth solicitor considered that he was the most senior and wanted a larger fee and that she needed more money to pay him.

Joan and I discussed the extra expense and contacted Mr. Smith at the bank and asked him to make the money available, which he did. Mr. Smith arranged for the money to be sent to Glasgow, which I think amounted to £500.

I seem to recollect that Barbara Hendry rang us again to say that due to her treatment at the hospital and as a result being under the influence of drugs she had got the amount wrong and another £400 was needed to pay the Solicitor. As a result I contacted Mr. Smith at the bank explained the situation and he made the money available. The money was sent to Scotland and Barbara contacted us to say that she had received it but I do not know who collected it.

Both Joan and myself were getting rather concerned about it all but we were constantly reassured by Barbara who told us that everything was going ahead as planned and would be alright, the money would soon be released.

Joan and I were trying to get all of the visits to the bank to see Mr. Smith in our dinner hours from work, which meant a quick walk into the city and back within an hour sometimes we got back to work a little late, which made things very difficult.

Barbara told us on the telephone around this time that a new solicitor was involved on her case by the name of Mr. Spiers who would be handling the cheque side of the estate and he would be travelling to Zurich to sort it all out. Mr. Spiers the solicitor had a lot of contact with the Bank Manager Mr. Smith but neither Joan nor I ever spoke to him. (All part of the deception as if either Ted or Joan had spoken to Spiers on the telephone they would have recognised the voice being that of Donald Hendry the partner of Barbara Hendry.)

The next money that was sent to Barbara by Joan and myself was as a result of a telephone conversation during which Barbara said that there had been a terrible misunderstanding, which had resulted with her being charged with theft and fined £350.

The circumstances were that Barbara needed a further £350 and it had been taken out of the petty cash by a Mr. Leggatt who was a solicitor and it had been taken to Barbara who at the time was in hospital. Barbara went on to say that she had been caught by her "Mummy" the Duchess attempting to put it back. Her mother had called the Police and Barbara had been charged with theft and fined £350. Barbara also said that there was a further debt and that all this needed to be paid before the inheritance could be released. We contacted Mr Smith who made the money available and it was sent to Barbara in Scotland.

It was about this time that we had contact with Doctor Jean Turner. I was at work one day and was called to receive a telephone call. Upon taking the call a woman introduced herself as Doctor Turner. She informed me that Barbara was very ill and asked if Joan and I were prepared to take care of Barbara at our house. We only had a small house but without hesitation I informed Doctor Turner we would do it. Doctor Turner explained that she was Barbara's doctor.

In another call Doctor Turner told my wife that Barbara would have to travel down to Lincoln in a private ambulance but the cost would be around £200. Upon hearing that this was the case we did not hesitate and immediately contacted the bank manager Mr Smith who after hearing the circumstances arranged the finance.

As it happened Barbara did not travel down as she was unable to secure the services of a driver due to the bad weather.

The next thing that happened was that Barbara contacted us and said that she would travel down by plane, which she did on the 16th January 1983. Mr. Smith from the bank came to our house on the day and collected Joan my wife in his car and they travelled to Kirmington Airport, collected Barbara and brought her to our house. I did not go to the airport I stayed at work that day.

I met Barbara that evening when I returned home from work.

Barbara stayed two nights but spent most of her time in bed, as she was not feeling very well. She told us later that she has bought a hotel in Southend on Sea that she was going to give our daughter in appreciation of what she had done to help i.e. lending money for us to send to Barbara.

Barbara was intending to travel down to Lincolnshire to stay permanently but before she left she received two letters from her son Kenneth who had told her not to open them until she got on the plane but she did. She told us that she opened them in the ladies toilet at Glasgow Airport.

Barbara gave those two letters to me on the Monday night and I went into the Trustees Savings Bank and showed them to Mr. Smith and he photocopied them. The two letters were each from a firm of solicitors in Scotland one being the firm of Joseph Mellicks and the other from a firm called Ross Harper and Murphy. The letter from Joseph Mellicks mentioned that in connection with the inheritance the sum of £1050 had to be paid to them for the work that they had carried out.

I discussed the matter with Mr. Smith the bank manager and he decided to advance us the money. Barbara also said that she wanted her taxi fare and the plane fare paying and on 17th January I went and got the £1250 from Mr Smith by increasing my loan at the Trustees Savings Bank.

After attending the bank I went home and gave the money to Barbara who took it back to Scotland when she returned the next day.

During her visit down to Lincoln Barbara was very reassuring that everything was falling into place especially now that she had got a new solicitor by the name of Mr Spiers involved in the Zurich end of things. She went on to explain the various delays that were happening involving the inheritance and how it was obviously the Argyll family that were causing all the problems in an attempt to thwart Barbara in receiving what was rightly due to her. Both Joan and I were confident that as a result of what was being explained to us that we were doing the right thing in helping Barbara financially.

A day or so after Barbara had returned to Scotland Mr. Smith the bank manager telephoned me at work. He said that Mr. Spiers the solicitor involved in attempting to get the cheque released in Zurich had just telephoned him and told him that he (Spiers himself) had been misled regarding the fees for the probate hearing and that the fees had been more that he had first been led to believe. He went on to say that until the fees had been paid all the estate would be held. Mr. Smith told me that the amount required as £1500. I asked Mr Smith to make this amount available in order to speed things up which he agreed to and as a result added the amount to my loan. The £1500 was sent to a bank in Scotland for collection. I later received a telephone call from Barbara confirming she had received the amount and that this would "obviously speed things up!"

A day or so later I received a further telephone call from Barbara Hendry she told us that a further problem had arisen. She said that payment of fees to an accountant for the final release of the estate needed to be paid urgently. I quickly contacted Mr. Smith the bank manager and outlined the situation and he agreed to advance the £600 needed to pay the accountant. Mr. Smith made the necessary arrangements and the money was transferred to a bank in Scotland and collected.

Around this time the solicitor, Mr. Spiers was travelling all over the country but he still kept in touch with the bank manager Mr. Smith. We all knew at this time that Barbara Hendry was extremely ill and in a nursing home in Newcastle. As far as we knew Mr. Spiers and Barbara Hendry were on their way to us but the next thing we knew was when Mr. Smith contacted us and said that Mr. Spiers had been in touch with him to tell him that Barbara Hendry had undergone a minor operation conducted by a surgeon who knew her mother the Duchess. We were also told that Barbara Hendy had taken an overdose because she thought that someone was following her. Anyway, Mr Spiers had said that he needed £800 to cover the nursing home fees and arrangements were made for it to be sent to a bank in Fareham. Mr. Smith asked me if I agreed which I did and the transaction regarding the transfer of the money was completed.

I received a further telephone call from Mr Smith around this time saying that Mr Spiers had contacted him to inform him that he had broken down in his car and had spent the night in a bus station and that he had contacted Mr Smith because he wanted £500 in expenses to pay for him to get back to Newcastle. I thought that we should do this, as things appeared to be so close to a conclusion and Mr. Smith said he would advance it to Mr. Spiers at a bank in Fareham, which I understand he did.

Over the next week or so Barbara Hendry telephoned us and said that she was feeling better and when she felt well enough to travel was going to come down. When I expressed concern she reassured me that things would be alright as she would be travelling with a doctor.

It was about this time that a man called Mr. Wilson came into the proceedings. Mr. Wilson was unknown to me but my wife met him during one of her visits to Glasgow.

Mr. Wilson, although I never actually spoke to him was supposed to be a security guard who had a security firm in Glasgow and Barbara made arrangements with him to travel down to Lincoln to bring the "cheque" a Rembrandt painting and a quantity of jewellery. I think that Mr. Smith at the Trustees Savings bank had some dealings with him. Mr. Smith was told by Mr. Wilson that Barbara Hendry had been rushed into hospital to have a blood clot removed from her spine. There was a lot of exchange of telephone calls between Mr. Smith and myself and Mr. Smith and Mr. Wilson made the security arrangements between themselves.

We continued to keep in touch with Barbara Hendry as best as we could throughout this on a regular basis as she always told us that settlement of the estate was not very far away.

During the early part of 1984, there were several dates when the cheque from the estate was supposed to be available. After Barbara had been in the nursing home and had the operation we were just about on permanent standby as Barbara was supposed to be coming down at any time to stay with Joan and I. Barbara had by this time returned to her flat in Glasgow from the nursing home and on several occasions we rang her there.

By this time Joan and I were getting rather concerned about the estate being settled. We had just about exhausted any further avenues that we could have approached to assist Barbara. It was never about making a profit but all about helping a friend. Barbara was consistent in telling us that the inheritance would soon be released and everything would turn out alright.

Barbara had previously told us about a civil dispute between herself and a woman called Margaret Simonette. She said that she was being sued by Mrs. Simonette for some money that she owed her and this had to be paid. Barbara said that if she ever was found to owe money and it became known to the Trustees who were involved in the estate, then it would contravene the terms of the will and invalidate it and Barbara would get nothing. She also said that if it ever came to light then everything would be frozen until enquiries had been made into her borrowing. This revelation caused Joan and me great concern and we discussed it between ourselves. We decided that if we could possibly raise the money we would assist Barbara to avoid any further complications.

On 9th or 10th March 1984, another letter arrived from Barbara when we opened it we saw it was another legal type document. I understood it to be a writ. It said the pursuer was Margaret Simonette and the defender was Barbara Ferguson known as Hendry and the amount involved was £890 including interest. Upon closer examination of the document I saw that it outlined parts of the will that Barbara had told us about such as not borrowing money. After reading it I understood it to mean that Simonette was seeking the return of monies loaned but Barbara was opposing it on the grounds that the monies borrowed didn't go to releasing the will but went to assist with medical expenses.. We were in a very agitated condition at this stage because we didn't want any more holdups, all we wanted was our money back and to be able to pay off our debts.

Because of Barbara owing this money to Mrs. Simonette, she again approached us and said that it had to be paid.

A certain amount of the money had to be paid into court by 13th March 1984 so we sent two packages of about £210 each to Barbara. We found it extremely hard to obtain the money and Barbara told us to approach the bank again but we were eventually able to borrow it from a friend.

Barbara again contacted us and told us that she wanted the remainder of the £890 sending to her urgently and after another struggle we obtained it and sent it to her. Barbara told us that an amount of interest had accumulated on the amount of money owed to Mrs. Simonette and this had to be also paid before anything could be done towards the release of the estate. We again struggled to borrow the money, which was around £250 and sent it to her.

Barbara again contacted us to inform us that there had been further unexpected expense as before the inheritance could be released an amount of tax had to be paid to the Inland Revenue, a total of £227. We raised this amount and sent it to her. This was the last money we were able to send to her as basically we could not borrow anymore from friends or relatives and the banks or loan companies would not deal with us any further.

Sometime in March 1984, a birth certificate arrived at our house from Barbara. She said that she had sent it to us to prove who she was and to show that she was related to the Argyll family. Upon examination I saw that it showed her father as John Ian Campbell (Duke of Argyll heir) and her mother as Margaret Wigham, who became the Duchess in later life.

My wife and myself's involvement with Barbara Hendry has stretched from 1976 to the present time and we have no reason to doubt anything that she has said. Both my wife and I firmly believe her to be the illegitimate daughter of the Duchess of Argyll and genuinely thought that as a result of what she told us that she had a large inheritance to come from her uncle. The Duchess (her mother) was continually blocking it and making things difficult for her in her attempt to release it.

Over the period of these years we have been assisting Barbara financially. We have sent her money, that to the best of our knowledge and belief, has been in the region of £50,000 and could even be as much as £60,000, including expenses incurred in sending the money as it cost £4.95 to send £100 to her in the early stages and in the later stages it was £6.95 taking into account that sometimes £600 or more would be sent on one occasion. Almost all the money sent to Barbara was for the purpose of her putting to the use of releasing her inheritance that was due to her but on occasions she did with our knowledge pay one or two electricity bills and some medical expenses.

I am not able to state the exact reasons on particular dates the various sums of money were used for but it was all sent in connection with legal expenses.

In the very early stages my wife Joan and I used our own savings to send to Barbara and also sent our earnings on a regular basis. At times her requests for money exceeded the amounts that we were able to provide so we turned to friends and relatives for their assistance.

The first person we borrowed money from was our daughter and she has at various times throughout the proceedings assisted us and the total amount she has lent us is £5000. Other friends have lent us about £3000. Since we encountered difficulty in meeting Barbara's demands in raising enough money we turned to my brother and his wife to assist us, which they did to the total of £5000 (at the time of approaching my brother Barbara was aware that he was suffering from cancer of which he died of shortly afterwards).We also borrowed £500 from my brother-in-Law.

As the years went by and the requests for money increased it became more difficult to provide Barbara with the amounts she required. We had borrowed as much as we could from friends and relatives and since Barbara was always telling us that the estate would soon be sorted out we naturally assumed that the next payment would always be the last.

We then approached finance companies to assist us. We obtained two initial loans from the companies one of £800 from Mercantile Credit to pay for our daughter's wedding and another £1000 from Lombard North Central to assist Barbara. I can say that we returned to these companies and borrowed further amounts, which have been sent to Barbara Hendry. We later approached the Trustees Savings Bank and obtained personal loans and an overdraft facility that together with other loans are still being paid off. At times the whole of our monthly wages went to Barbara Hendry.

There was one occasion that £600 was supposed to be used by my wife to pay for the burial of her mother, was sent to Barbara. This was done at a time when we considered it would all be sorted out very soon and the Co-op are at the time of my making this statement requesting payment. We even sold our car and the money we obtained was sent to Barbara and we obtained a further loan from HFC Trust for £400, which we sent to her. We also cashed in four insurance policies and sent Barbara the money.

In the past my wife and I have on occasions managed on £25 per week. We have sent Barbara packets of food to her, tea and soup as we were under the impression that she was really struggling financially.

If it had not been for our family helping us out at times I really do not know how we would have managed as we had to cut down on bus fares and rely on people at times to give us lifts to work.

At present we have two writs and judgments made against us for re-payment of loans and because of sending the money requested we have got behind with the rent for our council house and the council have obtained a repossession order. We have recently been able to make a payment to them.

It was not the fact that Barbara made us elaborate promises of a hotel for our daughter and a BMW car for us that made us embark on lending her the money but we seriously considered her to be a genuine friend over the years that was in a desperate situation, and we wholeheartedly wanted to help without regard for ourselves and now it appears it was to our detriment.

The only thing I wanted to happen was to be able to visit Canada one day and my my wife wanted was a small car but as it continued we disregarded these and just wanted our money back to pay off our debts. I cannot possibly say how long it will take for us to pay the money back that we owe and it appears that I will have to retire from work within the next two years.

I produce a breakdown of our income and commitments. If I had known that anything that Barbara said either wasn't true or the money was not going to the purpose of which she said she had wanted it for, then none of it would not have been sent.

Signed
E WARNER

The completion of the statement made for a very sombre moment. I just could not believe just what Joan and Ted had been through. My first thought was to attempt preserve their position and try and call in a few favours as having been a working detective in the City of Lincoln I have had a large amount of dealings with loan companies and local authorities and it was time to call and see a few people.

Since the statement was completed on a Friday evening that was a job to do first thing Monday morning when I would be banging on their doors and "re-introducing" myself. If one cannot pull in a few favours in circumstances like this then it's a bad job I thought to myself. I also thought that as I now had a statement from Ted if I could prove "Deception" and that Joan and Ted had been deceived I could charge Barbara Hendry and Donny Hendry with further offences in addition to the ones that they had previously been charged with. The recording of the statement of the statement took just short of two weeks, which could only be recorded and continued evening after evening when both Joan and Ted returned from work.

Over the following weekend I mulled over how I was going to progress the enquiry. As a professional investigator it is very difficult to put the matter under investigation aside, in fact some of the best lines of enquiry have suddenly flashed up like a light being switched on in the head whilst doing very mundane tasks whilst not at work such as digging the garden or on one instance the tiling of the bathroom or even whilst lying in bed.

Psychologists and Occupational Therapists often state that it is best to put these things aside whilst not working but it is easier said than done and anyway these things do require a lot of thought.

I still had a fair bit to do, and other witnesses to see least of all I would have to interview the friends and relatives of Joan and Ted from whom they have borrowed money from. What was at the fore of my mind was the fact that because of their lack of money they had been served with a possession order by the local authority as they had got behind with the rent on their council house. That was a situation I had to resolve first thing Monday morning.

Monday morning came and I was sat outside the council offices for when they opened. Upon entering I introduced myself and was taken to the department that dealt with the payment of rents for council houses. There I met the manager in charge and explained the situation. Because I was based at Marker Rasen in the event that the local council had any problems of a nature within that area that required a CID presence, it would be my services that they would call upon. Having made a play of working at Market Rasen I had the full and undivided attention of the manager.

I explained the situation that I was dealing with was a fraud and requested that Mr. and Mrs. Warner's were not pursued, as I am confident that in the future all arrears would be paid.

In the Police Force one learns that it is a folly to "stick one's neck" out and take people at their word. The nature of the business we are in dictates that there are a large number of Individuals whose word cannot be trusted they will swear on their lives, lives of partners or in one case "on a stack of bibles!" that they are telling the truth or that they will do or not do something. In my experience the worst offenders are drug addicts I have been caught out before like that so I have learnt to be very careful. And the biggest "lie" of all? The case in point being a number of years ago whilst in the process of executing a search warrant under the Misuse of Drugs Act we called at the house subject of the warrant and upon forcing the door and gaining entry was faced with the father of the house slumped in a chair semi-comatose with a rubber restrain around his arm having just injected heroin, his wife was sat at the table having injected amphetamines. Also sat at the same table was the daughter of the household aged about 15 years old with her exercise books on the table tying to complete her homework.

After the initial surprise of our attendance the house was searched and a quantity of drugs seized. The mother and father played up and were restrained and whilst in the process of removing her mother from the house the daughter began crying. Her mother turned to her on the way out and said, "Don't worry babe this is the last time, I'm going to stop the drugs!" Within 18 months the mother had died from a drugs overdose.

I had no reservation in assuring the manager at the council the arrears of Mr. and Mrs. Warner would be paid, as having dealt with them over a period of months their trustworthiness and integrity in my opinion was beyond reproach.

After a short conversation with the manager he said to me, "This all rings a bell."

I said, "How do you mean?"

He replied, "Somebody in the office has had dealings with this."

With that another member of staff approached and said,

"Is that the Warner account you are talking about?"

The manager replied, "Yes we are."

I explained that the Warner's had been subjected to a possession order and the reason for my visit.

"Yes, that is all being sorted out," He said.

I said, "tell me about it."

"Well," he went on to explain, " I recently received a telephone call from a Scottish Solicitor who explained that Mr. and Mrs. Warner were due to be in receipt of a large inheritance and when that was concluded all their arrears would be settled."

"You wouldn't happen to have his name?" I asked.

He returned to his desk came back and said that he could not recollect his name, but he had a very broad Scottish accent."

I immediately knew that was Donald Hendry, the partner of Barbara who had rung up the Council in an attempt to delay any repossession, but since there was to be no inheritance then it would only compromise the Warner's further.

I asked that the Council delay any proceedings, which they agreed to do. They also agreed to get all their paperwork together and I would return at a later date to record a statement.

I travelled back to Lincoln and went to one of the loan companies to visit a manager at the loan company I knew would assist.

Upon attending I was informed that the manager I had previously dealt with had moved on and was met with a rather small dapper man aged about 30 but was obviously attempting to look older and in authority. I did not think that his lack of height necessitated built up shoes but he obviously did.

I introduced myself and explained the situation and that the Warner's had received the loans and were no doubt struggling to pay.

"Yes?" The manager replied, "What do you expect me to do?"

I explained that I was requesting breathing space for the Warner's but he declined saying that "They've had the money and must repay it."

I accepted his point and told him I was confident that it would be repaid but not as quickly as agreed. I tried to reason further.

"There is nothing I can do, we will no doubt issue proceedings in the event of non payment of the loan." He replied.

I explained that there is every intention to repay the loan and that all I was seeking was a period of breathing space for Joan and Ted.

I was quickly beginning to dislike his attitude and I was not asking the world and gained the impression that if he had been 6 inches taller then he might not have got the attitude problem! All I was hoping for was that the company extended the period of payment thereby reducing the payments but extending the time to repay the amount owed.

It was not a regular habit to stick my neck out on behalf of complainants but I had total confidence that the amount due would be repaid by Joan and Ted. The only reply I got from the manager was "Can't be done!" I can remember thinking at the time it is amazing how quickly one can "go off" somebody and "What goes around comes around" I shall remember him!

Upon approaching a couple more loan companies that day and the Co-operative funeral directors (Joan and Ted had used money that they had put aside for a family funeral!) all were very sympathetic and very helpful but the vertically challenged manager at the first loan company was to be remembered. As the Chinese proverb goes "*If you sit on the riverbank long enough your enemy will come floating by*"

Having made a few calls I was able to stave off the imminent possession order and also obtain a bit of a breathing space for the finances of Joan and Ted. Don't run away with the idea that the Police will assist you with your finances when you are struggling but this was exceptional circumstances at the time and Joan and Ted were important witnesses that together with welfare issues prompted my decision to intervene. In hindsight this was no different to what family liaison officers practice today rather that abandoning the witness in a possible high profile case only to contact them again a while after their statement has been recorded and say "See you at Court tomorrow" or words to that effect. Not having given them any notice and not remained in contact. Having partially achieved my objective I returned to my office to reflect on my next steps. Both of the Hendrys were in custody so that minimised the potential of witness interference and with them temporarily out of the way I could get on with my job.

In any enquiry the investigating office has to constantly review their position and evaluate what further evidence is needed. To summarise, both alleged offenders had been arrested, Donald Hendry had partially admitted his part and had provided a voluntary statement. Barbara Hendry however had also partially admitted her involvement but was reluctant to elaborate when further questioned. She had also declined to make a statement. What one has to appreciate that at this time in the 1980's the interviews of suspects were not at this time tape recorded but a comprehensive note of the interview was prepared by the interviewing officers in their pocket books.

What was not uncommon was that the suspect could later appear at court and claim that the interviewing officers had made the whole account up and had in effect "verballed" the suspect up.

I knew that I would have to record further statements from witnesses who had loaned money to the Warner's but for the purpose of getting the case to court that is all that would be required. I was still slightly suspicious as it was quite an involved case but it seemed to be coming together rather easily. Considering the type of individual that we were dealing with either the amount of evidence at this stage was so overwhelming that she decided to make a clean slate of it (which I considered highly unlikely) or there was something else that I was missing. I would have to think further about that and bear it in mind.

During the investigation into the conduct of Barbara Hendry it was apparent that both Joan and Ted had been lied to and that they had sent large amounts of money to her in Scotland, what was needed was to prove this aspect to the standard required in a criminal court i.e. "Beyond all reasonable doubt" and to also establish the origin of the monies sent and that it has been obtained by borrowing from relatives and loan companies and the like. In the event of a subsequent "Not Guilty" plea then these issues would be explored and on occasions exploited by any defence counsel and need to be proved to the satisfaction of the court.

One also has to consider during any investigation especially lengthy ones that it is impracticable to follow every lead and to interview every witness in a case, as it can be poor use of resources especially if at the first appearance at court the offender pleads guilty and no further witness need to be seen. On the other hand however some offenders, no matter what the amount of evidence is that is available will always plead not guilty requiring the investigator to follow all leads available and interviewing all witnesses and then plead guilty at the eleventh hour.

At this stage in the case I would need to obtain evidence that supports the charge and not see all available witnesses, as there was a distinct possibility Barbara Hendry would, when faced with the evidence plead guilty but somehow I was not so sure about this but time will tell.

I decided to obtain witness statements from individuals that had loaned Joan and Ted money but that still left the question of just who else was involved. I was sure that I would not certainly be allowed to conclude the enquiry and answer all the questions but what still remained was the identity of the "Doctor" the story of the security guard and where all the money had gone. I would attempt to answer as many of these questions as I could.

I decided to trace Joan and Ted's only daughter who I knew had leant them money to give to Barbara, obtain her account and record a statement from her, maybe this would bring to the surface another angle to the enquiry.

On 2nd June 1984 I traced Elaine and spoke to her about Barbara Hendry. I also recorded a statement.

STATEMENT of   Elaine WARNER

I got married on October 27 1979 when I moved into my present address. Prior to moving into my own address I lived with my parents Joan and Ted Warner at Dunholme Near Lincoln and I worked at a local building society.

Whilst I lived with my parents, in August 1976, they went on holiday to Aberfeldy in Scotland. When they returned they told me that they had formed a relationship with a woman called Barbara Hendry and a man who she said was her husband Donny. Over the following few months my parents kept in touch with Barbara by both telephone and letter. Sometime during February or March 1977 my mum told me that Barbara was the illegitimate daughter of Margaret Duchess of Argyll. Due to the fact that I had never at this point met Barbara I didn't think too much about it. My mum also told me that there was a will in existence of which Barbara was the beneficiary and that she and my father were sending her £1000 at her request. A short time later, my parents informed me that they were sending money on a fairly regular basis to Barbara again at her request.

I understood that Barbara was using the money to release the estate with regards to the will. I had no reason to disbelieve this. I cannot say how much my parents were sending to Barbara in Scotland but I was aware that it was a large amount.

I never really had any involvement with the situation until about June 1977. Around this time I started giving my parents small amounts of money at their request, about £25 or £50 now and again. I realised that they were sending this money to Barbara. I cannot put a figure that I gave them or be specific about the dates. However this continued until the early part of 1978 when my husband and I purchased our current house.

The first time I ever spoke to Barbara was on the telephone on my 21st birthday. I also got engaged to my husband on that day. Barbara congratulated me on the phone and sounded like a very pleasant person. She also sent us a telegram wishing us all the best.

During the months leading up to my wedding I never gave my parents any money as I was spending it all on decorating my house and building an extension to it.

I first met Barbara the Christmas day after my wedding in 1979. My parents had gone to Scotland to collect her and Donny and on the day when they we due home I went to my parent's house to light the fire and prepare for their arrival. They turned up sometime during the evening.

A couple of days before Christmas day there was a telegram waiting for Barbara. After the introductions were over Barbara opened the telegram and remember her saying that it said "Congratulations you've done it!" or words to that effect. Barbara showed me the telegram and explained that it meant that she had won her court case and her estate would be released. At the time I did not know the amount of money she was due to collect.

I stayed and passed the evening away at my parent's house.

I got the impression that Barbara was very pleasant, a quite friendly type of person but for some reason I didn't really take to Donny. My husband and I spent Christmas day with my parents and the Hendrys and we had a super day. They were good company although I remember that during the afternoon, Barbara went quiet for a short time and complained that she was ill and that her stomach had swollen and ached.

Barbara and Donny went back to Scotland just after Christmas day and from then she used to ring me quite frequently at work and leave messages for my mum.

Sometime during early 1980, my parents asked my brother and myself if we would lend them some money for the purpose of assisting Barbara in getting the estate cleared. We agreed and over the next few months we gave them money when we felt that we could afford it. The money we gave to our parents came from our salary and although I cannot state the exact amounts or dates we were handing them small sums to help with the running costs of their home.

In early 1981, my parents again approached my husband and I and requested substantial amounts of money to help Barbara. Again we agreed and we closed our building society account, which contained our total savings of £585.31, and of that amount I sent £500 to Barbara at the request of my parents.

I believe that I wired the money to Barbara at a Post Office but I cannot remember the details of where it was. On the same day I opened another building society account for the specific purpose of keeping our savings in. Initially put £50 in to open the account, that was on 13th January 1981. My husband and I kept the account until May 2nd 1981, when we had a total of £250 in it. Again at the request of my parents I withdrew the £250 and handed £245 to Barbara personally. From what I can recall, that weekend, Barbara Donny and Robert (Barbara's son) had come down to visit my parents for a few days and Barbara actually waited outside the building society for me to withdraw the money. I came out and met her and handed over the cash. She thanked me for it – she often appeared embarrassed by money.

On 16th February 1981, my husband and I decided to get a personal loan from the Midland Bank in Lincoln. The reason was to send it to Barbara because she was requesting more money from my parents, which they could ill afford. I went to the bank and got a loan of £550, which I recall, I wired up to Barbara somewhere in Scotland. I still have a copy of the loan contract written up by the bank.

On 10th June 1981 sometime during the evening my mum called round to my house. She asked if I would increase my loan with the bank to £1100. She stated that Barbara was at her house on another visit and she had told her she needed another £550 to release the estate. I was a bit apprehensive at first because I did not know what my husband would say. I talked it over with him that night and he reluctantly agreed.

The following day being 11th June 1981 I went to the bank with my mum and had an interview with a view to increasing the £550 loan to £1100. The bank agreed to my request and handed me £550 immediately. I, in turn gave the £550 to my mum. I realised that she was going to hand it to Barbara. Again the bank wrote up a contract for me with regards to the loan, which I still have in my possession.

As previously stated I cannot be specific about amounts of money or dates until the last couple of occasions that I have handed money to my mum and dad.

On 10th March 1984, I took £125 from our account at the building society. I gave this money to my mum to help her with her general household expenses as she was using all her money to send to Barbara. My parents repaid this on 23rd March 1983. The last time I ever gave them any money in connection with Barbara was on 16th April 1984, when I withdrew £225 from my building society, which my parents have since repaid.

However during the time between my second loan on June 11th 1981 and 10th March 1984 when I gave them the £125, my husband and I have assisted my parents with their running expenses. I cannot put an exact figure on the amount we have given them but it has always been because they have handed their own money to Barbara to assist her with her inheritance. I would estimate that we have handed over about £4,500 altogether.

From the very beginning, when we handed money to my parents we always knew it was going to Barbara in order to release the money from the will. Barbara always promised that when this happened they would receive a substantial amount of money. However, for the past few years all my parents have worried about is paying all their friends and relatives their money back. My parents always had great faith in Barbara and almost idolised her. They would take anything said to them as being the truth and would not hear anything bad said against her. I went along with this to a certain extent because they are my parents and I would never hurt them intentionally.

Looking back over the years, it seems unbelievable how my parents kept up their payments to Barbara and the extent to which they went in order to do this but there was always some plausible explanation form Barbara when the monies from the will was not released and always what appeared to be genuine documents to back her story up.

Barbara always went out of her way to be pleasant and friendly.

Whatever money was handed to her she reacted with tears and said that we were her best friends for helping her and that everything would work out eventually. If I had the slightest inclination that the story she was telling to my parents had been untrue, I would have informed the police immediately but my parents were so adamant that it was true, I believed them.

With regards to my building society books I have referred to in this statement, I have them all in my possession and can produce them in evidence if necessary.

Signer E WARNER

Having seen and interviewed Elaine the daughter of Joan and Ted it was now necessary to start gathering further evidence to support the allegation that an offence of deception had been committed. In order to support a charge it was necessary to prove that money had in fact been sent to Barbara by Joan and Ted, under false pretences but also to establish that the money had in fact been raised and to show where it had in fact been raised from.

Since being shown in my view beyond doubt that they were being deceived both Joan and Ted had been of utmost assistance. They had explained where and how the monies had been sent and I decided to conduct enquiries on a more local basis at this stage. This had led me to another couple that were close friends and had loaned Joan and Ted monies.

I visited Dorothy and Bill Anderson on 3rd June 1984. Dorothy and Bill lived just around the corner from Joan and Ted in a very small and neat bungalow set at the side of a main road. Dorothy was a retired cook and Bill was employed locally. Having explained the situation of which they already had become aware of, I established that as a couple, they too had been approached by Joan and Ted to borrow money to assist them. It soon became obvious that they were very good friends and had willingly agreed to assist. I asked them to provide a statement. In the event it was Dorothy who agreed to make the statement.

Statement of Dorothy ANDERSON 64 years Housewife.

I live at the address provided with my husband Bill, I am a retired Cook but my husband still works as a plant attendant at a local pumping station but is due to retire from work in June 1985.

We have lived at our present address for the past twenty-five years and during that time we have become good friends with Joan and Ted Warner who live just around the corner. Joan and I are very close and she has always visited me regularly and confided in me. Ted and Bill aren't as close but they get on very well together.

During the summer of 1976, Joan and Ted went on holiday to Aberfeldy in Scotland. When they came back Joan came to visit me and she told me during a conversation that whilst they had been away they had met a woman called Barbara Hendry who was a waitress at the hotel they had been staying at. Apparently Barbara had befriended Joan and invited her and Ted back to her home where she lived with her husband Donny.

Soon after Joan had told me about Barbara she came to visit me again and she informed me that Barbara had stated that she was the illegitimate daughter of the Duchess of Argyll. I didn't really think anything of this at the time but I had no reason to disbelieve it. Shortly after that, I cannot say how long, I understood from Joan that she was sending money up to Barbara in Scotland. Apparently Barbara had requested the money and the reason that had been given was that there was a will in which a lot of money was due to Barbara. However, a lot of money was needed in order to release the estate.

At first it was small amounts I think but Barbara always seemed to need extra cash due to one reason or another that I never really understood, it was all very complicated but Joan is an extremely nice person, as is Ted and they truly believed that they were helping Barbara by sending her money. Joan often used to come to my house and use my telephone to ring Barbara. However once Joan realised how high our telephone bills were becoming she stopped using it.

During December 1980 about four days before Christmas I believe, Joan came to visit me. She asked me if Bill and I could possibly loan her £400 to give to Barbara in order that the money from the will could be released. I said that I would think it over and later that evening when Bill came home from work I discussed the request with him and we decided to help Joan and Ted. The following morning Joan brought Barbara and Donny to meet Bill and myself at our house. I remember Barbara saying to us that she was extremely grateful to us for lending her the money and that it would be the last time so that the problem could be sorted out. I cannot remember anything else what was said that day. I think that we just had a conversation about things in general.

After a short while we all went into Lincoln to the main Midland Bank in the precinct. Barbara, Donny and Joan waited outside the bank whilst Bill and I went in to see the Bank manager. We asked for a £500 loan, £100 extra had been requested to give Barbara some cash in hand to help her out. The Bank Manager agreed but we had to wait about three hours before it was handed over. During this time we all wondered round town. When we returned to the bank, we were handed the £500 cash (it had to be cash as Barbara had said the court would not accept a cheque). We handed the £500 cash to Barbara personally. We have since been paying that loan off in monthly installments of £18.48 and it will finally be paid off in November 1984.

The second time that I loaned money to Barbara was during late July/August, 1981. On that occasion Joan again approached me and requested a loan. Bill and I again agreed because we thought that it would help Joan and Ted out of their increasing financial difficulties. We borrowed £500 from the Mercantile Credit Company, which we again paid back in monthly installments of £44.00 starting on 4th August 1981. The last payment was made on 15th November 1982. I am in possession of the Mercantile Credit payment book for that particular loan and can produce this in evidence if required.

I believe it was shortly after Bill and I had finished paying off our loan when yet again Joan approached us and asked us to take out another loan. We agreed and took out a £300 loan from the same company, which we started paying off in approximately £34 monthly installments. I think that we only made one payment when after being asked by Joan we increased the loan to £500, thereby increasing the monthly installments to £36.00. I believe that we only paid off one installment when Joan insisted that we hand the payment book over to her so that she could continue making the payments. She did this because she felt guilty because we had not been repaid. Joan is still paying that loan off although it has remained in our name.

The final large amount of money that we have handed over knowing it was going to Barbara was in October 1983. I took £65 from my Burnley Society Account and I added £5 to it from my purse to make it £70. Then on 3rd October 1983, I took £200 from my Access account to make it a total of £270. I then went with Joan to the main post office in Lincoln where we sent the money to Barbara. I believe it was by registered post from what I can recall.

On top of the amounts that I have mentioned, Bill and I quite frequently handed £30 or £40 to Joan and Ted over the last six or seven years. I don't think that it was used for any other reason. As far as I can recall we have not handed over any more money to Joan and Ted for Barbara since late 1983. I cannot be more specific about amounts or dates because I have never made any accurate records of our outgoings to them.

Since the first time that I met Barbara and Donny, I think they have visited me twice more although nothing she ever said really stands out in my memory. She always said that she was very grateful to Bill and myself for all our financial help.

On one occasion, I received a bouquet of flowers through Interflora from a solicitor called McGrouther in Glasgow. There was a message with it which said something like "Thanking you for all your kindness to me and Joan and Ted".

If I had ever realised that my money was being wasted, I would have never have loaned it because Bill and myself cannot afford to just hand it out. We honestly believed that it was being used to help Barbara release the money from the will that was owed to her. On one occasion that she visited us she even brought what appeared to be some sort of legal document to back her story up. I cannot remember exactly what it was she showed me but it appeared very official whatever it was.

Bill and I estimate that altogether we have loaned £3500 to Joan and Ted Warner.

I was reasonably happy that it all seemed to be coming together and had time to mull over the mass of documents that had been produced by Ted Warner. It was obvious that I was dealing with a deception and could reasonably assume that all supporting documents sent by Barbara Hendry to Joan and Ted would turn out to be forgeries. Upon looking through the documents my attention was drawn to two documents in particular. Upon closer examination the letters both seemed to have been tampered with. At a first glance all appeared to be in order but upon closer examination the margins did not exactly follow the letterheads. I had obtained enough evidence at this stage to prove that money had been sent it was now time to demonstrate the depth of the deception that had been practiced upon Joan and Ted Warner. In order to do this I would have to prove that the documents provided to Joan and Ted by Barbara Hendry were in fact forgeries. The two documents I selected were one from a firm called A.R. MURRAY Messengers-at-Arms & Sherriff's Officers 166 Buchannan Street Glasgow. The letter went as follows:

Ref/92/F1035973   *4th November 1983*

Estate Settlement of the late James Campbell
In favour of Barbara Ferguson Hendry

Dear Mrs Hendry,
Referring to your Court Case in connection of the above (10.10.1983 – 14.10.1983).

The expected date of settlement in monies, investments and property to be settled on or before the 28.10.83 on your behalf, has been delayed by an oversight of a legal technical detail which I believe has arisen from E Astor whom is owing the sum of £500 and as all financial assets are at this time being transferred into the name of a third party appointed by you, in England, the Pursuer whishes payment before you establish your visit to England, also she states that you have a terminal illness and you have taken the precaution of transferring all of your assets to a party unknown to administer the above and is in fact the benefactor of all monies and property, and concedes she will not be paid once the estate is in the possession of the third party and feels it is her right to be informed of the third parties name and residence. If the monies due to her in a business transaction with you are not paid by the return date of 10th November a writ will be taken out against you. Until this has been settled we have to abide by the legal laws in Scotland as once the transfer is finalised to the third party you, in fact own no assets, which we went into detail last July. I would add to the above that also under the law of Scotland the name of the third party cannot be divulged (J. Warner of Lincoln) to anyone outside the chambers of this office or Court

I would advise you pay it as soon as possible before the date in question as it will delay all transactions.

As soon as we are in receipt of the above, finalisation will be about fourteen days from the date of receipt

Yours Faithfully
C Murray (Signed)

The second latter that caught my attention was a letter from a firm called Murdoch Jackson Solicitors and Notaries of Woodside Place in Glasgow The letter reads as follows:

To Mrs B Hendry   *31/10/1983*
10 Red Road Court   *Private and Confidential*

Balornock   *File MF/4046*
Glasgow

Dear Mrs. Hendry,

Re The Estate of the Late James Campbell

I as a friend and close business associate of Mr. McGrouther, asked me to investigate (very discreetly) the letter received by you, from Miss E. Astor, my findings are that it is a delaying method of preventing you being re-united with your friends in Lincolnshire, also a way of delayment to the financial arrangements already made by you in the interests of the third party to whom it is bequested in your will and in your lifetime to have control as Trustee, and complete control over all your interests which met with approval at Zurich. My advice to you is to pay her, the sum which I believe is £250 plus 50% this is the only way I see it to avoid you being subjected to more legal involvement. I must also add you have interest to add to the initial sum. I am sorry to say this but Mr. McGrouther and I are under the impression that your mother could be at the root of all this. The estate being of a considerable amount will be directed according to your wishes.

Please accept my sincere sympathy on hearing of your illness. Mr. McGrouther confided in me to establish urgency of the above matter in his absence.

This letter is in complete confidence; as you have to abide by the clauses set out in your late Uncles will although I admit he was a bit eccentric.

Yours Faithfully

William Jackson (Signed)

The letters to a layman without previous experience of the legal profession appeared to be professionally produced on headed notepaper, but to the trained investigative eye did not appear to be genuine despite the headed note paper there were slight grammatical errors and upon closer examination appeared to have been doctored. I decided that I would make contact with the alleged authors of the letters and see where it would take me.

After making the various phone calls I decided that I would have to again travel to Scotland to obtain the necessary evidence. I contacted my able and willing assistant Policewoman O'Connor and told her that we would be travelling north again to make further enquiries.

Chapter Eleven: All roads lead to Scotland

Having decided to travel to Scotland it was obvious that there were more enquiries to be made in addition to proving the letters produced to both the Bank Manager and Joan and Ted were forgeries.

I had made a number of telephone calls to Scotland to make arrangements to interview people who I thought could assist in my enquiries and the ones I could not contact I left with the Glasgow Police. I had arranged that I would travel up to Scotland conduct my enquiries in Glasgow and continue to Edinburgh. There was plenty do and many people to see. It was a long trip to Glasgow and we travelled on 4th June 1984 and arrived late afternoon by car. We received the usual high quality hospitality from the CID and were introduced to Detective Inspector Jim Cassells who had been conducting some enquiries on my behalf. Jim Cassells was a large man with a very thick Scottish accent he was also very jovial and nothing was too much trouble attitude. As with all of the Glasgow CID officers he was a very busy man and introduced us to his staff. We were taken to our accommodation, which transpired to be a distillery in the Clydebank area that was also a hotel. We were told that the local CID on duty would call and take us out to see the sights of the city as were going to be in the area for a number of days. (In the event I had to cancel the CID as after three nights I had had enough being the lightweight drinker I was and had to make excuses!)

The following morning I was we were up bright and early to conduct our enquiries. After having breakfast and being faced with a square portion of black pudding, which was politely declined, we went on our way to find the offices of Mr. Murrary the Sheriffs Officer from where one of the letters produced purported to have originated from.

We arrived at the premises situated on Buchanan Street and met with Mr. Murray as arranged by DI Cassels.

In the eighties there appeared to be a genuine desire to help police in conducting enquiries and police did not encounter such obstacles like *"If I disclose this information it could be seen as an abuse of their human rights"* or *"I'm sorry I cannot provide you with the information you are requesting as it contravenes Data Protection Legislation"*.

It was obvious that he was willing to assist. I showed him a copy of the letter that purported to have come from his office and he said, "I recognise that heading but not the content!"

Upon further examination a Reference number "Ref/92/F1035973" could be seen on the top of the letter and after a small amount of research the number was found to relate to a client of the firm of solicitors by the name of George Outram and Company Limited who were the publishers of the Glasgow Herald and Evening Times. It transpired that a customer of the paper by the name of R. Ferguson of 13/2 No 10 Red Road Court, Glasgow (which I immediately recognised as the address of Barbara Hendry) had allegedly contacted the Glasgow Herald and Evening News to place an advert to sell a car. The advertisement was obviously placed and payment was not made. As a result the Glasgow Herald and Evening Times had taken legal action for recovery against R Ferguson and used their own reference number i.e. 92/F1035973. The case was obviously taken to court and a judgement made. If payment was not forthcoming then the recovery was sent to the firm of A.R. Murray and Co to pursue recovery of the amount owed. During the recovery process A.R. Murray Sheriff Officers would have written to R. Ferguson on their headed notepaper using the same reference number.

It transpired that R. Ferguson had allegedly placed many adverts for selling vehicles but no payments had allegedly ever been made.

Upon hearing this I was feeling a sense of achievement as I now had concrete evidence that the letter sent to Ted and Joan Warner and produced by them to the Bank Manager Mr. Smith was a forgery.

Obviously what had happened was that a solicitor's letter had arrived at Hendry's flat for a member of the family and it had been doctored and used as part of the deception on Joan and Ted Warner. Upon closer examination the letterhead portion had been retained, photocopied and then a whole new content to the letter had been produced. The mistake being leaving the reference number at the top of the letter that enabled the letter to be traced back to the address of Hendry albeit under another name.

After recording a brief statement outlining the facts we departed and went to the purported origin of the second letter being a firm of Solicitors in Glasgow called Murdoch Jackson. The letter involved had again been sent to Joan and Ted Warner who had in turn produced the letter to Mr. Smith the Bank Manager for the purpose of corroborating their version of events. Barbara Hendry had sent the letter to Joan and Ted.

The letter was addressed to Mrs. B Hendry of 10 Red Road Court Balornock Glasgow and read as follows:

Re the estate of the late James Campbell
Dear Mrs. Hendry,
I, as a friend and close associate of Mr McGrouther, asked me to investigate (very discreetly) the letter received by you, from Mrs. Emily Astor. My findings are that it is a delaying method of preventing you being re-united with your friends in Lincolnshire, also a way of delayment to the financial arrangements already made by you, in the interests of the third party to whom it is bequeathed by you in your will and in your lifetime to have control as a trustee, and complete control over all your interests, which met with the approval of Zurich.

My advice to you is to pay her. The sum I believe is £250 plus 50% this is the only way I see it to avoid you being subjected to more legal involvement. I also must add you have interest to add to the initial sum. I'm sorry to say this but I and Mr. McGrouther are under the impression that your mother could be at the root of all this.

223

The estate being of a considerable amount will be directed according to your wishes.

Please accept my very sincere sympathy on hearing of your illness, Mr. McGrouther confided in me to establish the urgency of the above matter in his absence.

This letter is in complete confidence, as you have to abide by the clauses set down in your late uncles will, although I admit he was a bit eccentric.

Yours Faithfully (Signed)
William Rennie

Upon making enquiries at the firm it was apparent that the letter was composed on one of their letterheads, bore both the initials of one of their solicitor's together with the initials "MHH" that were the initials of the resident typist that would routinely type the letters. Upon showing the letter to Mr. Frame the solicitor "MF" he stated that that whilst recognising the letterhead he had no knowledge of the content of the letter. He did recall however that his firm had previous dealings over a debt on behalf of a client with a female called Barbara Hendry who lived at Burnside Bungalow on the Isle of Jura.

A statement was recorded.

Yet again it was proved that a letter sent by Barbara Hendry to Joan and Ted Warner in connection with the inheritance had been forged using a letterhead from a firm of solicitors that she had previously come into contact with. The evidence was mounting up but as I realised that to prove the offence in full and *"beyond all reasonable doubt"* there was still a long way to go......literally! It didn't cause me a great deal of concern as if necessary I would record statements for all hundred or so letters if I had to, that's what police work is all about especially fraud work! And that's why not everybody likes doing it. It is not about kicking doors down and wrestling with offenders, a majority of fraud work is meticulous painstaking enquiries sometime taking months and even years to complete, and lots and lots of reading. Not exactly sex drugs and rock and roll!

The next call was to The Sheriffs Court in Glasgow where I saw a Sheriffs Clerk by the name of William Ralston I had in my possession a number of documents that I had previously selected as being relevant. One document was a type of "Service Document" that had been sent by Barbara Hendry to Joan and Ted Warner. The document purported to show that in connection with an inheritance the amount of £890 required to be paid in to a court. I could see that it was a type of writ the pursuer being one Miss Margaret Simonette of 10 Red Road Court Flat 7/3. The same previous address as Hendry and the defender being Mrs. Barbara Ferguson known as Hendry of the same address but a different flat. The amount outstanding was £870. Upon the next page the document had an amount of typing in relation to an inheritance and a bank in Lincoln.

The document also displayed a case number of T128434 Glasgow Sheriffs Court. The document was shown to the Sheriffs Officer who recognised it as being a document he would use but again did not recognise the dialogue contained within it. *"Having examined the document I can say that the front page is in order except for the first calling date 24th February 1984 which appears to have been added to it.*

Page two of the claim bears no resemblance to the statement of claim for which my colleague Mrs. Stewart granted the warrant to cite and for the arrestment of the defendant. This form is a legal action for the recovery of payment instigated by Miss Margaret Simonette of Flat 7/3 Red Road Court Glasgow against a Mrs. Barbara Ferguson known as Hendry of Flat 12/1 Red Road Court Glasgow. The type and dialogue on page two I have no knowledge of.

I can say that additions have been made to the original document"

Yet again my suspicions had been confirmed and that Barbara Hendry has sent a doctored letter to Joan and Ted Warner.

The next person seen was the process server who actually delivered the summons that had been altered to the premises of Barbara Hendry in the first place. He was eventually traced and shown the altered summons he confirmed that he had served the summons on Hendry by leaving it at her address at Flat 12/1 10 Red Road Court.

For the purpose of evidential continuity it is necessary to trace the document that had been altered. So far we have established where the altered document had originated from, why it had been served on Barbara Hendry? by whom? And how it had come into her possession. What we had not yet established was who Margaret Simonette was and why the document had been created in the first place? We had to trace Miss Simonette while we were in Glasgow time allowing and get to the bottom of it. The tracing of potential witnesses would be left in the capable hands of Detective Inspector Cassels.

A further letter sent to Joan and Ted Warner purported to have originated from the Bank of Scotland, which was to be our next destination. The bank was situated at 110 Queen Street Glasgow. The letter was signed by a "Malcolm Riddell" It was confirmed that the Bank of Scotland did not and never has had an employee called "Malcolm Riddell" but the letterhead was of a type used by the bank. It was also observed that the "font" was not one used by the bank. Yet again the letter transpired to be a forgery.

The day had proved to be quite productive. We had shown that several letters sent to Joan and Ted by Barbara Hendry were forgeries and that evening sat and discussed our next move.

I was still curious to know what part the security guard Mr. Wilson had played and the reasons behind his conduct. I had briefly met him when Hendry was arrested and now wanted to interview him and see where it took us. We decided that the following day we would return to Red Road Court and track him down to get his explanation.

During the night Detective Inspector Cassels had traced the home address of our Security Guard Mr. "Wilson" and we went to see him. I had decided not to get a warrant for his arrest at this stage until I had decided just what his part in the whole scenario was.

Policewoman O'Connor and myself entered his house and sat in the lounge and by this time and after introductions I could not contain my curiosity and asked him directly. "Right Mr. Wilson, What has been going on with you and Mrs. Hendry?" to which he replied, "Nothing like that I can tell you!" That's a good start I thought I could believe that! We sat down and talked for some considerable time and whilst not fully convinced by his account decided to record a witness statement from him. The following statement would render him able to give evidence as a witness in any case against Barbara Hendry. At this time there was insufficient evidence to contest his account but would bear it in mind and re-visit his account if any other information became available.

Statement of Percy Wilson   Security Guard

I live sat the above address with my family. I am employed by Glasgow District Council as a Night Porter at No 10 red Road Court, Springburn Glasgow. I have worked there for the past two and a half years. The majority of the flats in No 10 are occupied by students but some of them are let to families. I know most of the people living in the flats through my job. I got to know Banette (Barbara)when they moved into their own flat, also in No 10 Red Road Court situated on the 12th Floor Flat number 1. They had previously lived with Banettes son for a short period in another flat.

I gradually got to know Banette and Donny whilst I worked as a Night Porter by lending them my paper during the early hours of the morning. They always seemed to go to bed very late. I start work about 1 am and work through until 9am. Before I used to finish my tour of duty I would go and collect my newspaper from Banette and Donny. On those occasions I sometimes used to stay and talk to them for a while.

During the course of those conversations I learnt various things from Banette. Once she showed me a birth certificate, which appeared to relate to Banette. I cannot recall her surname. However I do remember that the certificate stated that her mother was Margaret and the address was Oceanside in New York. Also mentioned on the certificate was Ian

Campbell who was referred to as Banette's father. The birth certificate was of the horizontal type. I have been shown by Policewoman O'Connor of the Lincolnshire Police a birth certificate showing the same details but it is of the vertical type and not the same one.

Banette always referred to her mother as "Mummy" and she once said that "Mummy" had asked her to go to Paris. Due to her various statements and the birth certificate bearing the name Margaret as her mother, I concluded that Banette was the daughter of Margaret Duchess of Argyll.

During the period that Banette and Donny lived at No 10 Red Road Court, I have got to know them very well and on occasions Banette showed me her correspondence and various documents. I can remember being shown by Banette a letter, which indicated that Banette was going to purchase a hotel in a resort somewhere on the south coast. The letter said that the banks Accountant had stayed at the hotel for six weeks and examined the books. From what I can recall the letter was from a bank.

Another letter Banette showed me appeared to be a summons of the civil type and I can remember that the pursuer was Margaret Simonette who I took to be the same Margaret Simonette who lives in the flats at 10 Red Road Court (I remember at the time thinking that's useful as up until that point we did not know where she lived!) The document mentioned something relating to furniture and also ten million pound assets. From what Banette told me and from what I have seen, I got the impression that she was related to somebody in the Scottish aristocracy. I remember her telling me that she had been brought up by her grandmother in Switzerland and that she had at some time attended an exclusive British school for girls, the name of which escapes me.

Banette also told me that she had previously been married to a man called Ferguson who she stated had been an Architect and that her divorce proceedings had been conducted personally by Lord Wheatley, whom she knew very well.

There was one occasion when I did not see Barbara for a few days. When she returned she said that she had been to the south of the country and that she had been taken ill as a result of which she had undergone some sort of back operation which she stated had been performed by a man she said was her uncle Fred, who was a surgeon at Carlisle and lived in Patterdale in the Lake District. Her uncle had apparently got her into a private nursing home where the operation was performed.

Sometime during January of February 1984 when the snow was on the ground either Donny or Banette mentioned that they had to hire a helicopter to bring Banette back from the nursing home where she had undergone the back operation. I understood that the reason for their journey south was to take various documents and a Rembrandt painting to a certain destination, which I do not know. Soon after Banette arrived home she told me that the Rembrandt painting and the documents were still in her flat due to the fact that she had not been able to deliver them to their destination because of her sudden illness whilst on the trip. I told Banette that I thought she was unwise to keep the painting and the documents in her flat if they were very valuable and that they ought to be in a bank for safe-keeping. In fact I even suggested I suggested a safety deposit box.

Shortly afterwards Banette told me that the Bank Manager Mr. Smith had telephoned her whilst a Doctor Turner had been with her and that he had requested to talk to Doctor Turner. Doctor Turner had then spoken to Mr. Smith and confirmed to him that Banette was ill. Banette then requested that I phone Mr Smith. She gave me the telephone number and from this I realised that Mr. Smith was the Manager of the Trustees Savings Bank in Lincoln. Banette asked me to ask Mr. Smith, which banks in Glasgow had facilities to store a Rembrandt painting and the documents. Mr. Smith suggested a bank in Millar Street. I did not know of a bank in Millar Street and I asked Mr. Smith if he meant a bank in Ingram Street, he agreed with me and stated that it was a suitable bank. It is a bank that is the Scottish equivalent of the Trustees Savings

Bank. I cannot remember the exact conversation I had with Mr. Smith but I gave him the distinct impression that I would deliver the painting, the documents and a watch to the Ingram Bank for safe deposit. I told him that as a result of what Bannette had told me. I firmly believed that was what she was going to ask me to do.

To the best of my recollection I only had one telephone conversation with Mr. Smith of the Trustees Savings Bank, Lincoln I was told by Banette after the conversation that she would get one of her sons to deposit the painting etc. at the bank instead of me. I now remember there was a second occasion when I telephoned Mr. Smith at Lincoln. I told him that the registered package had been taken to Rutherglen Post Office that morning. I cannot remember the date, and that there had been a "hold-up" at the Post Office. I knew this to be true for several reasons.

1. *Bannette had told me.*
2. *I had read it in the paper.*
3. *I had heard it on the radio.*

Mr. Smith enquired why the package containing the cheque had not gone into the post and I informed him that it was due to the fact that the Post Office was closed as a result of the "Hold Up". To save a lot of explanation I told Mr. Smith that I had been at the Post Office when the "Hold Up" had taken place and that I had been delayed by the police because I was required as a witness. The reason I told Mr. Smith this was because Banette had told me the story of what had happened at the Post Office and that in actual fact she said that it had been her son who had actually been at the Post Office during the "Hold Up", and I was telling Mr. Smith that it had happened to me and not to her son because I was genuinely under the impression that Banette was very ill and that by saying this I would prevent her from undergoing a lot of worry and stress.

A week or so later Banette told me that one of her friends called Joan was coming to visit her from Lincoln. I got the impression from Banette that Joan was in financial difficulties due to the fact that a close friend of hers, who was a dentist, had incurred large gambling debts. It seemed that Joan was visiting Banette to take the securities (i.e. the painting ect) back down to Lincoln with her. Banette told me that Joan did not like Donny and she therefore requested if my wife and I could put him up at our house during Joan's visit, However this did not materialise and I believe that Donny stayed at the flat.

Joan's visit took place one weekend and I believe it was on the Saturday lunchtime over the same weekend that Donny turned up at my house in a Taxi. He held the taxi outside whilst he came into my home. He said that Banette had sent him to ask me to return to the flat and say to her in Joan's presence (who did not know I worked at the flats) something to the effect that the securities were to be deposited at a bank locally and not kept at the flat. I went back to the flats at Red Road Court with Donny in the taxi and whilst Donny went to the shops I went to see Banette in the flat. Joan let me in and I went in. Banette was in bed and Joan and I went in to see her. Banette asked me some questions regarding the securities, I answered them in such a fashion that I stated what Donny had told me to say. Joan was in full hearing distance when I said this. I believed what I was saying to be true because I had no reason to doubt it.

I have an interest in the Conservative Party. I am Chairman of the Provan Constituency Association. We were due to hold a sale to raise money for election purposes on 10th March 1984. Banette had stated that she would like to donate goods to the sale for the purpose of selling. The night before the sale was due to take place I reminded Banette of her offer, she said that she had forgotten and that she would purchase some goods from the cash and carry store. The following day she borrowed a cash and carry card to use for this purpose.

The following morning, whilst I was on duty at work, Banette phoned me in my office, she asked me to look out for the Postman because he might possibly have a registered letter for her. In fact she asked me to ask the Postman if I saw him whether he had a registered letter for delivery to Banette. Banette had told me earlier if the letter did not arrive she wouldn't be able to donate anything to the Association. From this I assumed the registered letter contained money. The Postmen arrived with the registered letter. I informed Banette of this and the Postmen took the letter to her. Later that day Banette arrived at the sale at MacLellen Galleries in Glasgow, although I was not present. I understand she donated some goods and handed the receipt for them to my wife, who then handed it to me. The total amount of the goods was £80.94. I am able to produce the receipt if required. The goods were sold and the money raised went into the election funds.

During the time I have known Banette she has told me that she was receiving an allowance in money from a bank in Zurich. I was aware that she was receiving regular registered letters and therefore I assumed that they contained the money from Zurich. At one time I suggested that she should deal in cheques but she replied that the reason she dealt in cash was for tax purposes in relation to Zurich. The reasons why I spoke to Mr. Smith and told him what Barbara had told me to say was because I had no reason to doubt her, she always appeared genuine. Also I was concerned about her because of her illness and I did as she wished so as to pacify her and prevent her from worry. I have never received any money from Banette but she has given me gifts of the odd bottle of whiskey, however Banette has given gifts of this nature to other people.

Once I believe it was before Christmas 1983, Donny came down to the office where I work, Flat 1/4 and asked me whether he could borrow the office manual typewriter. I lent him the typewriter on that occasion for about or three two hours. As far as I can recall he also borrowed it the following day. I did not enquire what the typewriter was needed for but I got the impression that it was Banette who wanted to use it, not Donny. The typewriter is a very old one at least twenty years old.

On one occasion I went up to see Banette in her flat, on my arrival I saw that she was sat in bed, at about 9am, using what I presumed to be her own typewriter which was of a very old type. Banette remarked that she was typing something in connection with accounts. Around this particular time, Donny

approached me and asked where he could get some
photocopying done. I suggested that he could do this either at
the GPO or Central Station.
Signed
P Wilson.

Although not completely convinced I was satisfied with a
witness statement at this time. I also had to bear in mind that
Barbara Hendry had used the old typewriter that was situated
in the office at the Red Road Court flats. It may be the case at
a later date that I would need access to the typewriter for
forensic comparison with the typed letters in the event of a
"Not Guilty" plea, which in my opinion was a distinct
possibility. I did not consider that to be a problem and would
get it later. I decided not to make this an issue at this time as I
did not want it to disappear; besides Barbara Hendry was in
custody and was not going anywhere.

Later that day we decided to trace Patrick Phee who we
knew from the signed receipts had collected amounts of
money from the bank on behalf of Barbara Hendry. It would
be interesting to see what he had to say about what was going
on. We had previously established that he resided at Red Road
Court Flats on the 5th floor so it was back to Red Road Court
again to continue our enquiries!

We arrived at Red Road Court flats early afternoon. Upon
entering I had a discreet glance upwards just to check to see if
there were any falling paving blocks but my suspicions were
unfounded. It did not surprise me in the least that the lift was
not working and that we would have to take the stairs such is
my luck! After some huffing and puffing and carrying our
briefcases we arrived on the 5th floor and we soon located Mr.
Phee. After a short conversation it was obvious that we had
got the right Mr. Phee, he admitted knowing Barbara Hendry
and going to the bank to collect sums of money for her. I was
satisfied after speaking to him that he was yet again an
innocent "used" party. After the conversation between us a
statement was recorded.

Patrick Phee

40 years   Disabled
Flat 5ᵗʰ Floor, No 10 Red Road Court
Glasgow

I live at the above address with my wife and family. I am unemployed due to a disability I received whilst working. I have lived in the Red Road Court Flats for about two years.

Just before Christmas 1983 I was introduced to a woman who also lives in the flats by the name of Barbara Hendry, who lives with a man called Donny Hendry in flat number 1 on the twelfth floor.

On 12ᵗʰ January 1984 I was in my flat when Donny Hendry came down to see me. He said that Barbara or Banette as I call her, wanted to see me, so I went up to her flat at number 12/1 to see her and she was ill in bed. Banette asked me if I would do her a favour. I enquired as to what it was and she said she wanted me to go down to the Springburn Branch of the Trustees Savings Bank to collect some money for her.

She told me I had to put on a suite and look respectable. Banette said that she would telephone the bank manager and tell him that I was coming. She wrote a letter of authority out which she gave to me and I put the letter of authority in an envelope and went to the Trustees Savings Bank in Springburn.

Upon arriving at the bank I asked to see the manager Mr. Donaldson. I introduced myself and I went into the office and he gave me £850 in cash. I signed a receipt for it and went back to Red Road Court where I went to Banetts flat and gave her the £850.

She gave me £5 for going which I accepted.

The following day Donny Hendry came down to my flat again and told me that Banette again wanted some money collected.

I put my suite on and went to see Banette in her flat. She was poorly in bed again. I can't remember what she said but I went down to the Springburn branch of the Trustees Savings Bank. I didn't see Mr. Donaldson again, it was someone else, I think it was the Chief Cashier. I was given £300 cash after introducing myself and I went back to the flats and went up to Banettes flat and gave her the £300 cash. She did not give me anything for going this time.

Each visit to the bank I took my medical card and showed it for identification purposes.

I have been shown by Detective Constable Booth of the Lincolnshire Police one letter of authority. I identify this as the one given to me by Banette Hendry to take to the Springburn Branch of the Trustees Savings bank.

I have also been shown one written receipt dated 12.1.84. I can identify it as the one I signed on 12.1.84 when I was handed the £850 and can identify my signature on it.

I have also been shown on written receipt dated 13.1.84. I can identify this as the one I signed on 13.1.84 when I was handed the £300 at the Springburn Branch of the Trustees Savings Bank and can identify my signature on it.

I did not ask Banette where the money had come from and she did not tell me. Had I known anything was wrong I would not have collected it.

Banette one day showed me a birth certificate that she said was hers. I read it and saw that it said her father was the Duke of Argyll. I have been shown a Photocopy of a birth certificate by Detective Constable Booth and can identify it as being the one Banette showed me saying it was hers.

Signed
P Phee

I was reasonably happy with the way things were going as it was all coming together. We still had a lot of enquiries to make. We had to trace who played the part of Dr Turner and the doctor herself but I was sure that we would be able to complete our task. I had a rough idea who played the part of the doctor and just had to find her.

Since we were again at Red Road Court I saw it as an ideal opportunity to trace Margaret Simonette and establish how Barbara Hendry had got her hands on paperwork relating to Miss Simonette that she has used. We knew her address at Red

Road Court and crossed our fingers in hope that she was still living there.

We arrived at our destination, luckily Miss Simmonette was still resident at the flats, and we again familiarised ourselves with the stairs and went to the 3rd floor. Upon knocking on the door we were met by a female who after introductions identified herself as Ms Simonette we were shown into a tidy flat where we sat down in the lounge. After a short interview I decided a statement would be recorded from Miss Simonette.

Mary Simmonette

24 years   Unemployed
Flat 7/3 10 Red Road Court Springburn
Glasgow

I live at the above address with my brother I have resided there for the past twelve months.

Number 10 Red Road Court consists of numerous flats; I have a few friends in the block. My brother is friendly with a man called Robert Ferguson who lives at No 13/1 within the block and he introduced Robert to me.

It was through Robert that I met his mother who lives at No 12/1. Her name is Barbara Hendry and she lives with her common law husband Donny.

It was approximately 7 months ago that I mat Barbara and I became quite friendly with her. I used to visit her and have a chat from time to time.

During our conversations she told me various things about herself. She stated that she was the illegitimate daughter of the Duchess of Argyll and that not many people were aware of the situation. Although I found this statement hard to believe I never really thought much about it. She also told me that she had been married to a few men in the past but that she wasn't married to Donny. After I had known Barbara for about three months she approached me one day and asked me to purchase a living room wall unit for her. She gave me various reasons why she could not pay for it.

1. She said she had to be resident at any one place for two years before she could get hire purchase

2.   *She said that one of her uncles, whose name escapes me, had left her a will and that she had to pay to get the money from the will released. In relation to this she also said that she was paying taxes to Zurich. Although I didn't fully understand the business about the will, Barbara promised me that if I brought back the items of furniture for her she would pay me back once she had received the money from the will.*

I believed Barbara when she said that she would repay me and due to this we went into Glasgow shortly afterwards and I purchased a suite and a wall unit from Morris's, Trongate, Glasgow, for a total of £750. Barbara gave me £150 cash to pay the deposit on the furniture and I was to pay the remaining £500 in ten monthly installments of £50.

The first payment was due in January and I went to see Barbara to collect the £50. I politely asked her for the cash but she said it would be forthcoming- she did not pay me anything there and then. Barbara told me to get in touch with her lawyer if I wanted my money and when I asked her who her lawyer was she stated it was Patrick Wheatley who was a close friend of her family.

As a result of Barbara's attitude I sought advice from my father. He went to see Barbara and asked her for my money, but she again took an unreasonable attitude and told him that I should contact her lawyer.

In view of this I went to see my solicitor, Mr. Brown of Ross, Harper and Murphy, 232 St Vincent Street Glasgow. He instigated civil proceedings against Barbara. As a result of the proceedings I have recently re-possessed the items of furniture from Barbara and I intend to sell these to enable me to pay off the financial installments.

Barbara has never given me any money towards the furniture.

During my association with Barbara, she told me that she had a friend in Lincoln called Joan who works for the Social Services and stated that Joan did not like Donny.

I have been shown a Court Service Document from a Sheriffs Court and upon examination I see that the document

bears my name and address and although I have never seen it
before it is in relation to the proceedings I instigated through
Mr. Brown of Ross Harper and Murphy against Barbara.
  Signed
  M Simmonette

The evidence was slowly coming together as we now had identified where the altered summons had originated from.

The version that she was shown had come from Joan and Ted but the body of it had in fact been altered to relate to the inheritance. I was reasonable to assume that this was one of the documents that had been altered and photocopied.

After completing the statement from Miss Simonette we then went to find another witness by the name of Elizabeth McColm who also lived at the flats.

Policewoman O'Connor asked, "Where does she live?"

After checking my information, I said, "You are not going to believe this but it is on the 9th floor!"

We looked at each other and made our way to the stairs access door and began the ascent to the 9th floor. Whilst climbing the stairs we realised that due to taking statements neither of us had any lunch a fact that was not easily missed when in the company of PW O'Connor! We both decided to carry on and would get something to eat later.

We eventually arrived at the 9th floor and after a very "puffed out" introduction we were invited in and collapsed on a lounge chair and the settee. It was a very sunny day and the window to the lounge of the flat presented an excellent aerial view over Glasgow. We had just sat down and I was busy going through all the details for our visit when suddenly I was dazzled by a reflection of the sun, which caught me whilst sat on the settee.

"What is that?" I asked. The reflection appeared to be coming from a window of the block of flats opposite.

"Aye, It's them over there," she replied.

"What do you mean, who?"

"The people who live in the block of flats opposite," as she got up to draw the curtains shut. "You see on a day like this they use their window reflections to shine into your flat, If there is no response and you don't close your curtains they will come over knowing that there is no-one in and break into your flat, so we have to draw the curtains shut!"

I was half minded to tell her not to bother and wait and see who comes around to the flat to break in and arrest them for burglary, but I was forgetting where I was. Firstly I was there to gain the evidence against Barbara Hendry and secondly I was in Scotland and at that time we did not have the necessary powers to make an arrest in Scotland so I decided to carry on with my task tempting as it was!

I outlined our reason for our visit and explained that I wanted to ascertain what dealings Mrs. McColm had previously had with Barbara Hendry. After a short conversation I decided to record a witness statement.

Elizabeth McColm

Over 21 years   *Optical Worker*

9/1 10 Red Road Court Springburn Glasgow

I live at the above address with my husband. I am employed as an

Optical worker.

I have lived in the Red Road Court Flats since January 1982.

Also living in the flats is a Banette Hendry and Donny Hendry who live in Flat 12/1. I have known them since December 1983.

I got to know Donny Hendry first as I got talking to him in the lift (Obviously on a day when it was working!) one day about a children's party we were going to have as I told him I was very worried about it as we were having difficulty in selling the tickets. Donnie assured me we would have the party because he and his wife Banette were going to give a £50 donation and also items to put into a jumble sale and a raffle to help raise money.

A £50 donation was given by Banette Hendry to a neighbour Jesse Campbell. We had a jumble sale and the raffle, which was a great success, and Donnie and Banette came to it.

My husband and I went to Banette's flat and thanked her for the donation.

Just after the new year Banette came down to my flat with a man called Fred who she said was a Cardiologist, they stayed only a short while and Banette came back later and said that Fred and his wife had invited us to go and visit them for a long weekend to help my health in the Lake District at their house but I didn't go.

Banette told me all this after Fred had gone and she said that Fred was visiting her as he was executor of her Aunts will and that the Aunt had left Banette £4 million

Banette also told us that she had to go down to a bank in London to tie up things in connection with the will. Banette wanted me to go with her as she said we would be traveling in a private plane that belonged to Lord Wheatley's son's friend and that a man called Patrick who was Lord Wheatley's son and an Accountant would be traveling with us, but I didn't go.

Banette went and brought me some perfume and my husband some cigars. Banette also said that a friend called Joan from Lincoln was there as well and we learnt that a Bank Manager picked them up from the airport and drove them to the bank.

Early this year, I was in Banette's flat looking after her as she was very poorly with her nerves and I was nursing her, I had previously trained as a nurse and Banette was aware of this. The telephone rang and Banette and Donnie were both there, it rang twice and then stopped. Donnie didn't want to answer it and Banette got out of bed and rang back. Donnie told me it was Joan from Lincoln. I ordered Banette back to bed and I spoke to Joan's husband and told him I was nursing her and that I thought she ought to have some peace and quiet. I said I was nursing her but I didn't give my name. The man on the other end of the phone said "Thank you Nurse" or something like that and then rang off. The man asked to say goodnight to her but I told him that he couldn't as she had gone back to bed.

The following morning Banette telephoned me and asked me to go to her flat as Joan was arriving. I went up to Banette's flat and she told me to say that when I saw Joan I was to tell her that Banette and Donny were separated and that the family had to contact Donny, as she was so ill. I started to wonder about it when I got downstairs but Banette had earlier told me that Joan did not like Donnie and I thought it was something to do with that.

Later that day I was in the flat looking after Banette who was in bed sleeping and there was a knock at the door, I answered it and it was Joan. I didn't know her but I knew she was coming and Joan thought she had got the wrong flat. I asked her if she was Joan and she said she was and I told her it was the right flat and she came in. I told Joan that Banette was sleeping and not to be disturbed. Banette's son David was there but soon left. I noticed that Joan was not very happy about Donny being there and she asked how long Donny had been there. I told Joan the story that Banette had told me to say, that the family had sent for him and that he wasn't living there anymore. Donny then left and went downstairs and sat with my husband in our flat. An hour later Donny came back up again and started to make a meal and I left.

While I was there I tried to make conversation with Joan but she didn't want to talk much. I can't remember anything that was said.

I had previously told Joan's husband that I had been a Nurse and I was genuinely under the impression that she was very ill meaning Banette and I was very concerned about Banette's health.

I was under the impression Banette was a multi millionaire and that her mother was about 16 years old when she was born and that her father was the Duke of Argyll.

I realised that a lot of things that Banette said were not true but I did not intend to deceive anybody as I thought that Joan just didn't like Donny and Banette told me what to say to Joan when I saw her but I just thought I was helping out Banette who I thought was very ill.

A few weeks ago I got some tinted glasses from work for Banette and she paid me for them, after trying a number of pairs on Banette paid me for two pairs of sunglasses it was just before the Easter holidays. After I met Joan, I felt that I had been put in a very awkward position by Banette and I told her that I didn't lie for anybody and I fell out with her. It wasn't until recent weeks I put all these things together.

Banette showed me a letter one day that indicated that she had purchased a hotel in Southsea and that a Banks Accountant had looked into it and it was a good buy.

Signed

E. McColm

It was now later in the afternoon and we still had further enquiries to make. Due to the information I had received from the representative of the Trustees Savings Bank in early April I was aware that sums of money had been collected from a branch of the Trustees Savings Bank in Fareham which seemed a little strange to me, but never the less we would continue to make the enquiries and see where it took us. A Christine Cairney also of 10 Red Road Court Flats Springburn signed the receipts that had been signed by the person collecting the money in Fareham. We decided to trace her hoping that it would not be too high up the stairs towards the top!

We eventually found Christine Cairney on the third floor. There was no doubt before seeing her that I would be recording a statement from her whatever the reason for her collecting the various sums of money in Fareham. I was curious what the explanation would be and it would also tie up another loose end.

After a short conversation a statement was recorded.

Christine Cairney
Over 21   Civil Servant
13/3 No 10 Red Road Court
Glasgow

I live at the above address and am employed as a Civil Servant. I have lived at the flats at Red Road Court, Glasgow since October 1983 and shortly after moving in I got talking to a woman who lived in a flat opposite with her son Robert. Also living at the same flat was a man called Donny who I assumed to be the woman called Banette Hendry's husband.

I went into hospital with a complaint and when I came out Barbara wasn't well and I went down to her flat to see her as she had in the meantime moved down to flat 12/1 in the same block. Banette had previously looked after my young son when I was in hospital and while she was ill in bed I went down to visit her on a regular basis.

I had been told by one of her family that they were all going down to Portsmouth to visit Bannett's son who is in the navy and he was on leave over the weekend and Banette wanted to go and see him.

The day before they left Banette came to see me and since I was off work ill she thought it would do me good to go with them. She said I needn't worry about where to stay as she would put us up in a hotel. The following day Banette, Donny, Robert and his girlfriend, myself and my son travelled down to Fareham in Roberts car.

We didn't arrive until two in the morning as the car broke down in Birmingham (Repair receipt form recovered during search of flat) and Banette called out the RAC to fix it and since it was the started motor or something the RAC man took us somewhere and we hired a car in my name (car hire form found in flat during search showing licence used in the name Cairney) to travel on to Fareham arriving at 2am. Banette eventually booked us in at the Holiday Inn hotel for the first night and the next night we stayed at the Red Lion at Fareham. Banette paid for the hotel each time.

The following morning 23rd January, Banette came to the Red Lion in a taxi. She said that she had to get some money transferred from a bank in Lincoln to the Trustees Savings Bank in Fareham. Banette just said it was from an account she held in Lincoln and she said a man's name who was the Bank Manager in Lincoln but whose name I cannot remember but he thought she was in a nursing home in Yorkshire and was very ill and that he would be upset if he found she was in Fareham. Banette made out she knew him on a personal basis.

Banette also said that a Solicitor called Mr. Spiers was handling the transfer of the money and she asked me to telephone this Bank Manager in Lincoln and say that I had been authorised by Mrs. Hendry to collect some money on her behalf and he would know that I would be calling because this Solicitor called Mr. Spiers had told the bank manager. I rang the bank manager and during the course of conversation he asked me how much I was going to collect from the Bank in Fareham and I said I didn't know, he then said it was £820. There was a code word of "Campbell" used and it was either Banette or the bank manager who told me it.

The bank manager told me to go to the Trustees Savings Bank in Fareham and tell them who I was and if there were any complications to get them to ring him. That was the end of the conversation and I came off the telephone and told Banette and she said it was fine. She told me to go to the bank and collect the money.

I walked across to the Fareham branch of the Trustees Savings Bank and went in. I had to ask for someone whose name I cannot remember, and I ended up speaking to a young man. I told him who I was and he went away and came back and asked me if I had a code word. I told him the word "Campbell" and he went away and came back again to say there was a problem, as Mrs. Hendry did not have an account there. I told him to ring the manager at Lincoln, which they did and I signed a receipt and was given £820. I have been shown receipt from the bank and can identify it as being the one I signed at Fareham. I got the £820 and handed it to Banette.

The following day, 24th January 1984, Banette came to the Red Lion to see me and said she had very little of the money left and would I go to the bank again. She explained the car repairs would cost a lot and she had to pay the hotel bills. She said she would make arrangement for the money to be sent down again. I didn't need to phone anyone again as Banette made several phone calls from the Red Lion and almost immediately I went into the same bank again and saw the man who knew me and I signed a form and was given £500 which I went back to the hotel and gave to Banette.

I have been shown another receipt and identify it as the one I signed at the bank upon receipt of the £500 on 24th January 1984.

Shortly after giving Banette the £500 I made my way back to Glasgow as the weather was bad and it had been snowing up north and I had to get home as I was at work the following Thursday. I didn't want to get stuck at Fareham.

I wasn't asked by Banette to go anywhere else for her and she didn't pay me for collecting the money, anyway I didn't expect anything from her for doing it.

Shortly after my return I saw Banette a couple of times and then I didn't see her anymore and I was told she was on holiday visiting friends in Lincoln.

On the first visit to the bank in Fareham Banatte gave me an envelope to hand over the counter at the bank and said it was a letter of authority for the bank. I didn't open it.

When I was collecting the money I did not think anything was wrong as Banette had an explanation for why she couldn't collect it i.e. being in a Nursing Home. Had I known anything was wrong I would not have collected it.

Signed
C Cairney.

At the conclusion of the statement it was obviously that this was another individual that had "been used". I was satisfied there was no bad intention but what annoyed me was that Joan and Ted Warner were obviously running around in Lincoln to raise money to send to Barbara Hendry and all the time the money was being used to fund her lifestyle as on this occasion staying in hotels and even paying for other people and giving tips to hotel staff!!

The visit did however answer a couple of questions that had been of interest to myself. Firstly why was money being collected from a bank in Fareham as opposed to Glasgow both being more or less at opposite ends of the country?

As with all frauds, when the enquiry starts the investigator will be confronted a number of unanswered questions and it is only during the making of enquiries that these questions will be answered and the jigsaw begins to "come together" and the picture of what actually took place is gradually built piece by piece. The time spent on an enquiry is dependant on the complexity of the offence and the activity of the alleged suspect and this is the reason why offences of fraud can take such a long time to appear at court.

It was the end of a very productive day as we returned to our accommodation. We had traced to individuals who had been and collected money from the banks on behalf of Barbara Hendry.

One has to consider the points that have to be proved in order to corroborate any charges that may be made against both Barbara and Donny Hendry. As previously outlined in offences of Criminal Deception there has to be a victim that has been deceived by the conduct of the accused and within the offence and as a result of the deception practiced property has to be shown to have been obtained unless the offence is an "attempt".

In current case it has to be shown that the victim has been deceived i.e. by "words or conduct" and that the property i.e the money sent to Scotland for Barbara Hendry is as a result of the deception.

From the evidence gained there were other individuals that had been brought into the deception to give strength to the version of events being proffered by Barbara Hendry. The "security guard" had now been seen and interviewed, but the individual who played the part of the "doctor" had not. What was of interest to me was how could Barbara Hendry actually encourage or induce an individual who at this point of the enquiry did not appear to be involved for financial gain, to pose as a Doctor and speak to Joan Warner?

The depth that the enquiries go to in any offence depends on the conduct of the offender. If the offender pleads guilty then all the enquiries are not carried out but only enough to produce a "Guilty" plea and this was the stage that we were approaching. We had to make some more enquiries to tie up some loose ends and then see what happens. At this stage in the enquiry and at this time there one only one further issue that needed dealing with which was becoming rather urgent this was the issue of getting PW O'Connor fed and watered ready for another day of making enquiries, I was also very hungry too, but did not feel like climbing any more stairs, only to ones to my bed.

The following morning we were up bright and early and decided to go out and trace the woman who was alleged to have played the part of "Doctor Turner" we had been given a name but it was slightly wrong. In the end and after making a few further enquiries we ended up at Lennoxtown where we saw a woman called Elizabeth Carr. I was fairly satisfied that this was the right woman but was at a loss as to why she would actually pose as "Doctor Turner" and what was the story behind it.

We traced Elizabeth Carr and introduced ourselves. I found it rather hard to believe that she would have a good reason for posing as Dr Jean Turner but bearing in mind how fraudsters were able to manipulate individuals there was always a possibility that she did not realise what she was doing nevertheless I decided to initially interview her under caution which we did. After the interview I decided to "back my horses" both ways and record a witness statement that way I hopefully would not have to travel all the way back to Scotland again.

	Elizabeth Carr	Over	21
Housewife			
	Lennoxtown		
	Glasgow.		

I have lived at the above address for the past five years.

In July 1983 I took my children on holiday to the Isle of Jura.

I stayed with my brother at 2 Burnside, Craighouse, for a fortnight. The first day that I was there a woman who I now know as Barbara Hendry introduced herself to me. She said she was a friend of my brother and my father. I soon found out that Barbara ran her home as a boarding house and I became very friendly with her during that fortnight. She appeared to me to be an extremely pleasant person and was very kind to both the children and myself. At the time I appreciated this enormously because I had recently split up with my husband. I used to visit her regularly and help her around the house. She lived with a man called Donny Hendry and I was under the impression that they were married. She did not tell me much about her background, only that she had been married to a man called Ferguson.

Whilst I was on the Isle of Jura she left the island to go and see her daughter-in-law in Portsmouth who had had a baby. She stated that her daughter-in-law had had a difficult birth and was very ill. Whilst Banette was away I looked after her house for about ten days. At the end of this period I handed her keys to my father as Banette did not return and I had to go back home to Glasgow.

I returned to Glasgow and thought no more about Banette. However in October, 1983, my father who lived on the isle of Jura telephoned me to say that Barbara had moved from the island to Glasgow. Apparently Banette did not want my father to disclose to anybody her address in Glasgow, however she did give permission to my father for him to tell me her address and phone number. I therefore found out that she had moved to No 10 Red Road Court, Flat 13/2 Springburn. She had apparently moved in with her son Robert, at that address.

I telephoned her straight away because I regarded her as my friend who had been a great comfort to me on the Isle of Jura. Also I was concerned about her health because I understood from my father that she was ill and for that reason she was not going to return to Jura.

When I telephoned the flat I spoke to Donny who informed me that "Banette" had cancer for which she was receiving radium treatment in the Beatson Hospital Glasgow. On this occasion I did not speak to Barbara. Soon after I again telephoned and spoke to Donny. I arranged to visit Barbara at the flat about a fortnight later and Donny said that he would meet me off the bus.

I kept to the arrangements and Donny walked me back to 10 Red Road Court, after my bus trip from Lennoxtown. Whilst we walked Donny told me that he and Banette had got their own flat on the twelfth floor, flat No 1. On arrival at the flat I noticed that it had been fully carpeted and decorated throughout, also fully furnished. Banette was pleased to see me, and made me very welcome. She appeared full of vitality and looked well. After a cup of tea and general conversation with Barbara and Donny I went home.

After that my visits to Barbara became more regular, on average about once or twice a week. However, she never visited me at my home. When I started visiting Barbara on a regular basis she began to tell me a lot about her background. She told me that she had got twelve children and she filled me in about their lifestyles. She stated that she had previously been married to a Mr. Ferguson. She also told me that Donny had drinking problem. She said that in the past she had had a brain tumour removed from the back of her head and that she had had a hysterectomy. She also complained that at that time she was suffering from cancer of the stomach for which she was receiving radium treatment but it had to be stopped because of the adverse effects it had had on her. I was under the impression that the cancer had gone into remission. Up until Christmas 1983 Barbara always looked well but her appearance deteriorated after that and at times she looked genuinely ill.

Sometime during December 1983 Barbara asked me if I would telephone a woman called Joan Warner who lived in Lincoln. She told me that Joan was her longstanding friend and she told me to tell Joan that I was "Doctor Turner" and that as a Doctor I would telephone her again to confirm Banette's state of health in relation to her traveling to Lincoln. I did this whilst Barbara was present in her flat. Joan appeared concerned about Barbara. I made this phone call because I thought I was only reassuring Joan about Barbara's health and that I was doing Barbara a favour, although I *realised that I was wrong by stating I was a Doctor. I thought it was quite harmless.*

I continued to visit Barbara regularly and sometime during the first two weeks in January Barbara told me various things regarding a Mr. Smith whom she told me was the manager of a bank. Also a Mr. Spiers who Banette told me was a Lawyer. She also told me various things about Joan. I got the impression that either Joan or Mr. Smith or both were trying to get £25,000 out of Barbara illegally. According to Barbara Mr. Spiers was the only honest one!

Around this time Barbara asked me to make a number of phone calls, one of which was to Joan Warner. On Barbara's instructions I told Joan that Barbara was going to travel down to Lincoln in a private ambulance escorted by myself (as Doctor Turner). I also told Joan that Barbara needed money to pay for the private ambulance and the money also had to be sent up to Scotland. Whilst making this telephone call, I was also under the impression that Joan was a Trustee in a will.

It was also around this time that I made two or three telephone calls to Mr Smith who was the manager of a bank. During these telephone conversations I was always instructed by Barbara to tell Mr. Smith that my name was Doctor Turner. I was also instructed to tell him various things such as:

1.   That Barbara's visit to Lincoln would be to bring a cheque for £325,000 to be given to Mr. Smith.

2.   That Barbara would be flying down to Lincoln with me (as Doctor Turner) from Glasgow to Humberside.

I arranged for Mr Smith to meet us off the plane at Humberside so he could escort us to Lincoln. On that occasion I said that Mr. Spiers would also be accompanying us. Mr. Smith told me (bearing in mind he was under the impression he was talking to "Doctor Turner") that in all his years in banking he had never come across circumstances such as relating to Barbara and that he was not happy with them. He told me that Barbara was a very wealthy woman and that she had done business with his bank. He said that she had a Rembrandt painting and an oyster shell watch, a safety deposit box containing money and letters all belonging to Barbara. I took it from this that she had this property at his bank and I said that I had not been aware of this. He said that as " one professional to another" he was going to continue his sentence but I cut him short because when he said that it brought it home to me exactly how dishonest I was, purporting to be a Doctor. I then ended our conversation.

At that point I felt I was getting into a dishonest setup and I told Barbara how I felt. I felt dishonest and I told Barbara I was betraying Mr. Smith. Barbara became very agitated and sent Donny to phone someone. I then understood from her that she was going to phone Mr. Smith. However his line was engaged, she tried to phone Joan but her line was also engaged. I deduced from this that Joan and Mr. Smith were telephoning each other. At that time I decided that I would not make any more telephone calls for Barbara.

I remember that whilst making telephone conversations Mr. Smith mentioned the fact to me that Mr. Spiers was elusive and he asked me whether I had ever met him. I said that I hadn't.

Often whilst I was talking to Mr. Smith on the telephone Barbara would grab the receiver from me in an irate state and shout at him. She also did this on occasions whilst I was talking to Joan.

On one occasion, on Thursday, 12th January, 1984, Barbara offered me £5000 in cash which I refused to accept, She said that the money was in a safety deposit box and that there was £25,000 in it and at one stage she gave me two small keys which she told me were the keys to the safety deposit box. I gave the keys back to her.

The following day, Friday 13th January, 1984, I went to see Barbara at her flat. She told me that she did not buy friends and she insisted that I accept the £5000 but I again refused. Barbara went on to say that she had got a hotel somewhere in Southend on Sea called the Queens. Also that she had accounts in Switzerland and Hong Kong. She also mentioned the Rembrandt painting and an amount of jewellry which I took to be part of her Uncle James Campbell's will that she had previously mentioned.

On the evening of Sunday, 18th January 1984, Barbara telephoned me at home to say that she was setting off for Lincoln the following day, Monday. She asked me to go to Southend on Sea in order to attend to some business regarding the hotel if I got a chance during the future. She also asked me to meet her on 20th January 1984, at 2pm at Glasgow airport and to go on to Edinburgh with her, as she had to attend the probate court in relation to her late uncles will. I did not commit myself to any arrangements with Barbara.

I did not hear from or see Barbara again until around February time when she phoned me at home to tell me that she had two visitors from Switzerland staying with her. She said they were there in relation to her estate. She asked me if I would give her a hand with the meals but I did not want anything more to do with her and therefore I did not go.

From then on Barbara continued to call regarding minor things,

However, I did not have a lot to do with her until the end of March 1984 when she asked to see me. I visited her at her flat where she sent Donny out of the room. She quickly handed to me what appeared to be a cheque made out to me for £30,000. She told me to sign it quickly before Donny came back in. Due to this I signed it and she snatched it back off me. She gave me a card with the name Andrew P Gallen on it. She explained that this was the man who was investigating the will. (This looked a genuine card that a solicitor would produce which will form a further line of enquiry in the future) I now produce the card. I was told that the cheque would not be valid unless I signed the back of it.

During the earlier months that I was friendly with Barbara she asked me to go to the Glasgow library and try to obtain a copy of the book, which was the autobiography of the Duchess of Argyll. I did this but was unable to get one because the library did not have one. I then went to the Mitchell library in Glasgow which is just a reading library and there I found a copy of the autobiography of Margaret Duchess of Argyll and from this book I made notes about her on a piece of scrap paper.

At that point in time she told me she was the illegitimate daughter of Margaret Duchess of Argyll. I then went home where I received a call from Banette to ask me to find out the date of birth of Margaret Wigham (Duchess of Argyll). I rang the library for the answer then rang Barbara to tell her the result.

I now produce four pieces of paper with various details and telephone numbers written on them. These were written by both myself and Banette during the time I was making telephone calls on her instruction.

I also produce a piece of paper on which Barbara wrote details of the book from which she wanted me to get information from regarding the Duchess of Argyll. It was called "Forget Not".

Upon closer examination of the pieces of paper one of them seemed to ring a bell and I was of the opinion that I had seen it before. I was not certain at this stage but it was something to bear in mind for the future, as it could be an important evidential link.

That was the end of another productive day which when we returned to the hotel we reflected on and to discuss the itinerary for the following day.

The next morning I decided that we would trace a local landlord whose name had been used in correspondence between Joan and Ted and Barbara Hendry.

During the recording of their statement I had taken possession of a letter from a firm of solicitors called COCRAN DICKIE and MACKENZIE. The letter was on official headed notepaper and spoke about an amount of money that had been incurred by expenditure in connection with the "breach of duty as a Trustee" and that the amount of £750 should be paid. The letter went on to say that *"successful legal action had been taken against a solicitor but the expenditure had been incurred"*. The letter was addressed to Mrs. Hendry and further stated that *" If you wish to avoid any further delay as I understand your plans include I believe a holiday in Canada with family friends."* Upon reading this portion of the letter if I previously had suspicions about its authenticity then I was convinced it was a forgery after that. The reason being is that Ted Warner had made known it was his lifetime's ambition that before he died that he would visit Canada. Barbara Hendry was aware of this and its mention in the letter was a cynical addition to give Joan and Ted some degree of comfort to think that things were being sorted out.

There is a line of thought that in adopting this ploy with a victim, the victim with center on the facts in the letter such as a lifelong held ambition such as the "Trip to Canada" rather than centering on the authenticity of the letter and looking at it in further detail.

Upon visiting Mr Van Daal my suspicions were confirmed.

"About two years ago an approach was made to myself by a young man called Robert Ferguson who wanted some accommodation". After I had met him Mr. Ferguson was given a flat in Windsor Place Bridge of Weir Renfrewshire.

After a while, Mr. Ferguson became in arrears with the rent and I instigated legal proceedings against him after contacting my solicitor Mr. Marshall of Cochran Dickie and Mackenzie of Paisley.

I have been shown a letter and can identify it as a letter from the law firm of Cochran Dickie and Mackenzie. It bears my name but I have no knowledge of the content within it.

On one occasion I met Robert Ferguson's mother who gave her name as Mrs. B Hendry and she gave me her details as living at Burnside Bungalow, Keills Bridge, Isle of Jura Argyllshire.

It was again obvious that Joan and Ted Warner had been sent a forged letter and that somehow Barbara Hendry had got her hands on it and altered it then sent it to Joan and Ted. Yet again the evidence was mounting but we still needed to prove the offence.

We decided to go and find the original Doctor Turner and see what she had to say. We had made enquiries regarding her and we had established that she was a sort of legend in the Gorbals area of Glasgow the reason being that at sometime in the past she had held a medical practice locally and that one night whilst visiting her patients during her round in the Gorbals she had been mugged and badly assaulted.

We left Lennoxtown, and by this time it was late afternoon and again not having eaten we drove back towards Glasgow to a very well kept and quiet residential area and to the address of Dr Turner. An appointment had previously been made for early evening/ late afternoon and we knew we were slightly early. We called at the premises thinking that there would be no reply so that we could go off and get something to eat but the door was answered by a very well kept female with a peroxide / light coloured "Honor Blackman" type hair style. We were invited in and shown to the front lounge. We were offered a cup of tea, never known to refuse with the exception of one occasion, which is another story, while our host disappeared towards what I took to be the kitchen.

Dr Turner appeared shortly afterwards with a double layered type silver cake stand with an assortment of chocolate biscuits on the bottom tier and on the tier above a selection of cakes all looked very appetising! She placed the display on the table and busily rushed off to make the tea. Both my colleague and myself not having eaten all day drooled at the sight of the cakes and biscuits but not wanting to be seen as a "heathen" from south of the border waited until our host returned. I looked at PW O'Connor who was thinking the same as I was and no doubt "starving" I could tell by the look on her face what she was thinking and if given half a chance would have demolished the lot!

A few seconds later the Doctor returned with a pot of tea on a tray which she put down on the table in front of us, she took a look at the "untouched" cakes and biscuits and said "I'm sorry cakes and biscuits are not everybody's choice". She then proceeded to lift the plate and took them away to the kitchen. I looked at the face of PW O'Connor who was in complete shock at this, as she saw the plate of cake and biscuits disappearing into the distance! It took all my time not to burst out laughing but we are on a serious enquiry and would save that moment for later which I did!

We chatted to Dr Turner who was obviously a very busy Doctor carrying out her duties in a very difficult area. She was very amenable but had a very businesslike air about her. After chatting about her involvement with Barbara Hendry it was decided that a statement would be recorded from her, which she was only too agreeable to provide.

I decided that PW O'Connor could record the statement if only to take her mind from her pangs of hunger!

Dr Jean Turner   Over 21 Years   Medical Practioner
Charleston Street, Springburn Glasgow
I am employed as a Doctor and I have my own practice at the above address. I have worked there for about nine years.

Several of my patients are occupants in the flats at No 10 Red Road Court Springburn.

Approximately one year ago whilst working at the surgery I was called out to Flat 12/I also met a man called Donny Hendry – I therefore took the couple to be married.

On my arrival at the flat Mrs. Hendry was in bed and complained of general depression. She stated she wanted to lose weight to enable her to look nice. She requested that she became a private patient but I refused, telling her that I would only accept her as a National Health patient. I cannot really remember what prescriptions I gave to Mrs. Hendry, but I recall her telling me that she had recently moved to the flats from the Isle of Jura and that she had a large inheritance left to her by one of her uncles.

I did not see Mrs. Hendry again until a few weeks later when she attended my surgery. She appeared full of vitality, and although I cannot remember what her actual complaint was, it was relatively minor.

Whilst holding a conversation with her she informed me that she was going to buy a car and she took out a bundle of money from her handbag. I was genuinely shocked because I thought it was extremely unwise of her to carry that amount of cash around on her person, and I told her this. She appeared to find my advice highly amusing and then took a document from her handbag and showed me. To the best of my recollection the document mentioned a sum on money, which I think was four million pounds. Also on the document was a mention of a Swiss Bank. She inferred that she had come into a lot of money due to the inheritance left to her by her uncle but never really said how much.

With reference to Mrs. Hendry, I have no knowledge of a bank manager in Lincoln called Mr. Smith and I have certainly never telephoned anyone of that name or occupation for any reason. I have never made any contact with the Trustees Savings Bank and I have no knowledge of a Mr. and Mrs. Warner from Lincoln area or a Doctor Bell from Welton.

Signed

J Turner Dr

That afternoon at the conclusion of our enquiries we travelled south of the border and back to Lincolnshire where from my base at Market Rasen I would put the evidence together and submit it to the Crown Prosecution Service for the file. Both of the Hendry's were still in custody so there was no prospect at this stage of either of them interfering with any of the evidence. I was reasonably confident that the evidence would do the trick and would result in two guilty pleas, but I had a slight suspicion that the "fight" was not yet over.

Chapter Twelve: The case continues

Upon my return to Market Rasen the first thing I noticed was that the work had, in my absence been mounting up. I endorsed my file with the progress of my enquiries and then submitted it.

I had already agreed that as result of my enquiries Barbara Hendry would be seen in prison and the details of the new evidence should be put to her.

Now the avid and enthusiastic investigators amongst the readers will be thinking that she had already been charged and that you cannot put further questions to a suspect unless there are present very significant and urgent circumstances.

Barbara Hendry had previously been charged with offences of deception involving the banks in securing overdrafts by deception, as Ted and Joan Warner did not want to previously make a complaint. Now that Joan and Ted Warner were satisfied that it was all a deception they were willing to support a prosecution that would if the evidence was sufficient result in further charges of deception and the like. I knew I was on safe ground on this one, and I would make the most of it.

One thing I could not get out of my mind was the "cheek of it all" in that Donald Hendry had previously rang the Council to whom both Joan and Ted owed back rent posing as a Solicitor for the purpose of delaying their eviction. Since there would be no monies forthcoming then the eviction would still take place. This fact incensed me and I decided to revisit the Council and take the statement.

I attended and saw the member of staff involved who took the telephone call.

Statement of Wilfred Walker
West Lindsey District Council
1st June 1984

I am employed by West Lindsey District Council in the capacity of area officer. I work from the Council's premises situated at Park Street Lincoln. I am involved chiefly with the housing part of the department, and my duties include amongst other things bringing to the attention of the council bad debtors and instigate court proceedings.

The occupants of a council property at 25 Ryland Road, Dunholme Lincoln are a Mr. and Mrs. E.V. Warner. The Warner's have been in the property since April 1974, but our present records do not go back any further and indicates that they could have been in the property since 1960.

The rent for the property at 25 Ryland Road Dunholme is £18.50 per week, this includes the rates.

Throughout the period that Mr. and Mrs. Warner have been resident at number 25 I can say that the payment of rent has always been prompt and there has never been any cause for complaint, in fact they have been excellent tenants.

Around 26th May 1983, Mr. and Mrs. Warner began to get into arrears with their rent payments. On occasions failing to pay their weekly rent. The total amount currently owed is £453.36p.

At one point Mr. and Mrs. Warner did make contact with the council and say that there was a reason for failing to make the payments but did not elaborate on this.

Due to the fact that the arrears in rent were accumulating, I sent some letters to them bringing the matter to their attention and Mr. Warner wrote back saying he was experiencing certain difficulties but he would pay the amount in ten days time being September 1983. Payment was however not made.

As the arrears mounted up and payment had not arrived I passed the file to our housing manager who issued a notice seeking possession of the house occupied by the Warners. This was sent around 13th March.

At some time during my involvement with the Warner's, Mr. and Mrs. Warner came to my office and they said that they were expecting payment in full from Scotland and that I would be sent a cheque. They also mentioned something about a

Solicitor that was involved being in Zurich but did not elaborate on this point.

I can recollect that sometime during March, I cannot remember the exact date, a man with a Scottish accent telephoned and spoke to myself, he knew my name as Mr. Walker and knew that I had been dealing with the Warners. The man said that the Solicitor dealing was away in Zurich and the cheque settling the Warner's account would arrive in ten days time.

I know that this man rang on other occasions but I was not in the office and am unaware of what was said.

Signed
W. Walker

On 19th June 1984 and after preparing an interview of in excess of 500 questions together with Policewoman O'Connor I attended the Wold Newton remand center for women where I saw Barbara Hendry in the company of her solicitor whom I had not previously met. He was a very young man and I got the impression had recently qualified.

Barbara Hendry was already sat in the room with her solicitor when we arrived. She had not changed much in the intervening period and had not lost any weight. I got the impression that she had "settled" in. I introduced us for the benefit of the Solicitor who asked Hendry if she understood the reason for our visit. She turned and looked at her solicitor with that appealing "Basset hound puppy" look which appeared to me that she was playing the part of a persecuted woman. it was a look that made me at first feel sick and then after concealing my real thoughts got down to business.

What one has to remember is despite the circumstances and despite how you view somebody after the event it must never be forgotten why they are in the position they are in. Here we are faced with a very cold calculating female who has "conned" an elderly couple out of their savings and continued the deception over a number of years! One of the first rules of dealing with conmen or conwomen, don't be fooled!

As is the case with all fraud interviews where offences involve a large amount of paperwork the interview can appear monotonous and the documents need to be shown to the suspect to elicit any explanation they would wish to offer. As in this case a lot of the letters were handwritten and whilst the intention was to go through a majority of them, once admissions have been made regarding the first number or so that they have been written by the suspect then further denials are not a serious problem as the letters and documents can always be submitted for handwriting comparison to an expert at a later date it is always of assistance if they are all admitted but if they are not it is not the end of the world.

In current day fraud offences letters have been replaced by E-mail and hard drives there still is no supplement for the suspects to be actually shown the evidence in whatever format it may take.

The denials didn't really surprise me and whenever the questions were bordering on the difficult or probing they would be avoided or no answer offered.

Upon conclusion of the interview it was time to return to Market Rasen and get on with the job of detecting crime after the submission of the evidence to the County Prosecuting Solicitors Office.

The enquiries that took place were as always different and interesting even for a rural location. A few interesting burglaries took place in and around the area, Environmental activists targeted a local factory and attempted to destroy some fields of genetically modified crops and a church warden on a local patrol in a disused churchyard came across an additional grave that was not on the records (now there's another story!).

All in a days work!

One particular day I was working a late shift finishing at 10pm when I received a radio message to attend a burglary that had occurred during the day and had been discovered when the residents of the house burgled came home from work. Arrived at the premises around teatime and after knocking on the door it was answered by the lady of the house. She explained that her husband was on his way home from work and that she had discovered the house had been entered via a rear window. The burglar had forced the window to gain entry and once inside had searched the downstairs hen gone upstairs where the search had continued in the bedrooms. A quantity of jewellery had been stolen in a very organized search and missing from the bed in the master bedroom was a pillowcase obviously removed by the burglar to carry the stolen articles away in. The house owner was obviously very distressed and I commenced to record details of the property stolen I requested the attendance of the scenes of crime officer to see if there was any forensic evidence to be found and after completing the details of the stolen property I left the premises to conduct house to house enquiries with the neighbours to establish if they had seen anything.

There is a skill in obtaining information from individuals whether it be from a witness or a defendant and the object of either is being able to elicit the information required. In addition there are ruses that can be used to trigger an individual a certain way in order that they will take steps that have been provoked by the actions by the interviewer. For instance this is best demonstrated in a particular way on TV albeit slightly exaggerated. When watching the TV detective Columbo he will for instance interview his suspect and feed him information during the conversation that will make them think that they have made a mistake. The suspect will usually then take a course of action that has been prompted by what he has been told by the investigator i.e. Colombo. At the conclusion of the conversation Columbo will make to leave the room and just before going out of the door he will stop turn around and say something like "Oh, just one more thing that bothers me" or words to that effect and will drop a comment that will certainly get the suspect thinking and then Columbo will leave. This is what I call a "Columbo" moment. This can provoke the suspect into action such as cover their tracks, move the body, dispose of the murder weapon and the like.

After completing my house to house enquires with the neighbours I returned to the burgled premises and knocked on the door. The door was opened by a male being the husband who, in my absence had returned from work. I immediately recognised him as the manager from the loan company who had been very unreceptive to the plight of Joan and Ted Warner. I informed him that I had all the information I needed and would continue my enquiries with a view to catching their burglar. I was quite satisfied that he had not recognised me. After updating him I turned away to walk down the path and after a few steps I turned around and said to him, just one more thing Mr so and so I just wondered if you had any more thoughts on the plight of Mr. and Mrs. Warner and the possibility of extending the period of their loan to reduce the cost of the payments?"

Looking at the man I saw the instant sign of recognition on his face obviously remembering our previous conversation to which the man replied, "Er yes officer, I will deal with that first thing in the morning." And he did! That's what I call a "Columbo" moment!

Whatever I subsequently became involved in, the Warner scenario was always at the back of my mind. I knew that the additional evidence that was to be submitted would all be taken into consideration with regards to any further charges preferred against Hendry. It was also around this time that I was informed that Donald Hendry had applied for bail. I thought about it and decided that I would not really have any objection. He was another individual who had to a certain degree been deceived but that did not absolve him in my view from his actions. I didn't think he would cause a problem. Donald Hendry was released on bail to reside at a probation hostel in Lincoln and to be fair I knew that I would be able to keep an eye on him and if he did misbehave I wouldn't have far to go to get a grip of him, but I didn't think that I would have to!

I resumed my duties and kept in touch with Joan and Ted who although desperately disappointed did express a degree of relief it was all over that is despite the debt that they had got themselves into. I was satisfied that they would do all they could to repay those who had assisted them with loans.

One evening I went round to see Joan and Ted and during the conversation mentioned that I had become a father. A week or so later on another visit Joan presented me with a very elaborate knitted shawl for my newly born son. I initially decided that I could not accept the gift but after looking Joan in the eye accepted it, as I knew that both she and Ted would be offended. I was fully aware of how tight their finances were at this time but it was something that she obviously wanted to do.

All went quiet for a few months until I received correspondence for the CPS. The report was sitting on my desk early one morning. The situation had not changed much in the interim period. Barbara Hendry was still in custody but her husband Donnie had been bailed to a hostel in Lincoln and was living there. At least with her in custody I was confident that there would be no witness interference.

The report made various recommendations with regards to further evidence that needed to be obtained but the final paragraph made me read it again in which the words "The defendant Barbara Hendry intends to plead NOT GUILTY."

For me this meant that the gloves were off. It did not come as a surprise and deep down I realised that this was the opportunity to obtain further evidence so that the whole story would come out. The downside however was that if Hendry maintained her plea of not guilty then both Joan and Ted would have to give evidence, a situation with which I was not entirely happy with given the deterioration in Ted's health. This placed an increased responsibility on myself in that the additional evidence needed would have to be so compelling that Hendry would change her plea to guilty thus removing the need for both Joan and Ted to stand in the witness box and give evidence against her, which could transpire to be a most challenging ordeal. I knew what I had to do and decided that I would pull out all the stops to achieve the objective no matter how long it would take or how difficult it would be.

I made the necessary arrangements and went off to make my enquiries. The Crown Prosecution memo had outlined a number of further enquiries to be made but I had already instigated enquiries in Scotland regarding the birth certificate that Barbara Hendry had provided to Joan and Ted that purported to show that she was related to the Duchess of Argyll. I was pretty happy that the certificate was a forgery but as usual this matter would have to be prove "beyond reasonable doubt". I had contacted Detective Inspector Cassells who had made the necessary enquiries and had sent me a statement from a Registrar of Births and Marriages. The records showed that the birth certificate was indeed false. It did however contain details such as place of birth that gave it credibility such as "Oceanside New York" but it also displayed an NHS number that predated the creation of the NHS System by two years. Countless number of times fraudsters have let themselves down by being slightly inaccurate or missing certain details, the art of the investigation of fraud is being able to spot the details where mistakes have been made and sometimes this can be very difficult but as they say in the TV programme "Through the keyhole" "the clues are there".

During process of interviewing witnesses and especially from Joan and Ted came the information that Barbara Hendry had travelled down to Lincolnshire in a Mercedes Limousine by chauffeur. As best as recollections could recall the name of driver was a man by the name of Duncan Henderson. I had previously provided this information to the ever-reliable Detective Inspector Cassells who had assured me that if this man did exist then he would find him. Sure enough shortly before Christmas 1984 an envelope arrived on my desk and within it was contained a statement from Duncan Henderson. I sat back and read what he had to say. Another piece in the jigsaw had fallen into place.

Statement of Duncan Henderson
Sub Postmaster, Taxi Operator
Tarbet
Argyll

Dated 15th December 1984

I am the Sub Postmaster for the town of Tarbet Argyll. In addition to these duties I also operate a Taxi business.

I have known a woman called Barbara Hendry for about 5 or 6 years. Initially she lived on the Isle of Jura, which is off the coast of Argyll. Bannette as she was known locally, used to phone me regularly from her home on Jura and hire my taxi to meet her at the ferry terminal and drive her to various destinations. She always seemed to have plenty of money and from my conversations with her I formed the impression that she was related to the Campbell family and the Duke of Argyll whom she referred to as "Lorne"

Sometime in 1981, perhaps February or March of that year I received a telephone call from Bannette Hendry on Jura asking me if I could meet her the following morning as she got off the ferry and drive her to Lincoln.

Next morning as requested I met her and drove her to Lincoln in my Mercedes limousine taxi. During the journey she told me that she was going to visit her friend 'Joan' and also to make business calls on her legal advisors and her bank manager. She also talked of having loaned Joan a large sum of money in order that Joan's daughter could buy a house but she believed that the money was being mis- used, she intended to demand it be returned to her.

I arrived in the town of Lincoln about 8pm and Bannette directed me through the town center out of the town for a bit and then into a private housing estate. During this journey Bannette gave me £20 and told me to book a hotel after I dropped her off and I agreed to accept this money after telling her it would be deducted from the final bill.

On Bannette's instructions I stopped outside a house and I saw a woman greet Bannette warmly. I now know this woman to be called 'Joan'. I carried the bags and cases into the house and was invited to stay for tea, which I did.

Joan and her husband seemed to be very nice people and they insisted that I sleep in their spare room rather that book into a hotel. I asked Bannette if this would be alright with her and she agreed so I accepted the offer. The two women said that since I was staying the night perhaps I could take them into the town center about 9.30pm. I drove them both into Lincoln.

Joan asked if she could be dropped off and Bannette said that she was hungry. There was a fish and chip shop nearby and I brought two portions which we sat in the car and ate. About thirty minutes later Joan was picked up from where I dropped her off. We later returned to Joan's house. While Joan was away Bannette told me in confidence that Joan was off to meet a man with whom she was having an affair. (This revelation took me by total surprise but bearing in mind who we were dealing with didn't believe it and did not find any evidence to support this during the enquiry)

About 9.30am, the following morning Bannette and Joan got into the car and directed me to Lincoln town center again. I stopped in a car park adjacent to a light grey municipal building with sloping lawns on which there are public benches. I parked the car and both women left saying they would be back in an hour. I arranged to leave the car and meet them later and went for a walk to pass the time.

Upon returning to the place where I had parked the car I saw the women. Bannette said that the man that Joan had arranged to meet had failed to turn up and Bannette got into the car while Joan went off to see if she could find him. Almost immediately I saw a middle aged man, 5'9" in height average build wearing a camel coat and maybe a hat get out of a red car and speak to Joan. Both of them walked off through an archway and out of my sight.

Bannette sat in the car with me. She was very agitated and twice asked me to go and see what was keeping Joan. On each occasion I looked through the arch and saw both of them sitting there on a bench in animated conversation, the man was waving his hands about a lot. I returned to the car. After a while I saw Joan approach the car and I said so to Bannette who left the car hurriedly and spoke to Joan about 5 or 6 yards in front of me. They had a brief discussion and I saw Joan hand to Bannette an envelope measuring approx 9" x 4". I am sure of the size because I handle quite a lot in my business. As soon as this was handed over Bannette gave Joan a brief embrace, both women said their farewells and Bannette got back into the car and told me to drive back to Scotland.

I told Bannette that I would have to fill up with diesel and drove into a filling station. Bannette said that she would settle up with me there and then and asked how much she owed. I also told her it would cost £190 less the twenty pounds she had given me the previous night. She told me to forget that and I saw her tear the end from the envelope which she took from her bag and count out twenty ten pound notes one at a time. I would estimate that there was about £2000 in the envelope in ten-pound notes. I handle thousands of pounds each day and am sure of my estimate.

Bannette during conversation told me that she had managed to get £1800 of her money back. I assumed she was referring to the money she had loaned Joan to which she had referred to the previous day.

I then drove back to Tarbert, Argyll, where Bannette booked into a hotel and the following morning I drove her to the ferry terminal where I saw her board a ferry for Islay and Jura.

Shortly after this I refused to do business with Bannette as it became difficult to obtain payment and in fact I had to take legal action to obtain payment of outstanding bills to me.

D Henderson.

With the man Henderson traced and his statement recorded it was not time to concentrate on strengthening the case for the prosecution. I had previously made enquiries to trace the parents of Barbara Hendry without success whilst I had been in Scotland. I received a telephone call again from the Scottish police to the effect that an individual who they believed to be the mother of Barbara Hendry had been traced. Without further delay I travelled to a small place in Dunbartonshire called Loch Garelochead where I saw an elderly woman called Janet Bain. I recorded a statement, which again I knew would prove useful in the case thereby completely dispelling the myth that Hendry was related to the Duchess of Argyll.

"I am the mother of Barbara Elizabeth Wright BAIN or HENDRY who was born to myself and my second husband James BAIN at Glasgow on 17th January 1930. Neither my husband nor myself have any connection with either the Duke or the Duchess of Argyll and for Barbara to claim that she is the illegitimate daughter of the Duchess of Argyll is a complete fabrication.

Barbara has no expectations of any trust funds set up for her in any banks in Zurich.

I produce a Photostat copy of the record of Barbara's birth.

I was satisfied with the result of my enquiry and that the statement would "nail the lie" but the answer would only be revealed if Barbara Hendry changed her plea to guilty. I would have to wait but in the meantime would continue with my enquiries.

I was still of the impression that in order to do what I could to try to prevent Joan and Ted Warner having to give evidence I would have to gather all the evidence available so that Barbara Hendry would plead guilty. I had formed the opinion that I did not like her one bit and that I would not put it past her just to plead "not guilty" out of spite by the fact that she had been caught and her scheme exposed.

I had always considered Barbara Hendry to be very cold and calculated and would never underestimate the depths to which she would plunge to save her own skin. My theory was confirmed when I received information that she had married her common-law husband Donny whilst on remand in prison.

It was known in those days that a married spouse was, in the capacity of a witness against his/her spouse was "competent but not compellable" to give evidence. Having interviewed Donny who was now on bail I did not think that he would marry her bearing in mind just what he had got into with her but I decided to check anyway.

To my surprise I discovered that on 8th August 1984 one Donald Hendry had in fact got married to Barbara Elizabeth Wright Bain in the registry office in the district of Durham Central. Donnie giving his occupation as Mashman/ Stillman whilst the occupation given by Barbara Hendry was left blank (Probably due to the fact that she was on remand in prison at the time of the ceremony!). What typified the character of Barbara Hendry to myself was that fact that she had given her address as 32 Finchall Avenue Brasside Durham, this being the address of Durham Prison!

To my mind the reason she had got married to Donny was that she was under the impression that if married he would not be able to give evidence against her in any forthcoming trial.

Chapter Thirteen: The Hunt Continues

I had decided that as a result of the entire goings on I would record statements from whomever I could just to put this situation to rest. Joan and Ted were getting very agitated at the thought of having to give evidence and I felt it my duty if possible to try and prevent that scenario from happening, after all they were the victims in this case!

Having assessed the evidence so far I had to decide what other evidence would assist my case. There was the alleged "Rembrandt" painting I could have an expert take a look at that and then there was Margaret Duchess of Argyll who could finally be seen. I had made a few enquiries about her and found out that she was very well known and to say the least had a somewhat colourful past. There was controversy over her marriage followed by the controversy involving the photograph of the "Headless man" (the head of the man allegedly performing a sex act had been removed from the photograph making identification impossible).

There was also the matter of identifying which typewriters had been used to type the invoices and some letters sent to Joan and Ted Warner.

There were still a number of lines of enquiry that could be pursued during the process of investigation. The danger for any investigator is to go off at tangents and conduct enquiries that whilst relevant to the offence can often take the place of other enquiries to be made. This is where in a larger enquiry such as murder or kidnap that the role of the SIO (Senior Investigating Office) becomes important, the reason being is that one of the responsibilities of the SIO is to keep the enquiry on track and not to let it become bogged down with peripheral issues and enquiries.

The investigating officer also has to consider during his investigation the evidence that has to be obtained in order to prove the offence being investigated. For instance in offences of deception one has to prove that some one has been deceived (or a misrepresentation has taken place under the new fraud legislation) in previous cases individuals have purported to have been relatives of members of the Getty family in order that a deception can take place. A more recent case involved an offender assuming the identity of the former Director of Public Prosecutions Keir Stamer QC in order to his deceive victims.

In the early seventies I was in "Digs" or lodgings in a small market town in Lincolnshire called Louth. My landlady was a very friendly elderly lady whose husband had died years before and who liked the idea of providing lodgings for a young police officer as a bit of company having to cook and look after someone else not to mention some form of security. Unfortunately this custom has all but died out. Anyway at this time I was not an avid reader of newspapers but did like to have occasional look at the Daily Express that the landlady had delivered. I can recollect reading the gossip column of one William Hickey whose regular feature covered political scandal and gossip and on a not infrequent basis featured articles on one Margaret Duchess of Argyll. I gained the impression that she had an interesting background including some scandal and knowing what little I did about her was looking forward to meeting her if I could arrange it.

I had a discussion with my Detective Chief Inspector who reluctantly agreed that for completeness the Duchess should be seen. I did not tell my work colleagues as I was convinced that I would never hear the last of it and would be subject to ridicule for years to come.

I had made a few enquiries and located a relative of the Duchess who lived in the south of Lincolnshire and had provided to me her telephone number.

One day in the office I rang the Duchess whom I knew was resident at the Grosvenor House hotel in London.

It was fortunate that the relative involved had informed her of my interest and when we spoke she knew a little about what I needed and we arranged a convenient date between ourselves for me to visit her.

On 9th January 1985 I travelled down to London to see the Duchess. I had with me my briefcase, which inside contained all the detail's I would need to put the Duchess in the picture. From the previous enquiries I had made about the Duchess it had been said she could be rather prickly and difficult to deal with but the reality was that I did require a statement from her and that was the objective.

I arrived at the Grosvenor House Hotel and stood outside for a minute looking up. It is an imposing place far removed from the streets of Market Rasen in Lincolnshire.

I entered the hotel and into the lobby looking around I notice that I was being observed by some sort of Commissionaires stood there in his what I took to be a top hat. I saw the lift and walked over to it and went in. I looked first at the buttons knowing that the Duchess lived in a flat on the upper floor. I pressed the button waiting for the door to close but nothing happened. Thinking that I had either pressed the wrong button or in fact not pressed it hard enough I pressed it again. Nothing happened.

I was then faced with the Commissionaire poking his head in the lift with a "Can I help you Sir?"

I said, "Yes you can, I am trying to get to the upper floor."

He replied in a rather suspicious tone, "And why would you want to go up there Sir?" He spoke in the tone of an old police sergeant who had come across a drunk in the street making his way home.

"Well I have some business up there," and was just about to explain what business it was when he retorted, "And what business would that be then?" I was getting the impression that we have here a frustrated commissionaire who wanted to be either a Police officer or was a member of the Stazi in a previous life.

I replied, "I have an appointment to see the Duchess."

"And who might you be then?" he asked.

I replied, "Lincolnshire Police CID," I replied. I did not tell him Marker Rasen as I was confident that in his mind anything north of Watford probably did not exist to him!

"Have you any ID then?" He asked.

At this point I felt like the escaping officers from Colditz that had escaped and arrived at the local railway station only to be met and caught out by the local Gestapo after answering a simple question.

I reached into my jacket pocket and pulled out my identity card that had been made the previous night by Donald Pleasance under candlelight wearing his "jam jar bottomed glasses" hoping that it would satisfy the local "Stazi". He looked at the ID card and said, "Lincolnshire, where that?

"North of Watford," I replied.

The lift started moving and I arrived at the correct floor. The doors opened and I was faced with a very bland looking landing and corridor and a few doors. I found the door that I wanted and knocked. An elderly and who appeared to be a well-kept female opened the door. I was of the opinion that the Duchess at this time would be between 70 and 80 years old and the first thing I noticed was her skin which gave the impression of being very pale and porcelain like without a blemish.

"Don't just stand there officer come in." She said.

I moved from the door way into what I could see was a very well furnished flat. I sat down opposite what appeared to be a very ornate and carved Chinese looking drinks cabinet.

"Right then." She said "Sit down and tell me all about why you are here." I had just sat down taken an intake of breath ready to recount the story when the Duchess said,

"Does the press bother you officer?"

"I'm sorry?" I replied.

"Does the press bother you officer?" she again asked.

"No," I replied. With that she called out the name "Alfonse." and in came bounding a black poodle type dog and with that the Duchess said, "Come along officer we are going for a walk," and she picked up a dog lead.

I had not travelled down from Lincolnshire for the purpose of taking a poodle for a walk but I did need a statement from the Duchess but was thinking that I would probably be photographed by a journalist from the Daily Express being seen arm in arm with the Duchess taking her poodle for a walk. If this came out I would never hear the last of it. Still in the pursuit of crime one has to make sacrifices and so be it.

We went to the lift and descended down to the lobby where the first individual I laid eyes on was the local "Stazi" with his top hat on and grinning from ear to ear!

We walked out of the hotel and a distance down the road to let Alfonse sniff around a bit and then returned to her flat.

I started to explain the reason for my visit and the Duchess interrupted saying, "I don't know how people can be so stupid," a comment which I could have easily taken exception to.

I continued the story and by the end of it she had mellowed conceding that Barbara Hendry had really gone to some trouble to execute her deception.

During the process I happened to mention that I was unable to obtain a copy of the biography "Forget me not" written by the Duchess and with that she went into another room and returned with a book.

"Here officer you can have this copy".

I informed her that at the conclusions of any case I would return it but she insisted that I should keep it.

Upon looking inside the book I saw that written in it was *"To Mr(s) Walden with best wishes Margaret Argyll October 1979"*

The Duchess provided me with a telephone number that was different to the one I had. I queried the number and she said, "Use that number "she then opened the drawer to the desk and removed a telephone saying, "I will always answer this phone when it rings." She then returned it to the desk drawer and closed it.

I then requested of the Duchess that I record a statement to which she agreed.

Statement of Ethel Margaret Campbell (Duchess of Argyll)
69 years Bn 1.12.15
C/o Grosvenor House Hotel Park Lane London.

I live at the above address and I am the Duchess of Argyll.

In 1951 I married Ian Campbell, Duke of Argyll (11th).

I do not have any children by marriage to the Duke of Argyll, but have two children by my previous marriage to Charles Sweeny.

The children are the current Duchess of Rutland Francis Helen Manners and Brian Sweeney who lives in Putney.

I do not know Barbara Elizabeth Wright Bain alias Ferguson alias Campbell alias Hendry and for her to purport to be my daughter illegitimate or otherwise is complete fabrication.

I have no knowledge of the title Countessa De Leonie.

I have been shown by Detective Constable Booth of the Lincolnshire Police, Police Item EVW 136A copy birth certificate. I have never seen it before but I can say that my maiden name is Wigham, and my second husbands name was Ian Douglas Campbell, not John Ian Campbell as shown on this birth certificate. His title was 11th Duke of Argyll whose family titles also include Marquis of Lorne.

My husband at one time was a university student and went to Oxford. I produce to Detective Constable Booth of the Lincolnshire Police a copy of my autobiography entitled "Forget not" which was published in 1975.

Anyone purporting to be a relative or my illegitimate daughter or whoever would be able to find details of my history or background from my book.

I would like to add that the birth certificate I have been shown is obviously false.

Signed
Margaret Argyll

I completed the statement from the Duchess and returned to Lincolnshire to add it to my ever-mounting file of evidence and from thereon in the Duchess would be more than a name in a paper.

I had enjoyed the visit to see the Duchess and it was nice to put a face to a name. In reality she could not have been more helpful, all in a days work.

For the following few days I kept an eye on the newspapers but nothing was ever printed, obviously the maids (Journalists) "day off!"

Having obtained the statement from the Duchess it was again time to review the evidence obtained and the evidence available. I was satisfied with the evidence gathered with regards to the birthright of Barbara Hendry but now had to decide what other evidence was available. She had admitted writing the letters and evidence was also available and had been obtained showing that either she, or other persons on her behalf had collected the money from banks and delivered it to her. Basically her story was a lie and she had obtained monies from Joan and Ted Warner by using it. The only other evidence that was available was evidence that the typewriters used by her had been used to type the letters sent. Also there was the Rembrandt painting that was obviously in my view a forgery and there was also the "trust fund" documents given to the Warners by Barbara Hendry.

The "trust fund" document was elaborately written in longhand and to the untrained eye appeared to be very elaborate. It outlined details of the alleged trust fund also giving details of the" Trustees" who had been given the task of administering the estate which was alleged to run into millions of pounds. There were several well-known "Trustees" mentioned in the document being Maurice Chavalier, Lord Wheatley being Lord Chief Justice for Scotland and Nicholas Fairburn a very well-known and slightly eccentric Scottish Member of Parliament.

I had previously decided that I would obtain all of the evidence available to be had. There was the obvious reason of putting Barbara Hendry in an impossible position that she would have no alternative but to plead guilty but there is another reason that when an investigator has the time and the resources is that all relevant and interesting statements should be recorded. In the prosecution of a case the Prosecution is not obliged to use all the evidence available (these days subject to conditions it has to be "disclosed to the defence) but if a statement has been recorded the prosecutor will, despite not using it will have hopefully read it which will provided a better and more thorough picture of what occurred.

I decided that I would make enquiries into the "Trustees" first and made an appointment to travel down to the House of Commons in London and interview Nicholas Fairburn the Conservative MP.

Chapter Fourteen: Piecing the jigsaw together

On 27th February 1986 and by prior appointment I travelled down to London from Lincolnshire. The purpose of my visit was to interview Nicholas Fairburn and also to visit the Art experts Sotheby's to obtain a professional opinion on the "Fake Rembrandt" that I took with me. Upon my arrival at Kings Cross I deposited the painting at the British Transport Police office for collection later. I then made my way to the House of Commons where after identifying myself I was shown into a large lobby to await the arrival of my witness. After about 15 minutes I saw a very dapperly dressed male approaching whom I recognised to be Nicholas Fairburn MP. Upon his approach I saw that he was wearing the loudest "Tartan" designed jacket and trousers I have ever seen in my life!

He approached and introduced himself. We walked to a bar area nearby where we could talk in private and I could elaborate on the reason for my visit. I explained the situation and he asked that since he could not recollect anybody by the name of Barbara Hendry did I have a photograph of her as in his role he met so many people some of whom he knew by sight only.

Upon showing him a photo of Barbara Hendry he burst in a loud bout of laughter saying, "If I had met her, I would have remembered it!" a fact that I totally believed as he stated he did have a good memory for the female form!

I asked if he would provide a statement, which he readily agreed to do.

A short time later after consuming a much-welcomed cup of tea I recorded a statement from Nicholas Hardwick Fairburn.

I am the Member of Parliament for Perth and Kinloss and have been so for many years.
On 27th February 1985 I was shown by Detective Constable Booth of the Lincolnshire Police, one colour photograph of a

woman (Police Item KNB4). I can say that I do not know this woman and I have not, to my recollection ever seen her before.

I do not know any woman going by the name of Barbara Hendry, Banette Hendry, Barbara Morrison or Bain and for this person to profess to be a friend of mine is incorrect and untrue

Signed

Nicholas Fairburn Q.C M.P.

Upon leaving he House of Commons I returned to Kings Cross where I collected the painting and made my way across London to Sotheby's still lugging the painting along with me.

Upon arrival I was met by a lady who was a renowned paintings expert and asked for her professional opinion. She took a very detailed look at the painting and stated that she was of the opinion that it was as I has suspected a forgery. It only yet again confirmed my suspicions the next step was to obtain a statement.

Paintings Expert
Sotherby's
34/35 New Bond Street London

I am a paintings expert and I work at the premises of Sotherby's situated at 34/35 New Bond Street London.

On Wednesday 27th February 1985, I was shown by Detective Constable Booth of the Lincolnshire Police on framed picture of a self-portrait by Rembrandt (Police Item JL11)

Firstly, I am satisfied that this is not a painting as such, as it is not comprised of paint on canvas. It is a reproduction made by some form of processing of which I am unable to say.

Upon looking at the picture I can see it is meant to be a Rembrandt self-portrait and I am satisfied it is a forgery.

I would like to add that I specialize in studying and working with old master paintings.

Signed

Now with the statement completed it was another evidential nail in of Barbara Hendry so to speak. I returned to Kings Cross and caught the train to Lincolnshire after another successful day. I realised that I would still have to make further enquiries to disprove the authenticity of the trust document and would have to visit the other "Trustee" being Lord Wheatley in Scotland. Further issues to be considered were the official solicitor's letters that had been produced by Barbara Hendry to both Joan and Ted Warner and Mr Smith the bank manager.

I was satisfied that they were forgeries produced by Barbara Hendry to support her fraud and needed to establish for evidential continuity where they had been produced and what typewriters had been used in their preparation. I had established that she had at times used a typewriter belonging to the security guard at the Red Road Court flats and would need to seize it in due course I had already seized a typewriter from the Hendry address upon their arrest but suspected that Hendry in an attempt to further her fraud had used other typewriters so that the forged letters would appear to have been typed on different typewriters in an attempt to avoid any suspicion. After putting all the evidence obtained at this point it was sent to the Crown Prosecution Service for their information and to add to the existing prosecution file.

I returned to Market Rasen to continue with my duties to await any further instruction. I was also aware that further enquiries had to be made on the Isle of Jura where Barbara Hendry lived previously in the early days of her fraudulent activity as there were further questions to be answered. I had to make arrangements prior to my visit to inform the local police that another police force would be making enquiries within their police area as was, and still remains the existing protocol.

Chapter Fifteen: A visit to the Islands

Fraudsters are basically "users of people" in that they will identify individuals that they consider will be of "use" in pursuit of their objective i.e. the fraud being perpetrated. The fraudster will appear to be needy on occasions to foster sympathy; the fraudster can convey an image of being of valued assistance or can ingratiate themselves to an individual at the expense of more valued relationships by the victim. The latter is more common where the fraudster becomes involved in family or well-established relationships, which often can result in the division of the family unit.

I have encountered fraudsters who in the past have weaved their stories "He was in the SAS you know but didn't like to talk about it" or "she's had a sad life been very unlucky!" On one occasion I encountered a fraudster who had told the victim he was wanted by the IRA but "You can't tell anybody as my life will be at risk!" The stories know no bounds. Since the Hendrys had resided on the Isle of Jura for a period of time during the commission of the fraud against Joan and Ted Warner there was no doubt in my mind that evidence of use would be found on the islands. The intention was to find people that had been "used" by Hendry and further build the case against her and her husband. The main issues in my mind were the administrative side of the fraud such as preparation of the fraudulent letters used, photo copying typewriters used and anything else that would be of assistance.

On 9th March 1985 together with my colleague Policewoman O' Connor we travelled to the Inner Hebrides the final destination being the Isle of Jura. Not a lot was known about the Hendry's whilst they were living on the island but it was an important period being the early days of the fraud. It was also important to identify individuals who knew them and to build up a picture.

Before actually going to the Isle of Jura I had a couple of potential witnesses to see if we could pull them in on the way in the Glasgow area then travel to Jura. One of the next steps was to conduct further enquiries around the handwritten will that had been handed to the Warner's by Barbara Hendry. The will had been witnesses by two individuals it was time to go and find them to see what they had to say. I had briefly conducted some enquiries and had established possible addresses. The first call was to Dumbarton an area of Glasgow where we were hoping to see another alleged "witness" to the will. We attended an address in Castle Green Street where we saw Thomas McLoughlin and who turned out to be a very nice gent only too willing to help. After a short conversation during which the situation was explained a short statement was recorded.

Thomas McLoughlin   *Retired*

I have lived at the current address with my wife Kathleen.
On 8th March 1985, I was shown by Detective Constable Booth of the Lincolnshire Police one colour photo of a woman Police Item KNB 1). I can say that I have never seen this woman before. I do not know any woman by the name of Barbara Hendry, or Banette Hendry or Barbara Morrison or Barbara Ferguson or Barbara Elizabeth Wright Bain.

I have also been shown a written will (Police item EVW 90) I can say that I have not seen this document before. I can say that I do not know a James Mc Lovogin or any name similar (McLovogin was a witness to the will and his address was shown as being 37 Castle Green Street Dumbarton).

My wife and I have lived at 37 Castle Green Street for seven years. We have a large family but none are called James and none are employed as a solicitor.

With Mr. McLoughlin having lived with his wife at the address for 7 years it supported the view that the witness to the will was "made up" and didn't even exist. Of course the defendant can always provide details of the alleged witnesses to the will but I considered it highly unlikely!

After recording the statement from the alleged witness to the will we went by plane from Glasgow to Arran then by ferry to Jura. It was whilst on the ferry the member of staff approached and said to me.

"You'll be the police from the mainland then?"

"How do you know that?" I asked.

"Everybody knows that you are arriving today." Obviously a well-kept secret I thought but not a problem.

We departed from the ferry and travelled to the Jura hotel on the island where we booked in.

After getting settled in we went down the bar and had a much-welcomed drink.

I spoke to the barman and asked him, "There doesn't seem to be many cars about on the island?"

"No." He replied, "There won't be, it's because everyone knows the police are on the island."

I said, "Why would that be of any concern?"

"Well," he replied, "the locals are all worried because nobody has any tax or MOT's on their cars and they done want to get done!"

After a short laugh I replied, "They have no need to worry bout that as it is not the reason why we are here. We are making enquiries into a fraud. Motoring offences are not my concern." With that a telephone call was made and cars started to appear and the ice was broken. After a short conversation we established where Hendry lived and who her immediate neighbours were. As the night progresses the bar filled up and an enjoyable evening was had with the locals. Basically the majority of people are basically honest and hardworking individuals always willing to assist and have never encountered a "Detective" or been involved in a police enquiry certainly not a fraud investigation and during a very social evening we were soon able to find out who on the island could provide typing facilities photo copying and the like.

The following morning after an early rise we went out to trace potential witnesses.

Statement from "Nancy"

I currently live on the Isle of Jura and have done so for a number of years. My husband runs the local bus and is also responsible for delivering the milk, papers and mail on the island, which has a population of just over 250. I help him from time to time when he goes out on his delivery runs.

About ten years ago I cannot remember the exact date a man and a woman came to live on Jura two or three doors away from us. Being a small close community I soon came to know the couple as Banette and Donny Hendry whom I initially assumed were married. My husband and I delivered their milk, mail and papers and I started to get to know Banette although I never got really friendly with her. Now and again, on the deliveries, I would pop into her house for a cup of tea and a chat but it wasn't on a regular basis.

Banette used to tell me various stories about herself and her background. She initially told me she was Swiss and she used to put on a fake accent, which she dropped over the following months. Before long Banette began to get behind with her milk bills and on three occasions she paid her account with cheques, which subsequently "bounced", She ran up a bill of over two hundred pounds and I never got the money from her. She used to promise me she would pay me the money when it came in at the end of the month but on two occasions when I visited she was sat up in bed and took out a wad of money consisting of ten and twenty pound notes. I estimated that these wads were about £2000 each and he said that she would be spending the money on the mainland. She never said where the money came from although I was aware that she collected the money from the Islands Post Office. (If you the reader were conducting this investigation where would you conclude the money in her possession had come from?) you don't need to be an ace detective to figure that one out!)

She had plenty of nice clothes and often wore expensive jewellry so I presumed that was what she spent her money on.

Banette never had a telephone at her house and I was quite happy to let her use ours. On several occasions a woman called Joan rang her and I fetched her from her house to speak to her. Banette also used to make calls from our house but she always shut herself away in the room so I never heard any of the conversations she held. She never asked me to make any phone calls for her.

I met Joan and her husband once or twice when they came to visit Banette. I took a liking to Joan she seemed a very friendly type of person. They appeared to be good friends. I never knew whether to believe Banette because some of the things she told me were a bit far-fetched. She said she was a friend of Lord Wheatley and I remember her saying she was related to the Duchess of Argyll. <u>Banette also used to borrow my typewriters one being a very old one and another one being more up to date. She never used them at my house but took them back to her house to use.</u> More often she sent her husband to collect them. I think she broke the first one but then used the other one after that. She told me she needed them to type letters to the council but I never questioned it. I am still in possession of both typewriters and can produce the modern one of the two in evidence.

As with all enquiries nuggets of evidence can appear from the most unlikely places. The lady interviewed was able to state that Barbara Hendry whilst living nearby had borrowed her typewriter and it was reasonable to assume that it could be one of the typewriters that have been used to produce the forged solicitors letters. I was allowed to take the typewriter for evidential purposes and would in due course have it forensically examined to establish if it was the typewriter used. The statement also confirmed the connection between Barbara Hendry and the Warner's and went on to say that they had visited the island.

Statement of Sandra

I have lived on the Isle of Jura since 1968 but have only lived at my current since October 1984. The island is small consisting of a population of about 250 so everybody knows everybody else. During the months of 1976 a couple moved into the bungalow next door. Initially I believed the couple were married but as I got to know them I understood that they were living together and that they liked to be known as Banette and Donny Hendry. I never had much to do with them for the first six months because they did not attempt to make conversation with me or anybody else. The couple left the island around July 1983.

During the time that Donny and Banette lived near I never really trusted them. Banette acted strangely and always gave the impression that she had something to hide and was out to impress people. When she eventually started talking to me she gradually told me various things about herself. She told me that she was the illegitimate daughter of the Duke of Argyll and that her mother had given birth to her and she had been brought up by a person in Garelochead. She also said that she was good friends with Lord Wheatley and in actual fact on one occasion I was at a neighbours house called Chrissie Kingbury when I answered the phone and was told it was Lord Wheatley himself and he wanted to talk to Mrs Kingbury. I got Chrissie to the phone because the gentleman calling was quite adamant even though he was polite. Chrissie was quite old at the time and has since died. I thought that I recognised the voice on the phone as Donny.

Banette also told me that she had a grandmother in Switzerland.

As I got to know Banette she started to use my phone to both make and receive calls. Several people used to ring her including a woman called Joan from Lincoln. Apparently Joan and Banette were supposedly the best of friends but in spite of that when I used to fetch Banette sometimes to take a call from Joan, she informed me that she was ill and could not come to the phone even though I knew she was in the best of health. Donny also told me she was ill but I knew otherwise, it was obvious to me that Joan thought the world of Banette and I couldn't understand why Banette wanted to avoid talking to her. I got the impression that Banette just couldn't be bothered to make the effort.

Banette always wore expensive looking rings, necklaces and watches. She told me that she got them from Kilmans on Islay, but it always turned out that she got them on approval and *took them back after she had worn them. Sometimes she was in possession of large sums of money. I was in the Post Office one day when Donny drew out £800. Barbara said it was her allowance and I have been in her house a few times after her phone was connected and been present when she has rung the Post Office to see if her allowance has been wired through. Towards the last few months of her living on the island she appeared to be receiving amounts of £800 to £1000 each month. I don't really know where Banette used to spend all her money I never really questioned it. She told so many stories I never knew whether to believe anything she said. One explanation I got was from Donny who said that the money was being sent by Lord Wheatley who was supposedly being blackmailed by Banette.. The story went that Lord Wheatley had visited a brothel in Edinburgh when Banette and her mother had been "society whores" <u>Upon hearing this nothing surprised me anymore with the stories that I knew she had been propagating in the past!</u>*

Banette was always complaining of ill health but I never believed any of it. To tell the truth I was glad when she left the island. I was always very wary of her because although she appeared to be a nice person on the surface, I did not believe she was a genuine person and was always putting on a front, which hid her true character.

After recording the statement we went further around the island to trace individuals whom we believed could assist us further. It was whilst recording a statement on the island I looked out of the lounge window from the house and onto a pebbled beach where I saw two sea otters playing. I can recollect thinking to myself that taking statements doesn't get any better that this! The scenery was stunning, the locals extremely friendly it was and is a very beautiful place the type of place ideal to get "away from it all" There have not been many occasions in my career where I have recorded a statement sitting in the lounge of a cottage and seeing two otters playing on the beach across the road!

Statement of "John"   Occupation Deer Stalker

I have lived on the Island of Jura for the past twenty years. About three years ago I got to know a woman called Banette Hendry and her husband Donny. I didn't get to know her well but she would come to our hose and use our telephone. The house where I live is a tied cottage and it is owned by Lord Astor as I am employed by him as a deer stalker. Banette only used the phone two or three times but I can recollect that on one occasion when she was in my house the MP Nichols Fairburn came on the TV and Banette made comment that he was a good friend of hers. (That's not what Nicholas Fairburn said when I recorded a statement from him at the House of Commons!)

At the conclusion of the statement it showed how Barbara Hendry was using the name of individuals such as Nicholas Fairburn to impress people. We had also during our stay identified an individual who had facilities on the island for the purpose of printing and photocopying but he was not available and this would have to wait until a later date. I would leave a message for the local officer who would hopefully be paid a visit and establish if it was worth recording a witness statement. It was time to leave the beautiful island and travel to Glasgow to collect further evidence.

After another enjoyable night in the Jura hotel and early rise was the order for the following day. After a rather late night, a short drive, a ferry trip and a plane flight we arrived in Glasgow yet again!

The next on the list was the witness P Bryson Hamilton with the address of Dharling Road Kirn Dunoon. Later the same day we arrived at the address shown on the will. After a knock on the door it was answered by a rather distinguished looking gentleman and after a short explanation we were invited in. After sitting down and elaborating on the reason for our visit a statement was recorded.

James Bryson Hamilton   Doctor

I am a Doctor by profession and practice in the Dunoon area of Scotland

On Monday 11th March 1985 I was shown by Policewoman O'Connor of the Lincolnshire Police one handwritten copy of the will of Barbara De Leonie of Burnside Cottage, Isle of Jura. Upon examination it can be seen that the will has been witnessed by P. Bryson Hamilton of Dharling Road Kirn Dunoon Argyll. I can say that I have no knowledge of this document and have never seen it before or signed it despite that I live at the same address as shown. I have also been shown one colour photo of a woman (Hendry) and I can say to the best of my knowledge I have never met or had anything to do with this woman. I have no relatives with the surname of Hamilton whose Christian name begins with a "P"

As far as I was concerned the statement again nailed the lie of one of the witnesses that had witnessed the will to false, as he had no knowledge of the will or of Barbara Hendry and the signature on the will provided by Barbara Hendry had been forged. Further enquiries were to be made in relation to the will, which were to be made the following day in Glasgow.

The will provided to the Warner's was endorsed "Copy at Tilsons Solicitors and with that in mind and by prior appointment went into Glasgow to pay a call. We were met with the usual hospitality at Tilsons solicitors where a statement recorded nailed another lie in the fraud. The purpose of the visit to Tilsons was establish if they did have a copy of the will in their possession. I was satisfied by this time that it was totally fraudulent but evidentially it has to be confirmed as such.

William MacLaurin   Solicitor

I am the senior partner in the practice of Tilson and MacLaurin Solicitors in Glasgow On 12th March 1985 I was shown by Detective Constable Booth of the Lincolnshire Police one handwritten will of Barbara De Leonie of Burnside Bungalow, Isle of Jura. I can say I have never seen this *document before. It can be seen that typed on the will it states that the original copy is lodged with Tilson and Co, since I am principally involved in executory work with our firm I can say that a copy of the Leonie will is not lodged with this firm. I can further state that I have not signed the document and it does not show a signature on it that bears any resemblance to my own. I have also been shown a colour photo of a woman (Hendry). I can say I have never seen this woman before to the best of my knowledge and belief.*

After concluding the statement the next destination was Edinburgh to further enquire into the handwritten will.

Again this statement served to show the will produced to Ted and Joan Warner by Barbara Hendry was not "as stated" lodged with the solicitors Tilson and Co and that the solicitors had no knowledge of it.

The case was coming together in my view we were showing the depths of the lies spun by Barbara Hendry during the commission of her fraud. I was satisfied that we had proved that the handwritten will was a total fabrication that had been created by Barbara Hendry in furtherance of her fraud and designed for the sole purpose of deceiving both Joan and Ted Warner. It would appear to me that Hendry's cruelty and dedication to her fraud knew no bounds and that she had carried it on with Joan and Ted for nearly seven years! It was finally coming to conclusion but there was still work to do!

As with all frauds the offence is built on a tissue of lies and deceitful activity. The object of the investigation is to disprove the version of events and accounts provided to the victim by the fraudster. In the current case enquiries have established that the birth certificate provided by Barbara Hendry to Joan and Ted Warner to be false.

Looking at it I could see how it would have been accepted by them. The Duchess of Argyll has been shown the birth certificate and provided a statement. The two alleged witnesses to the hand written will also provided have been seen and have not seen it before and have no knowledge of it. The solicitors who were   allegedly supposed to be in possession of a copy of the will have no knowledge of it and obviously stated that they do not hold a copy of it. Casting one's mind back earlier in the investigation the witness Elizabeth Carr stated that she would attend the library in Glasgow and obtain personal details about the Duchess and her life and give them to Barbara Hendry and at the time Barbara Hendrys flat was searched hand written details about the Duchess were found on a piece of paper obviously extracted from her biography.

There only remained one further line of enquiry from "up north" Barbara Hendry had made large play to various individuals that she was very friendly through her "society" connections with Lord Wheatley who at the time and still is a very distinguished "Gentleman of Law (as she put it) in Scotland and that he had allegedly acted for her in a legal capacity in connection with the will. I had absolutely no doubt this fact was another lie but decided to disprove it.

Actually seeing and interviewing the Lord Chief Justice for Scotland is not an easy thing to arrange believe it or not! Being a very senior judge and a very busy man does make life difficult for a junior detective, however it was time to turn to, and seek the assistance of Strathclyde Police finest the very reliable Detective Inspector James Cassells. A quick telephone call was made and arrangements were made to secure a visit.

The following day I attended the Central Criminal Court in Edinburgh where I was shown into the Judge's chambers at the court. I only had to wait a couple of minutes or so when I was confronted by a very impressive figure of a man all "robed up" being one Lord Wheatley. It would be safe to say that I was rather conscious that the statement had to be right and also wanting to give a rather professional impression of both the Lincolnshire Police and myself.

To be fair one could not hope to find a more helpful individual in such a senior position. I was immediately put at ease and outlined my story. Lord Wheatley provided a short statement outlining the fact that he had never heard of Barbara Hendry, had never met her and had certainly never acted for her in any legal issues. The statement recorded it was time to head back to Lincolnshire. I had not seen all the people I needed to interview but I knew that I could rely on both the local police from Islay and Jura and the Strathclyde CID who had provided every assistance in my enquiry.

It was time to return to Lincolnshire but before final departure down south there was one more thing that needed dealing with and that was to return to Red Road Court flats and collect the typewriter from the security guard's office that had also been allegedly used for the purpose of typing the forged letters by Barbara Hendry that had been given to Joan and Ted Warner. A swift detour and the typewriter was collected.

Chapter Sixteen: Preparation of the file

Upon return to Market Rasen the work had not stopped coming in but fortunately things had been covered in my absence by my ever reliable colleagues. It was time to further prepare evidence that had been collected during the trip to Scotland. I prepared a submission report for the typewriters that had been obtained during enquiries to have them forensically examined against the legal letters that had been handed to Joan and Ted Warner by Barbara Hendry during the fraud. I now had three in my possession one that had been removed from Barbara Hendry's flat, one from a witness on the Isle of Jura and one from the security guards office at Red Road Court flats. Upon completion of the report I travelled to Birmingham to deliver the letters together with the three typewriters to the FSS (Forensic Science Service) for comparison purposes.

As previously stated the investigator can never have enough evidence in support of a case the only thing that limits it these days is expense and time spent on an enquiry. Allegations of crime can always be supported by real evidence be it by fingerprints or more recently by DNA. Sometimes lines of forensic enquiry can be disregarded as the investigator can all too readily dismiss these lines of enquiry as a "Waste of time" or too much of a "long shot and I would suggest that these lines of enquiry really have to be seriously considered. I would also suggest that there are investigators who silently after acquittals at court wish that they had gone that extra mile with forensics and mull over the thought that if they had the case may have ended with a conviction.

A case in the mid-seventies demonstrates that long shots do on occasions tend to "pay off". In Humberside (previously Lincolnshire) and on the outskirts of a town called Brigg lies a place called Pingley camp. The location during the war served as a detention center for both German and Italian soldiers.

More recently it has fallen into dilapidation but one can guess its previous life.

During the seventies it provided accommodation for individuals employed in the local agricultural industry. The warden in charge was a foreign national by the name of Charles Spasik who was responsible for the running of the camp, which at that time provided accommodation for Polish Slavics and Yugoslav workers. It was rumoured that he kept large sums of money in his hut and this no doubt gave rise to the fact that he was found brutally murdered at nearby Bigby Hill. He had been fatally injured by persons at that time unknown with a pitchfork and a bottle which locally became known as the "Pitchfork murder."

At that time Pingley camp came within the force area of the Lincolnshire Police but later due to boundary changes came under the force area of the newly formed Humberside Police. Upon the body being discovered a murder investigation was mounted by the Lincolnshire Police under the supervision of an established and much regarded police officer Detective Chief Superintendent Miller Patrick. A large number of Detectives were seconded to the murder team (not so much these days!) It soon became apparent that the murder was" local" and two Yugoslav workers came under the spotlight but enquires revealed that they had made good their escape. Due to the location of Brigg being close to Hull and Grimsby a line of enquiry was launched to investigate the possibility that the offenders may have taken a ferry from either Hull or Grimsby to make their way back to Yugoslavia.

Detectives were dispatched to the ferry ports and all of the embarkation cards for the ferries were seized for examination. In the meantime other enquiries had revealed the names of the possible offenders and for the first time ever UK police officers conducted enquiries behind the iron curtain. The offenders were eventually returned to the UK by the Lincolnshire Police and charged with the murder of Charles Spasik. The two offenders received terms of imprisonment of ten and twelve years.

The interesting point of this offence is that Detectives returned to the murder incident room with hundreds and hundreds of embarkation cards from the ferries covering the suspected departure dates of the suspects. Despite it being a very long shot indeed the fingerprints of one of the suspects were found on one solitary embarkation card!

During the following months and after having spent a large amount away on the fraud enquiry it was time to return to getting on with my local work and wait for justice to take its course. I had left requests for statements to be recorded from witnesses that I had been unable to see and was waiting for any replies. In my absence there had been a number of burglaries at large houses on the patch that needed looking into, I still had the enquiry to pursue where an "additional" grave had been discovered by a gardener in a local graveyard and I had also been given an enquiry to look into about some very suspicious "goings-on" and a very large country house in the north of the patch. Gossip was rife about women being chased around the very large gardens of the premises scantily clad, chauffer driven cars arriving at all hours of the day and night being let into the premises which were guarded by very large metal gates. I decided to go and take a look to see what was going on, and when I approached the gate was met by a very large male with no neck who when I enquired as to who lived there was told in no uncertain terms to "Piss off!" not a good move really by the man on the gate it only served to feed my appetite as to what was going on.

I had not introduced myself for fear of compromising any future enquiries but as it turned out the premises were owned and being used by a multi-national company as a "knocking shop" where executives would no doubt take advantage of the pleasures on offer to ease the process of any business negotiations! The premises later featured in a national corruption enquiry involving a well-known national company.

The burglaries being committed on the patch were proving to be a challenge but I was confident that we would get there in the end and we finally did.

The weeks went by and carried on with my duties and as promised there was a slow progression of statements arrived at Market Rasen that had been recorded by my colleagues in the Strathclyde Police especially my contact Detective Inspector Jim Cassels.

Statement of Helen Donald   Registrar

I am the Registrar for Inveraray, Argyll.

On Monday 25th June 1984, I received from Detective Inspector Cassels of Clydebank Police office, on behalf of Police at Lincoln, a document that is a photocopy of a form used by the Registrars but the contents are very obviously false, for the following reasons:

1)   On the form the district No was given as "Argyll". This should have been a number, never a place name.

2)   The box headed Entry No bore the figures 47538 which bore no reference whatsoever to my business.

3)   The box headed NHS is completed but as the birth was allegedly registered in 1930 there was no National Health Service at that time it could not have possibly been completed

4)   Entry boxes 3 and 4 of the form indicate that the alleged birth occurred on 17.1.30 at the Lodge House Inveraray. If this were true, the only place that the birth could be registered would be at my office. I have searched my records relative to the date in question and no such birth is registered.

5)   A date of birth for the mother is shown in box 5. This is never shown in true extracts

6)   The same applies to box 8 where the date of birth relative to the father is shown.

7)   At the bottom right hand corner of the document, there is an oval shaped stamp. No such stamp to my knowledge is used at Inveraray.

8)   The document is signed by a Francis M Stewart, Registrar and according to my records, no such person exists.

9) The form used is one which only came into being after 1965 and anyone requesting an extract would be supplied with a replica of the from on which the original birth was registered, in this case a long narrow form.

10) In conclusion I must state that there is no doubt the document is question is a forgery.

I always had the deepest suspicions regarding the birth certificate that was given to Ted and Joan Warner by Barbara Hendry in March 1984, there was obviously something wrong about it but to a normal member of the public it was acceptable. Its purpose was to support her story about being related to the Argyll family. It did contain accurate dates of birth. We had now evidentially proved it to be a forgery and another large step to proving the whole scenario was just one big fraud committed over 7 years or so.

In the following weeks I visited various loan companies to document the details of the monetary loans that Joan and Ted Warner had taken out to pay to Barbara Hendry to assist her financially with regards to the bogus inheritance. The amount actually borrowed actually came as a surprise and I did wonder just how they were financially surviving. The loan companies up to this stage had been very understanding in assisting with their situation but at the end of the day the monies loaned did need repaying the only alternative was for Ted Warner to declare himself bankrupt. I did not think that Ted would find the option very favorable but it had to be considered.

I would during my other enquiries "pop in "and see how Joan and Ted were doing. I would always be offered the utmost hospitality despite them by this time being of very limited means. I did note however that Teds health in my opinion had started to deteriorate further and he was starting to lose weight a matter I found of great concern. I was always asked by both Joan and Ted what was the likelihood of them having to give evidence in Crown Court at a later date and told them that it was always going to be a possibility but with the weight of the evidence Hendry would plead guilty to the charges, deep down I knew that I had to obtain such a plethora of evidence that a "not guilty" plea would not be an option. At a point when I was satisfied the time was right I did mention the possibility to Ted about declaring himself bankrupt to alleviate the debt problem. His reaction was "I've borrowed the money and somehow I will repay it."

I can honestly say that I felt really sorry for the predicament that they found themselves in. I had visited to loan companies involved and unbeknown to Ted had renegotiated their repayments thus not clearing the debt but extending the time needed to pay and reducing the weekly payments but this had not yet filtered through. The loan companies were extremely understanding with the exception of one that needed, shall we say, a little encouragement! especially if the manager involved wanted his burglary at his home address solving!

Time was passing by and the legal cogs slowly turned. A few weeks later I received an envelope from the forensic science service. Upon opening the envelope it enclosed a statement from the scientist who had examined the typewriters and made comparisons with the forged letters given to both Joan and Ted and the bank manager at Lincoln. The result was that it was proved that all three of the typewriters could be shown to have been used in the preparation of the forged letters beyond doubt. The evidence was mounting up and the following day I received a further statement from the fingerprint department stating that the fingerprints of Barbara Hendry had been identified on some of the receipts signed for collection of monies at the banks. (Get out of that one I thought to myself!) Fingerprints had been identified on exhibits provided by the witness Clay DRC 1 DRC 2 and DRC 3 being receipts from banks.

I decided I was time to tie loose ends up and record statements from the respective loan companies where loans had been taken out by Joan and Ted

Statement of Mr M   *Branch Manager*

C/o Mercantile Credit Company Limited
Clasketgate Lincoln

I am employed by Mercantile Credit Company in the capacity of Branch Manager and I currently work form the company's premises at Clasketgate Lincoln.

Mercantile Credit is a company that amongst other things loans monies to both companies and individual customers.

I can say that present customers include one Mr. and Mrs. E V and J Warner who live at Ryland Road Welton Lincolnshire.

The Warners approached our company in 1980 for a loan and after initial enquiries were provided a loan of £1,100.00 that required payments of £59.13 per month to be made. The loan a was repaid in December 1980 by way of a settlement figure being given to Mr and Mrs Warner and another loan was taken out for £1576.00 in January 1981. The installments for this loan were £84.71 per month.

In September 1981, Mr and Mrs Warner borrowed a further £400.00. The installments were £20.67 per month

In July 1982 the second loan for £1576 was settled and replaced in August 1982 by a loan of £994.00 to be paid at £51.57 per month.

In March 1983 the £400.0 loan was paid off and replaced in June 1983 by a loan of £50.00 to be paid at £28.28 per month.

In July 1983 the £994.00 loan was paid off and replaced in August 1983 by a loan of £1222.00 to be paid at £65.18 per month.

In September 1983 the £530.00 loan was paid off. In October 1983 it was replace by a loan of £897.00 to be paid at £47.84 per month.

In September 1983 the £1222.00 loan had been paid off and replaced by a loan of £1485.00 in October 1984 to be paid at £79.20 per month.

To date Mr and Mrs Warner are in debt to the Mercantile Credit Company to the amount of £2856.96 and through legal action judgement it has been agreed that they will now repay at a rate of £30 per month.

Statement of Mr B   Branch Manager
Lombard North Central Lincoln

I am employed by Lombard North Central PLC in the capacity of Branch Manager and I work from the company's premises situated in Lincoln.

Lombard North Central is a finance house, which amongst other things provides personal loans to customers.

I can say that amongst the customers using the company' facilities are Mr Edward Warner and his wife Joan Warner, both of whom reside in Dunholme Near Lincoln.

On 2nd October 1979 Mr. and Mrs. Warner approached Lombard North Central and were granted a load for the purchase of a motor car costing £1895 with a deposit of £895 and a £1000.00 advance over two years costing £53.33 per month.

The loan was paid in full on 2nd September 1981.

On 24th April 1981 a £500.00 personal loan was granted jointly to Mr. and Mrs. Warner working out at £28.96 a month for two years. This loan was paid in full on 9th September 1981. On 20th August 1981 a new loan of £998.00 was added to the outstanding balance of £492.00 over a further two-year period at £85.29 per month. This loan ran until 29th July 1982 when a further advance of £494 was added to the settlement of £1,106.00 resulting in a payment of £88.33 to be made on a monthly basis over a period of rtwo years.

The current loan of £595 together with the outstanding amount of ££1,115.00 was taken out on 13th July 1983. This was to be paid at a rate of £91.67 for the next two years.

Due to the fact that the payments ceased, the matter was passed to the company's legal department and legal action was commenced.

During the enquiry it became apparent just how much money Joan and Ted Warner were borrowing to support Barbara Hendry in her bogus plight concerning her "inheritance". They had borrowed as much as they could from relatives and had turned to loan companies to meet the fraudulent demands. Unfortunately because *of* the "secret" element of the fraud Joan and Ted had not informed their close relatives of their approaches made to loan companies. I could see how they had been unable to make the necessary repayments to the various loans they had taken out but that did not deter Barbary Hendry who persisted in her demands to request further monetary payment to assist with her alleged legal fees!

Time and time again innocent victims become involved with fraudsters who will take them for all they have.... Literally! And this case was turning out to be no exception. While Joan and Ted were seriously struggling financially Barbara Hendry was up in Scotland spending their money until it ran out and she would make further unsubstantiated demands for more. In all fairness the loan companies involved had on the whole been very understanding and although it was too much to ask for them to write off the loans but generally they had been in agreement to re-negotiate the monthly repayments to make the loans easier to manage for Joan and Ted who by this time had been seriously struggling financially.

After recording the statements from the loan companies I again called in to see Joan and Ted to see how they were managing. Ted I observed seemed to be a shadow of his former self. He had lost weight and was becoming fragile. We talked about the actual fraud and he thanked me for getting involved, which I informed him that it was my job and I was very sorry the way things were turning out. Barbara Hendry was still remanded in custody and was not going anywhere and I had to monitor things just in case she was able to make contact with hem from inside prison. This was going to be difficult for her as Joan and Ted were not on the telephone.

Ted reassured me that should any contact be made or attempted he would be in touch.

One thing I had learned about Ted over this period was that he was as good as his word. During our conversation apart from his financial worries something else was troubling him.

"Ted," I asked, "What is worrying you? Have you got something to tell me? "

Ted replied, "I know that I have been stupid in falling for this and I appreciate all the work you have done and I apologise for not agreeing to help you earlier but will Joan and I have to give evidence in Crown Court?"

My suspicions had been confirmed. I had always suspected that giving evidence would be of concern.

"Ted," I replied, "I cannot guarantee that you will not have to, but I will be there to support both you and Joan. If I can accumulate enough evidence then hopefully both she and Donny will see sense and plead guilty but I can't guarantee it of course".

Ted replied, "I understand."

I sit here as a seasoned fraud investigator and do not criticise either the victim or the relatives. Time and time again relatives are left unaware of what has been happening until the very last moment. This case is no exception, in fact the fraudster concerned added and element of "secrecy" to ensure that Joan and Ted did not inform relatives of just exactly what was going on. "If the trustees find out I have been borrowing money it would contravene the will and invalidate it and I (Barbara) would get nothing and everything would be frozen." So any relatives should not feel guilty and I can relate to this from personal experience. Bearing in mind that I have been involved in fraud investigation over many years. Recently a close relative of mine an auntie died. Her and her husband were not particularly wealthy but led a comfortable life. Their flat was full of nick-nacks and various items, she used to enjoy playing bingo at nearby coastal resorts on holidays and obviously accumulated items consistent with her "hobby" ornaments and the like…. A lot of them!

Shortly after she died the unenviable task of clearing the house and sorting the estate out fell to our family. Upon clearing the house I was very surprised to find that she had accumulated a large amount of paperwork relating to alleged lottery wins, fortunes being read, palm readings and horoscope readings. Upon looking at the paperwork it was obvious that large amount of money had been sent to these fraudsters and charlatans which was unknown to the wider family including her husband! I was surprised this activity had been going on without anybody knowing. So it just goes to show that these circumstances can even occur to a relative of an accomplished fraud investigator!

Statements continued to arrive at Market Rasen Police station, which I always opened with interest.

Statement of John Sproat   Flight Navigator

Although I am a flight navigator my hobby is printing and I have a small workshop at my home on Jura. About six or seven years ago I was approached by a Mrs Hendry who had recently moved to Jura. She asked to borrow my typewriter. I would not let her take it away but she used it at my house. I have no idea what she typed.

Subsequently from time to time Mrs Hendry approached me, this time to have some photocopying done these were official looking letters, which had different titles. One was the Royal Bank of Scotland, Islay, the Sheriff's offices in Oban and Solicitors in London and Glasgow. These letter headings had obviously been doctored, I noticed that the letter headings had been stuck on the top of other letters. I think one of the other letters was to a couple in Lincoln stating that Mrs Hendry was buying the Doctors house in Craighouse. Another letter was to the County Planning Office in Lochgilphead. I remember her saying that her friends in Lincoln were helping her financially.

They told me that some of the letters were to do with Mrs. Hendry's divorce and maintenance payments. At first it was Mrs Hendry who came to have copying done but latterly it was her husband Donnie.

I never read the contents of the letters I only checked that they printed alright as it is an old photocopier using prints on a negative. It was the negative I was checking so I was reading it backwards. Mrs. Hendry always offered to overpay me for the copying, for example she offered £10.00 to have three copies of an article. I normally only charge 20p per copy. She often arrived at my house by hire car. I continued to do this work once every two months up until Mrs. Hendry left Jura.

The last one I copied it was Donnie who brought it to me. I became unhappy about copying this type of letter and told him to try the hotel for his copying, as it was a newer and better quality machine. I thought this would stop him coming to me. About two years ago Mrs. Hendry brought to me a silver tea service and a gold ring. She asked for them to be initialed by engraving. I cannot remember what the initials were but she said it was for her son. I do not know which one.

In all crime enquiries it is very important for the investigator to keep their "eye on the ball" and restrict the statements recorded to individuals who have something relevant to say. Investigators will no doubt interview witnesses who are obviously of good intention but what they are offering up as evidence has no relevance to the enquiry or what they are willing to provide is already known to the investigator or has already been documented, if this is not strictly adhered to then the investigation will become bogged down with too many repetitive statements. Throughout the current enquiry other individuals have been seen but statements were not necessarily recorded.

Upon reviewing the statements already recorded I was quite happy that the relevant lines of enquiry had been dealt with, the will produced had been proved to be a forgery, the individual that had played minor parts such as the Doctor and the Security Guard had been traced and interviewed and the identity of the "bogus Solicitor" had been resolved. I was quite happy but silently suspicious that things had been going really well.

Chapter Seventeen: The Final Furlong

A court date had now been set for 2nd April 1985 when hopefully the whole matter would be concluded. Up to this date no indications had been received as to how either Donny or Barbara Hendry would plead. As soon as I was notified of the date of the case I visited Joan and Ted to inform them. Upon sitting down in their lounge I sensed a degree of apprehension from them both. I explained how the case would progress if it went to trial and if the defendants decided to plead guilty. I also sensed a degree of relief that it was all coming to a close. During our conversation both Joan and Ted expressed their disappointment at how they had both been treated by someone whom they had considered a genuine friend and for how long they had been taken advantage of. Ted was struggling to pay back the monies that they had borrowed both from friend's relatives and loan companies and was determined that all monies obtained would be repaid in full. With the co-operation of the loan companies the repayments had been made easier but it still remained difficult for them both.

During the following few days and prior to the court date I continued to visit Joan and Ted offering support but the main question to be answered was, were they going to be required to give evidence at the trial? I had concerns for Ted as the case was starting to take its toll. He had become rather frail but he was very resolute. If he was required to give evidence then so be it. This scenario had been 7 years in the making and we were in the last few days.

The day of the court case arrived and I as the officer in the case attended Lincoln Crown Court which is situated in a very historic setting within the castle walls, the inside of the court building can be quite intimidating to a person who is not familiar with the setting but all in all it is quite impressive.

I registered my arrival with the local Crown Prosecution representative to be told that Joan and Ted Warner had not yet arrived. I decided to have a quick walk round to see if I could find them and located them both sat together in a rather isolated spot adjacent to the court. Approaching them from behind I could not do any other than feel great sympathy with their situation. As soon as I made my presence known both stood up and welcomed me and shook my hand after which they enquired if there had been any intimation of a plea of either guilty or not guilty from the Hendry's. I informed them that I was unaware of any pleas but would obviously keep them updated as the day went on. It was obvious to me that both were very concerned at the prospect of having to give evidence, I was happy that I had done the best job possible and would have to wait and see what happens.

The morning went by and from the enquiries I had made both defendants were in conference with their legal Counsels with regards to the progression of the case.

The court adjourned for lunch I and I went to see Joan and Ted to appraise them with regards to the lack of progress both were obviously disappointed and went off to have their lunch. I was summonsed to the court as both Donald Hendry and Barbara Hendry had both been given bail for over the period of lunch and as Barbara Hendry left the confines of the court I was dispatched to basically follow her during her "walkabout" with her Solicitor during lunch. I also did not want Joan and to meet her during this period.

Both Barbara Hendry and her Solicitor took a walk around the Bail area of Lincoln finally returning to court an hour or so later discreetly followed by myself. The purpose being in case she decided to make good her escape never to be seen again. I considered this highly unlikely but have also been proved wrong in the past!

Upon returning to court both defendants again went into conference with their Barristers only to return later and myself being informed that both Barbara Hendry and her husband Donald had decided to plead "Guilty". This was extremely good news to hear and as far as I was concerned that another of my objectives had been achieved, neither Joan and Ted would be required to give evidence. I immediately went to find them and did so in exactly the same place in the castle grounds as they had been before. I approached them and saw the worry in their eyes.

Upon telling them that both Donald and Barbara Hendry intended to plead guilty the relief on their faces shone through as if a major burden had been lifted. Joan's eyes started to well up and Ted hugged her reassuringly. I informed them that if they wanted to sit in the back of the court then they could do so. Both agreed that they would like to.

An hour or so later the court re-convened. Sat in the in the dock were to very somber looking individuals Barbara and Donny Hendry. Sat at the back of the court were Ted and Joan Warner. The proceedings commenced and I was requested to enter the witness box the answer some questions and read out the antecedents of the defendants, a task which I duly relished as we were now approaching the end of a seven year saga for Joan and Ted.

After the case was outlined by the prosecuting Counsel the defence Council stood up and gave their mitigation which to my mind was irrelevant. The Judge Edwin Jowitt QC said of the Warners *"It may be their only hope is bankruptcy- with the humiliation that will bring them. You traded on their sympathy and trust"*. Barbara Hendry was sentenced to four years after she admitted obtaining property by Deception and her husband was sentenced to two years imprisonment with 16 months suspended. I was commended by the Judge for bringing the offenders to justice always nice to receive but not the motivating force. Both were taken away to start their terms of imprisonment.

There's something very satisfying about hearing a guilty plea and then in the event of a prison sentence being given watching the offender being "taken down" and then being placed in a prison vehicle and taken away to start their prison sentence and wondering how they are coping with their first night in incarceration.

The day proved to be a great relief for Joan and Ted after finishing at court that day I later visited them and they were sat at home wondering what the future would hold. I had informed them that there was little hope of recovering any of the money stolen. They had really accepted that but were still bewildered at how someone who they had considered to be a real friend could ever do what had been done to them over the period of seven years. They thanked me for what had been done and apologised for not believing that it was all a fraud earlier. I told them that an apology was not necessary and then left them to carry on with their lives as best that they could. Ted did say that he intended to repay the money if full which I totally believed he would ….. and he did!

Epilogue

The months went by after the conclusion of the case. Barbara Hendry was declared criminally bankrupt as was the legislation of the day but nothing was ever recovered. Things would be different these days with the introduction of the proceeds of Crime Act 2002 and beneficiaries of the fruits of her fraud would have had to account more fully. Joan and Ted carried on with life and I occasionally visited them whilst passing but was conscious that it would have to come to an 'end as whatever they said and however welcoming they were during my visits I only served to be a reminder of less happy times.

I was convinced that Ted's health had suffered towards the end of the fraud and that he was becoming a shadow of his former self together with the worry of repaying all the money that he had borrowed.

I was informed during a holiday abroad on 2nd August that Ted had passed away and I was unable to attend his funeral. He had continued, and finally repaid all his debts. I had by this time concluded my visits and carried on with my career.

Around the start of March 2003 I received a message from a colleague at work that Joan would like me to visit her. A day or so later I called in to see her and as always was given a warm welcome. I did notice that she was extremely chatty, she was looking well and getting on with life. After general talk and a cup of tea I got up to leave when she said, "Kim you won't forget our agreement will you?"

I thought for a second trying to remember what it was we had agreed."

Joan said, "The book."

I said, "What book?"

Joan replied, "About the whole story."

It was during a very rare, lighter period whilst recording the statement from Ted that he said "Do you know this would make a good book you know." At the time I laughed it off but then realised he was being serious.

Ted said, "It is important that people should realise two things, firstly that it is so easy to become a victim of fraud and secondly it is important that people should realise that we are not fools. The only thing I ask is that if you do write our story that it should be done after we have both died."

Upon realising Ted was serious I replied "Ok Ted I give you my word."

Joan died on 8th March 2003, a few days after I visited her.

And so you have it that's the story. My objectives were achieved, Ted and Joan finally supported a prosecution of the Hendry's, the fraud was stopped, enough evidence was collected to as best as possible to ensure a "Guilty Plea" and thereby avoiding the necessity for Joan and Ted to give evidence and finally the book has been completed.

Never underestimate the effect of fraud on the victim and never become lulled into a false sense of security "I never thought it could never happen to me" is a phrase I have heard so many times as believe me the fraudsters are still out there looking for their next victim. Make sure it's not you, a relative or a friend or a loved one.

*

Printed in Great Britain
by Amazon